SPECIAL MESSAGE TO READERS

THE ULVERSCROFT FOUNDATION
(registered UK charity number 264873)
was established in 1972 to provide funds for research, diagnosis and treatment of eye diseases. Examples of major projects funded by the Ulverscroft Foundation are:

- The Children's Eye Unit at Moorfields Eye Hospital, London
- The Ulverscroft Children's Eye Unit at Great Ormond Street Hospital for Sick Children
- Funding research into eye diseases and treatment at the Department of Ophthalmology, University of Leicester
- The Ulverscroft Vision Research Group, Institute of Child Health
- Twin operating theatres at the Western Ophthalmic Hospital, London
- The Chair of Ophthalmology at the Royal Australian College of Ophthalmologists

You can help further the work of the Foundation by making a donation or leaving a legacy. Every contribution is gratefully received. If you would like to help support the Foundation or require further information, please contact:

THE ULVERSCROFT FOUNDATION
The Green, Bradgate Road, Anstey
Leicester LE7 7FU, England
Tel: (0116) 236 4325

website: www.ulverscroft-foundation.org.uk

MURDER ISN'T EASY

While other children were devouring the works of Enid Blyton and Beatrix Potter, Carla Valentine was poring through the pages of Agatha Christie novels. It was this early fascination that led to her job as a pathology technician, trained in forensics and working in mortuaries.

Nearly every Agatha Christie story involves dead bodies, and for a young Carla, a curious child already fascinated with biology, these stories were perfect puzzles.

Of course, Agatha herself didn't talk of 'forensics' in the way we use it now, but in each tale, she writes of twists and turns with her expert weave of human observation, ingenuity and genuine science of the era. Through the medium of the 'whodunnit', Agatha Christie was a pioneer of forensic science, and in *Murder Isn't Easy* Carla illuminates all of the knowledge of one of our most beloved authors.

CARLA VALENTINE

MURDER ISN'T EASY

THE FORENSICS OF AGATHA CHRISTIE

Complete and Unabridged

CHARNWOOD
Leicester

First published in Great Britain in 2021 by
Sphere
An imprint of Little, Brown Book Group
London

First Charnwood Edition
published 2022
by arrangement with
Little, Brown Book Group
An Hachette UK Company
London

A catalogue record for this book is available from the British Library.

ISBN 978–1–4448–4833–5

Published by
Ulverscroft Limited
Anstey, Leicestershire

Printed and bound in Great Britain by
TJ Books Ltd., Padstow, Cornwall

This book is printed on acid-free paper

For my brother, Ryan, who I love with all my heart

Contents

Introduction

The Scene of the Crime

'It's quite easy, you know.'
'What is?'
'To get away with it.' He was smiling again – a charming, boyish smile.

— *Murder Is Easy*

As a pathology technician who worked in a mortuary, the question I'm asked most often is, 'How on *earth* did you end up working with dead bodies?' The answer — that I'd wanted to do so ever since I was a child — rarely satisfies. But the reason for this early fascination is simple: I fell in love with forensic science after I fell in love with the books of Agatha Christie: books which I began borrowing from my local library aged just eight years old. Coincidentally, Agatha describes me exactly via the twelve-year-old character Pippa in her 1954 play *Spider's Web*. When Jeremy Warrender, the house guest of Clarissa Hailsham-Brown, asks Clarissa's stepdaughter Pippa what her favourite subject at school is, we're told that her answer was 'immediate' and 'enthusiastic'. She says, 'Biology . . . It's heaven. Yesterday we dissected a frog's leg.' The application of biology to crime can loosely be described as forensic pathology, and it's something I was surprisingly aware of, and enamoured with, from childhood.

Of course, Agatha herself didn't talk of 'forensics' — it's a relatively modern term. But every one of her stories is an expert tapestry of human observation and ingenuity, threaded through with the emerging sciences and detection methods of the era; and it's this attention to forensic detail that really enthralled me at that young age. Included in her repertoire are mentions of fingerprints and document comparison, blood spatter analysis, trace evidence and firearms. There is a proliferation of poisons — perhaps the weapon most associated with Agatha's books — since she spent time working as a dispenser in a pharmacy during both World Wars and incorporated that knowledge into her fiction with immense success. Also, critically, every Christie detective story involves one — or more commonly several — dead bodies. For a curious child already fascinated with biology and pathology, these stories and their corresponding bodies were the perfect puzzles.

* * *

A quick synopsis of the chapters of Agatha's own life, for those who aren't familiar, reads just as intriguingly as one of her books. She was born Agatha Miller in 1890 in Devon, UK, and became the world's most commercially successful novelist, outsold only by the Bible and Shakespeare. In 1952 she wrote *The Mousetrap*, a play which has had the longest initial run in history (in fact, after 67 years, the only thing capable of suspending performances of *The Mousetrap* was the Coronavirus outbreak of 2020), and in 1971 she was made a Dame of the British Empire. However, before her incredible literary successes she mucked in like the rest of the population during the First World War (as she did again in the Second) by working for her country as a nurse and then a pharmacist — roles which would become pertinent in many of her future stories. Some people are aware of the unfortunate end of the marriage to her first husband Archie Christie, in 1926, and her subsequent disappearance: it hit international headlines at the time, when after eleven days she was discovered in a hotel in Harrogate, suffering with possible short-term memory loss — although the incident remains somewhat of a mystery, and she didn't mention it in her autobiography. Thankfully, her second marriage four years later, to the archaeologist Max Mallowan, was much happier, and stayed that way until her death in 1976. This second union even inspired in Agatha an interest in archaeology which provided yet another talent towards her rapidly growing repertoire to be drawn upon in later books. And 'drawn' is the operative word here; Max encouraged her to attend sketching lessons so she could record the finds at various excavations for posterity, and after meticulously cleaning and illustrating them she became a bona fide member of the dig team.

Despite creating such enduring sleuths as Hercule Poirot and Miss Marple, Agatha didn't only author crime fiction. She also wrote six romance novels under the pseudonym Mary Westmacott (a pseudonym which remained a secret for nearly twenty years), several works of non-fiction, including her autobiography (published posthumously in 1977), and numerous short stories and plays.

But it's evident that what Christie knew best was crime. She wrote sixty-six full-length whodunnits in her forty-five-year career, along with a prolific amount of short detective stories. She was the first person ever to receive a Grandmaster Award from the Mystery Writers of America, and she was a founding member and president of the Detection Club in 1930 — a society of crime-fiction writers whose members were required to follow rules about writing detective fiction specifically, and swear an oath of allegiance upon a human skull called Eric, in a rather tongue-in-cheek ceremony.

I'm interested in the fascinating history of forensic science, and an avid reader of murder mysteries: Agatha Christie's books are the perfect combination of the two. Her desire for procedural accuracy, and the developments in criminology and medicolegal sciences her writing tracks, show clearly the progression of forensics into the field of study it now is.

⋆ ⋆ ⋆

The term 'medicolegal' — and the more archaic 'medical jurisprudence' — are designations which were once slightly more common than the word 'forensic' we currently use — although they refer to almost the same topic. Medicolegal means 'encompassing both medical and legal aspects', so specifically involves the medical sciences; while forensic means 'relating to or denoting the application of scientific methods and techniques to the investigation of crime'. Forensic, in origin, means 'relating to the courts of law', derived from the Latin *forensis* ('of or before the forum'), and *law* is really the focus here: in Roman times, someone accused of a crime would have to present their case before a group of individuals in the Forum, just like in our courtrooms today. However, it seems that the word 'forensic' has recently become synonymous with 'careful investigation' or 'in-depth analysis', and is used in a much broader context. I'm thinking here of headlines like 'Forensic analysis of rugby match between Wales and England' or 'Forensic examination of Egyptian mummy'. Often the techniques talked about, particularly on television, can simply be described as in-depth, analytical or scientific, and neither the rugby teams nor the Egyptian mummy are being accused of a crime.

Medicolegal was the preferred term before forensic science ascended as a subject in its own right, particularly once it had made its mark on popular culture. I studied forensic science at university, when it was in its infancy as an educational topic, before going on to assist pathologists during forensic autopsies for ten years. I subsequently moved on to repair and restore historical body parts in a museum setting, which requires a similar level of attention to detail as the autopsies did. This gives me a unique perspective on both the historical and modern practices of forensic science.

Currently I conserve over 5,000 anatomical specimens at Barts Pathology Museum in London. The sub-group of specimens known as the Medicolegal Collection consists of pieces of preserved human tissue illustrating such injuries as poisonings, gunshot wounds and judicial hangings; the earliest dating from 1831. However, those specimens in the same sub-collection acquired since 1966 became known as the Forensic Medicine Collection, the alternative name illustrating the more modern turn of phrase.

It's difficult to say for certain when one description fell from the vernacular and others became more common, as there is certainly some overlap. However, it is possible to look at the timeline of criminalistics, or forensic science as we know it today, and see how the discipline developed — in some cases from as far back as the thirteenth century! — regardless of which name was used.

Perhaps one of the most famous names in *modern* forensic science is that of Dr Edmond Locard (1877–1966), a French criminalist who established the first police laboratory in Lyon, in 1910 — not long before Agatha began her illustrious writing career. At this point it's worth noting the difference between 'criminalist' and 'criminologist', as the two words often appear in Christie's works. A criminalist is more like what we'd call a 'forensic scientist' nowadays, whereas a criminologist studies the psychology and sociology of crime and criminals, perhaps what we'd call a 'forensic psychologist'. (In Agatha's books Hercule Poirot, for example, seems to veer very much between the two.) In his childhood Locard had been an avid reader of Conan Doyle's Sherlock Holmes stories, as was Agatha Christie, and later in his forensic career he even wrote a book titled *Detectives in Novels and Detectives in the Laboratory*. He is responsible for formulating what is known as the fundamental tenet of forensic science, the simple phrase: 'Every contact leaves a trace.' This basic rationale, now known as Locard's Exchange Principle, expresses the fact that the perpetrator of a crime will inevitably bring *something* — some sprinkle or spray, some smudge or smear — into the crime scene. They will also leave with something from it, unbeknownst to them, and both can be used as forensic evidence. Christie was fully aware of this principle, whether she knew it as

Locard's or not, as she understood the concept of evidence linking killers to victims and to crime scenes.

Perhaps, after Agatha's success in 1920 with her first book, *The Mysterious Affair at Styles*, she wanted to further her research and picked up a brand-new copy of Locard's *Detectives in Novels* . . . when it was published in 1922. It would have seemed made for her! She certainly could have even obtained a copy of the original French edition — a language she read in although, according to Charles Osborne, couldn't speak very well. It is notable that she uses the word 'trace' in her stories after the publication of her 1923 novel *The Murder on the Links* — which is coincidentally set in France — but not before. In this book, about a suspicious death which occurs on a golf course while poor Poirot is trying to relax, the official local detective assigned to the case, Giraud, is describing Locard's principle when he says:

'The men who carried out this crime were taking no chances . . . They counted on leaving no traces. But I'll beat them. There's always something! And I mean to find it.'

By the time Locard released his *Traité de Criminalistique* (Treaty of Forensic Science) in 1931, the discipline of forensics as we now know it was born — early on in Christie's career and during the 'golden age' of detective fiction.

* * *

Because of her unique placement as a writer during extensive advances in medicolegal history, and her meticulous attention to detail, the burgeoning science of forensics can be studied through Agatha Christie's works. Agatha is said not to have used real people as the inspiration for her characters, for the most part, because they wouldn't become real *to her*. She had to invent them because she needed them to do whatever she wanted them to do; a bit like puppets. If they really existed, she would have an idea of their character traits and thought processes which might be quite at odds with how she wanted them to act in her books. In her autobiography she states that she 'decided once and for all that it is no good thinking about real people — you must create your characters for yourself'.[2] That said, she was inspired by real-life stories and overheard conversations. 'Her rich imagination was stimulated from studying newspaper reports of true-life crimes. Almost daily, distressing incidents of killing, vandalism, robbery and assault provided inspiration for plots.' We can certainly see this in her books: the infamous Jack the Ripper case from 1888 was referenced several times in *The ABC Murders*, and the Great Train Robbery of 1963 inspired part of the plot of *At Bertram's Hotel*, published only two years after the robbery, in 1965. Throughout her canon she mentions well-known cases such as those of Edith Thompson, Dr Crippen, the 'Brides in the Bath' and Lizzie Borden as well as more obscure crimes like the Brighton Trunk Killings and the Hay Poisoner. But if art imitates life, then life may also — horribly — imitate art, and this was the case when several sets of 'Alphabet Murders' — similar to Agatha's fictional *ABC Murders* — occurred from the 1970s onwards. First, in Rochester, New York State, three pre-teen girls were sexually assaulted and strangled between 1971 and 1973. Each of the girls had first and last names that started with the same letter, and their bodies were discovered in towns which also began with the same letter — an uncanny parody of the methods of Christie's ABC Killer, which saw Alice Ascher killed in Andover, Betty Barnard murdered in Bexhill and Carmichael Clarke killed in Churston. The real-life Rochester victims were Carmen Colon in Churchville, Michelle Maenza in Macedon and Wanda Walkowicz in Webster.

Then, coincidentally, across the country in California, more double-initial murders took place in 1977 and 1978, and later in 1993 and 1994. The victims, older women who were said to be prostitutes, were Carmen Colon (bizarrely the exact same name as one of the upstate New York victims), Pamela Parsons, Roxene Roggasch and Tracy Tofoya.

In 2011 a man called Joseph Naso was eventually arrested for the California crimes. He was a photographer and a native of New York who travelled between the east and west coasts of America for decades. He was sentenced to death for the West Coast murders in 2013. DNA evidence didn't support his involvement in the Rochester Alphabet Murders, so officially that case remains unsolved.

Similarly, in South Africa between 1994 and 1995, a series of murders known as the ABC Murders were perpetrated by Moses Sithole. Within that short time period, Sithole killed 38 people in a spree beginning in Atteridgeville, continuing through Boksburg and ending in Cleveland.

There is, of course, absolutely no evidence to suggest that these murderers were inspired by Agatha's works at all; although these killings have echoes of Christie's plot, the perpetrators never named her as an influence. But it does show that real-life crime can certainly be stranger than crime fiction, and that anyone who perhaps considers Christie's work far-fetched and unrealistic might do well to delve into the world of true crime . . . And why not? As Poirot points out to Katherine Grey in *The Mystery of the Blue Train*, 'Fiction is founded on fact.'

Conversely some criminals unfortunately *did* name Christie's books as a source of inspiration.

In 2009 in Qazvin, Iran, a 32-year-old woman called Mahin Qadiri became Iran's first female serial killer. She claimed she had been inspired by the books of Agatha Christie which she read after they were translated into Farsi. She murdered five elderly women by drugging and strangling them, then stole their money and jewellery. According to an article by Robert Tait, 'Mahin in her confessions has said that she has been taking patterns from Agatha Christie books and has been trying not to leave any trace of herself.'

This certainly isn't Agatha's fault, and she never wrote about anyone who utilised this modus operandi; if murderous intent exists within the hearts of man they will find a way to carry it out whatever the inspiration may be. Christie alludes to this herself in *Evil Under the Sun* when she quotes Ecclesiastes 9:3: 'This is an evil among all things that are done under the sun, that there is one event unto all: yea, also the heart of the sons of men is full of evil.' But thankfully, with forensic science, we have the means to investigate evil.

* * *

When reading Agatha's books I am always struck by the tremendous amount of forensic accuracy, which isn't so surprising considering Sir Richard Attenborough — who was part of the original cast of *The Mousetrap* in 1952, and who later acted in a 1974 film version of *And Then There Were None* — described her as 'a stickler for things being absolutely right'. He knew her for forty years and, presumably, very well indeed, so this character observation is valuable. Despite admitting to having little knowledge of the implements she often employed as murder weapons (apart from poisons), she researched enough to make her work believable and authentic. According to her husband Max, Agatha used to take endless trouble over getting her facts right. She would consult professional authorities on police practice, on the law and on procedures in the courts. Perhaps she felt she *had* to be very accurate in order to avoid criticism. Tellingly, in *Mrs McGinty's Dead* (one of her later books, from the 1950s) Ariadne Oliver, Christie's crime-writing character who appears in several Poirot books, says, 'Sometimes I think there are people who only read books in the hope of finding mistakes in them.' Cathy Cook, the author of *The Agatha Christie Miscellany*, noted:

> It gave her great satisfaction when a solicitor once wrote complaining of her ignorance about the law of inheritance. She was able to write back and demonstrate that the lawyer himself was outdated, that the law had been changed, and that her statement was correct!

Agatha also indicated in her writing that she was aware of the impact that her stories — and detective stories in general — could have on the layman's knowledge of crime, in effect opening up this elusive science to a wider public, and her attempts to replicate crimes for her readers gave them a taste of what was previously privileged police knowledge.

In her short story 'The Idol House of Astarte', the character Dr Pender laments the fact that he and a friend moved a dead body into the safety of the nearby house. He says apologetically, 'One would know better nowadays . . . owing to the prevalence of detective fiction. Every street boy knows that a body must be left where it is found.' This is what we think of when we consider Christie stories: *bodies*. We imagine a woman's pale, cold fingers curling up from an oriental rug on a library floor; a drained champagne glass lying next to her, her lips turning blue as her eyes slowly close. Or we envisage a man slumped forward over a crimson stain spreading slowly across the blotter of a mahogany desk, a silver blade sticking out of his back, reflecting the flickering firelight. Both of these vignettes are puzzles to be solved using investigatory methods and clues found at the scene.

* * *

Agatha is said to have 'abhorred violence'[6] and she wasn't enthusiastic about detective fiction which included savagery and brutality. This may explain why she never gratuitously depicted the physical impact of murders in her books. In real life, she didn't think she could personally look at a 'really ghastly, mangled body' and in her novels she rarely described a corpse in gory detail. This doesn't mean that she wasn't capable of writing about it, or that she never did. In her autobiography she is very matter-of-fact about gruesome scenes she witnessed while nursing in the VAD, including helping a new nurse dispose of an amputated leg and its associated blood and gore. In her authoritative biography of Christie, Laura Thompson elaborates on this with information from Agatha's own diaries. Describing an amputation surgery and the discarded limb which resulted from it, Laura wrote that Agatha had to 'clean up the floor down there — and stuck it in the furnace myself'.

In her fiction, though, her deliberate avoidance of gory detail works in her favour as she often only points out the salient features about the victim, leaving much to the reader's imagination . . . which can sometimes be worse. In *After the Funeral*, one of the characters is violently murdered with a hatchet, and the injuries to her face are enough to make identification nearly impossible. In *The Body in the Library*, the corpse of a young female victim is burnt beyond recognition after her murder, and in *One, Two, Buckle My Shoe* we have allusions to the disfiguring nature of decomposition on top of savagery. We can imagine the effects of these awful crimes without having to be told in detail the resulting injuries, and that in itself is enough to give us nightmares.

Agatha's investigations often start with anecdotes from witnesses, and some of her fictional murders are solved by the sleuth characters in the *absence* of a body. Sometimes the detective only enters the story days, months or even years after a victim has been killed, and they solve the case retrospectively, avoiding any interaction with the body: typical 'armchair detectives'. But often they do see a corpse at the scene of the crime. In fact — according to the game show *Jeopardy!* — Christie is credited as being the first person to ever use the phrase 'the scene of the crime' (in *The Murder on the Links*, published in 1923, where it is even a chapter title). But perhaps even *more* impressive is her apparent prediction of the need for what many of us know as a 'crime scene examiner's kit' or 'crime scene bag', which is now such a staple in both fact and fiction you could easily imagine they have always been employed. This isn't true. In real life, it was eminent golden-age pathologist Sir Bernard Spilsbury — someone we'll encounter frequently in this book — who noticed that even at the scenes of the most gruesome murders police officers weren't furnished with the basic protective equipment they required. They were removing chunks of human flesh from between paving stones with their bare hands, and wiping up spilled blood with their personal cotton handkerchiefs. Items such as envelopes, tweezers, pots and gloves — to be used to capture evidence, and to avoid the officers as well as the scenes being contaminated — were often improvised and not available as standard. It wasn't until 1924 following the appalling killing of Emily Kaye, known as the Crumbles Murder, that things changed. The Crumbles was a shingled beach on the coast of Sussex which was unfortunately the location of two separate murders. The first was the 1920 bludgeoning of Iris Munroe, when she was only seventeen years old, by two men with a motive of simple robbery.

The second, four years later, was the more notorious gruesome slaying and dismemberment of the pregnant Miss Kaye by her married lover Patrick Mahon. What made the crime so sensational was the fact that Mahon stowed the body parts of Emily Kaye in a large chest in one room of their bungalow, and had the gall to invite another woman, Ethel Duncan, to stay at the bungalow with him over a long Easter weekend . . . while the various severed limbs were decomposing there. Christie references this case in *Murder is Easy*, the 1939 book after which mine is named, although she calls it the Castor case:

> 'You'll remember the Castor case sir — and how they found little bits of the poor girl pinned up all over Castor's seaside bungalow . . . '

It was this grisly scene which inspired Spilsbury to introduce the 'murder bag' that morphed into the crime scene examiner's kit, which contains all the typical investigation implements we're now so familiar with: gloves, evidence bags, tweezers, sample tubes, etc. However, in *The Mysterious Affair at Styles* — published four years before the murder of Emily Kaye — Hercule Poirot appears to have a CSE kit of his own! He wanders about collecting evidence in 'test tubes' and 'envelopes', and states, 'I will put down my little case until I need it', showing that he even has specific apparatus for the purpose. At that time it was a novel idea, if you'll pardon the pun.

* * *

Although the crime scene is of utmost importance, there are many different aspects to forensic investigation. In *Towards Zero* solicitor and criminologist Frederick Treves laments the fact that detective stories begin with the murder, and feels that it is in fact the *end* of the story and not the beginning:

'The story begins long before that — with all

the causes and events converging towards a given spot . . . *Zero Hour.* Yes, all of them converging towards zero.'

I want to try to honour the above quote with this book, insofar as forensic evidence goes. The story of a murder victim begins at the scene or scenes, and all of the evidence converges towards the body — *towards zero*. Like an investigator who appears once the body has been removed to the mortuary, I will begin analysing 'causes and events' metaphorically at the scene of the crime, scrutinising footprints, fragments of paper and spent bullets. Only then will I arrive at the body to examine wound patterns, toxicology and other artefacts noted at autopsy. Here we will experience the finale to our investigation — the denouement, the book's conclusion: *Zero Hour* — which will tie all of those forensic threads together into a neat little investigative knot.

1

Fingerprints

And yet I had an uneasy feeling that the sinister old creature had seen something in my hands. I looked down at my two palms spread out in front of me. What could anyone see in the palms of anyone's hands?

— *Endless Night*

Ten black, smudged ovals on pale rectangles of card — inky facsimiles of the tips of criminal fingers — are synonymous with the history of detection. The fingerprint, with its distinctive pattern of lines and curves, has become a universal embodiment of crime. Countless films, documentaries, games and podcasts have used an image of a fingerprint to represent crime and forensics. It's a pattern so characteristic and specific it tells a story almost without the need for explanation. A fingerprint at a crime scene, usually called a finger-*mark* by today's crime scene examiners, surely places a person there; as Hercule Poirot says in Agatha Christie's first novel *The Mysterious Affair at Styles*, 'Then how do you account for the fact that you left the unmistakable impress of your finger-prints . . . ?' A person can't leave their fingerprints on a permanent object at a scene unless they were present — or their finger was removed somehow and *it* was present instead!

Because of this iconic status, and the relative ease with which prints can be lifted from a scene, they became a frequent trope in detective fiction, and Agatha Christie utilised them as much as the next writer, in various ingenious ways. Whether placed there accidentally or planted on purpose, whether smeared on glass or pressed into card, fingermarks are peppered through Agatha's entire canon. She certainly understood their forensic value, and there are more mentions of prints throughout her novels than any other forensic science. Given that Scotland Yard's fingerprint bureau was established in 1901, Agatha had around fifteen to twenty years' worth of information about the development of this pivotal 'new' technique to draw upon when she embarked upon *The Mysterious Affair at Styles* in 1916. Even so, she goes into a surprising amount of fingerprint detail in her debut considering the country wouldn't have been awash with the forensic documentaries and police procedurals we are all used to today. Before she published her first book, though, we can assume Christie certainly read around this topic in newspapers, and perhaps even sought new information out.

In truth, crime fiction was one of the main ways this type of specialist knowledge was imparted to the general public, and for Agatha — who was an avid reader of Arthur Conan Doyle's detective stories in particular — Sherlock Holmes would have provided lots of material to work with. Also, more general fiction such as *Life on the Mississippi* and *The Tragedy of Pudd'nhead Wilson* by Mark Twain included fingerprinting information. Golden-era writers of crime fiction would largely have been supplied with scientific facts by newspapers, and later on perhaps by books like *Modern Criminal Investigation*, first published in 1935. But that wouldn't be an average source for the public; it was really for more specialist circles.

With this in mind, it's interesting to note that Arthur Conan Doyle was part of a society called the Crimes Club, formed in 1903, which was described as 'A small group of men who shared an interest in murder'. The Crimes Club was a circle of men — and it was *only* men — interested in crime, but from various different 'loosely legal' backgrounds. Their aim was to learn more about a topic which they felt at that time was largely owned — and sensationalised — by the media. The group included writers as well as law men, coroners and surgeons, and during their very private meetings they frequently hosted guest speakers including the eminent Bernard Spilsbury, already mentioned, a pathologist whose cases were particularly inspiring to Christie — and who invented the 'crime scene examiner's kit' or 'crime scene bag' that Agatha had cleverly anticipated in the world of fiction before it became fact. The exclusive Crimes Club met (and still do meet, although under a different name) several times a year for 'supper and crime' . . . and I'm happy to report that I'm privileged enough to be a member as it's no longer a men-only society.

Another group, the Detection Club (the one which required its members to swear an oath upon Eric the Skull), came later, founded in 1930, and was always open to both women and men — but these were all writers of detection fiction only. Anthony Berkeley was instrumental in its founding, basing it on the idea of Conan Doyle's Crimes Club, and its first president was G. K. Chesterton, who penned the mystery novels featuring the sleuthing cleric Father Brown.

Agatha Christie is often cited as being a founder member of the Detection Club, in that she was very likely present at Berkeley's earlier, intimate dinners which began around 1928 — consisting of just detective fiction writers — and which spawned the idea to create an actual club, with rules, meetings and membership votes. She continued attending and became more and more involved, especially since her marriage had tragically ended two years before. (Martin Edwards, the club's current president, wrote a whole book about this interesting club's inception called *The Golden Age of Murder*, which I highly recommend.) Agatha, as the world's most popular detective fiction writer, was its president from 1957 right up to her death in 1976, although she did have a co-president as she was very shy and didn't want to carry out too much public speaking — the duties were split with a couple of other members, a bit like a job-share, over the period of her reign. Given that Eric the Skull had to be touched as part of the initiation into this club, I wonder how many illustrious fingerprints are on *him*!

In this club, Christie would have discussed very similar topics to the ones addressed by the earlier Crimes Club — including ingenious uses of fingerprints — with her fellow writers, in the same way as Conan Doyle had with his. We know this because Berkeley's letters of invitation to join the club sent to other crime fiction writers said that they should dine together at specific intervals 'for the purposes of discussing matters concerned with their craft'. Subsequently, in 1936, seven of the Detection Club members released a collection of comprehensive and meticulously researched essays on true murder cases under the title *The Anatomy of Murder*. Martin Edwards, who is also the club's archivist, says in his introduction to the 2014 reissue that 'discussion of real-life murder cases was a feature of Detection Club meetings', indicating this may have been where Christie and her contemporaries found much of their inspiration. How I wish I could have been a fly on the wall during the club's golden-era existence!

Suffice to say, the Detection Club would prove an incredibly important resource for Agatha's work going forward as it allowed her to converse with other writers — about crime and fiction — from what was effectively the early stages of her career. They bounced ideas off each other and challenged each other's craft, and even wrote books together and collaborated on radio broadcasts, earning money to sustain the club and pay for its lavish suppers and ceremonies. And as well as providing this professional benefit it was a valuable personal resource for such a shy and retiring woman, who relished being able to just be herself amongst friends.

* * *

It's amazing to think that the physical purpose of ridge detail on the fingertips is simply to provide some mammals with friction on surfaces which would otherwise be too smooth for gripping. It's purely incidental that the patterns created as a by-product have become one of the best forensic identifiers we have.

Fingerprint patterns are formed on the foetus in the early stages of pregnancy. Beginning around week 10 and completed by week 17, the prints a baby is born with remain unchanged their whole life. The exception is when deep tissue damage occurs to the finger pads — such as burning or scarring — which may alter the prints in an unnatural way. Not only are they formed before birth, fingerprints also happen to be one of the last features which remain after death and bodily decomposition, meaning a positive identification can often be made of someone who died several years earlier.

It's this durability which makes it possible to fingerprint the decomposed dead in a process known colloquially as 'gloving', a seemingly gruesome procedure which requires an autopsy or crime scene technician to remove the sloughed-off skin of the fingers or the entire hand of the deceased, wear it over their own latex-clad hand — like a second glove — and 'print it' with the correct contours of a fingertip. The technical name for this is a bit of a mouthful: it's called the Indirect Cadaver Hand Skin-glove Method.

In *The Secret Adversary*, Agatha Christie's second published novel and rather unexpectedly a thriller rather than a murder mystery, the leader of a communist gang tells one of his henchmen, 'You will wear gloves with the fingerprints of a notorious housebreaker,' presumably so that misleading fingerprints are left at a scene. Although Agatha doesn't elaborate on how these gloves would be created, it's possible that a dead man's sloughed off hand skin was what she meant when she described them. It's oddly clairvoyant, since she wrote this book in the early 1920s and yet the first time this procedure was ever mentioned in real life was at a fingerprint conference in 1936, when the method used by the Buenos Aires Police was being described. During this presentation, the pieces of epidermis which had sloughed off the dermis of the corpse were delightfully referred to as 'skin thimbles'. We're told: 'The operator places these 'skin thimbles' on his own fingers, protecting himself with rubber gloves. Now the operator acts as he were fingerprinting himself.'3

Because facial recognition can be nigh on impossible in decomposition cases, fingerprinting by using the gloving technique is pivotal in ascertaining the identity of the body, since the process creates an image of the fingerprint just as it appeared in life. It's particularly useful when the decay process of the deceased involves dehydration and their fingers become desiccated, unmalleable and wrinkled — like the puckered ends of a salami sausage. These are then rehydrated using a mixture of water and fabric softener, a trick known to many forensic practitioners but very infrequently discussed in polite circles. Add this titbit of knowledge to the fact that we also use biological washing powder to strip soft tissue from bones in the lab, and it can really change the way you experience popping on a wash load.

What is Fingerprint Analysis?

The science of fingerprint analysis is also sometimes called 'dactyloscopy', a word devised by another forensic pioneer, Juan Vucetich. He was a criminalist originally from Croatia who immigrated to Argentina in the 1880s, and in 1892 was the first person ever to solve a murder using fingerprint evidence. Vucetich's influence is perhaps why the Argentinian police were so advanced, and were giving instruction on using skin thimbles as early as 1936. The term 'dactyloscopy' comes from the Ancient Greek *dáktulos* which loosely translates as 'finger'. A recent question on the quiz show *The Chase* was 'What is the common name for a 'dactylogram'?' and the answer was, of course, a fingerprint. You just don't know when you'll need this kind of knowledge!

In its most basic sense dactyloscopy is an alternative word for 'fingerprinting' and involves recording or retrieving an impression left by the friction ridges of a human finger. The reason it's possible to attribute particular prints to specific individuals lies in the fact that the patterns of these friction ridges have never been found to be the same on two different people, even identical twins. This type of evidence which has unique, individualising characteristics and can point to a particular object or person is termed 'individual evidence' or 'individual characteristics' — as opposed to 'class evidence' or 'class characteristics'.

The patterns on our finger pads have evolved through primates' tendency to swing from branches and hold food. It's incredibly difficult to calculate the chances of two people having the exact same prints, but fingerprint features are highly discriminating and those people employed as examiners are extremely accurate when reaching an identification. They are 99.8 per cent able to 'tell people apart' as prints are made up of such an arbitrary combination of several features:

Ridges — The full term is 'friction ridges' and these give traction to our fingers. They may seem uselessly minute but paired with the increased number of sweat pores in this type of skin they stop us from being incredibly clumsy. It is these ridges which effectively 'stamp' the pattern of a finger pad out as a fingermark.

Furrows — The furrows, conversely, need to exist in order to ensure the friction ridges are raised, but they also create channels for the sweat pores' secretions to run through so that our fingertips don't end up too slippery.

These ridges and furrows loop and weave across the surface of our finger pads, creating distinctive random patterns which can't be duplicated. I remember a craft project in my childhood which involved pouring several colours of oil paint onto the surface of a wide tub of water, swirling them around with a wooden stick, then laying a blank sheet of paper over the top. The resulting marbled image transferred to the paper was intricate, completely haphazard and impossible to exactly replicate. This is how I imagine the formation of fingerprints. It's their uniqueness that informs the science of 'ridgeology' which categorises the patterns that are created when the ridges and furrows are generated on any volar surface (that is another name for the ridged surfaces of fingers, toes, palms and heels — even lips have ridges which can give rise to prints in a process called 'cheiloscopy'. These have been analysed in a few criminal cases, so think twice before you seal that letter with a loving kiss, especially if that letter is a ransom note . . .).

The Murder of Roger Ackroyd, written by Agatha in 1926, is perhaps the most quintessential golden-age murder mystery ever written in absolutely every way — except one. But it is this one spectacular difference which sets it apart from other books of the era, and which catapulted Agatha Christie into the upper echelons of the genre. In fact, as the ending was so unorthodox and apparently 'broke the rules' of the Detection Club's oath — tongue-in-cheek though they were — there was a movement to expel Agatha from the club entirely! Only a vote by fellow female crime writer, Dorothy L. Sayers, saved her. If this doesn't make you intrigued to read the book, you don't need to just take my word for it — in 2013, nearly ninety years after its publication, the British Crime Writers' Association voted it the best crime novel ever, calling it 'the finest example of the genre ever penned'. It features typical golden-era elements within the text, such as a floor plan of all the rooms of the house and heavily buried clues, and I'm of the opinion that the only way to do this particular book justice is to read it. Don't watch an adaptation, don't listen to an audiobook, don't even use an e-reading device and deny yourself the pleasure of the rustling pages peppered with nuance: buy a copy of the book and *read* it. It's the only way you can 'read between the lines' of this clever tale.

In the book, we're told that Inspector Raglan — who is attempting to solve the stabbing of the unfortunate Mr Ackroyd — examines various enlarged photographs of fingerprints with the characters in the book, and then proceeds to 'become technical on the subject of loops and whorls'. This effectively tells us that Agatha, too, was familiar with this uniqueness of fingerprints created by the patterns on them, namely loops, whorls, arches and various combinations thereof:

Loops — A loop is made of ridges which flow in from one side, and create a distinct ovoid shape by circling round and leaving via the same side. Because they point one way or the other, a fingerprint will either have 'radial loops' (which point to where the radius bone ends: the thumb) or ulnar loops (which point to where the ulna bone ends: the little finger or 'pinky'). Loops make up about 60 per cent of pattern types.

Whorls — A whorl looks like a whirlpool or swirl, often with a series of complete concentric ovals or circles in the middle. Whorls make up about 35 per cent of fingerprint patterns.

Arches — An arch is like a wave, smooth and rounded at the top, flowing across the finger pad. Just as a doorway or window may have a pronounced, pointy arch or a curved, flatter one, so do fingerprints. Arches can be described as 'plain' or 'tented', and tented arches — as the name suggests — rise into a much more pronounced point than the plain, flatter arches. These arch patterns make up only 5 per cent of all fingerprints.

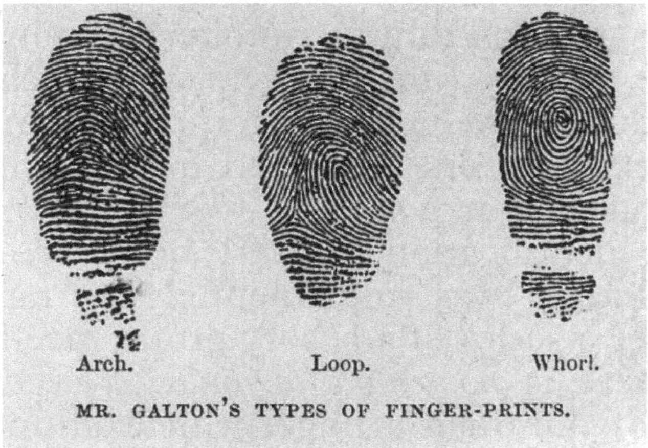

A basic image of whorls, loops and arches

Take a look at your fingerprints now — it can be quite engrossing! You'll discern a combination of all these features spread across your ten finger pads. Since loops are the most prolific, you may notice them more than you notice arches, but you may not. Everyone is completely different. These three basic designs can also combine into sub-sets like twinned loops (called double loops in the US), or may be something else entirely, known as 'accidental': a pattern that does not conform to that of the arch, loop or whorl and yet possesses characteristics common to all three types. These combinations of ridge endings and bifurcations create endless varieties of patterns across your fingertips.

While it's certainly possible that one person's fingerprints may contain elements that are the same as those in another person's print, it is the *whole* which is taken into consideration within fingerprint comparison. Initially twelve identical features were required for two different prints to be considered 'a match' — that is, a piece of *individual evidence* — and it was Edmond Locard who proposed this number, known as the 'minimum number of minutiae', in 1918. He surmised that if there were twelve details that matched between two fingerprints — in the most obvious example one extracted from a crime scene and one taken from a suspect — it would prove to be a positive identification. In 2001, however, a non-numeric standard was implemented in England and Wales after a series of advisory group meetings. This means there is *no simple formula* to ascertain the number of minutiae a fingerprint examiner has to find before concluding that two fingerprints 'match', and it's certainly no longer twelve — it's a process involving experience, statistical knowledge, a discerning eye, computer technology and much, much more. Fingerprint comparison isn't just a qualitative assumption; probability models and statistical techniques are also used to clarify the likelihood that two prints came from the same person.

* * *

In *The Mysterious Affair at Styles*, during a conversation with stalwart friend Arthur Hastings, Poirot asks him if he is a decent judge of 'finger-marks', and Hastings admits he knows that no two fingerprints are alike, but that's as far as his knowledge goes on the topic. Poirot, always the more experienced of the two men, elaborates: 'I will not describe to you the special apparatus, dusting powder etc which I used. It is a well-known process to the police, and by means of it you can obtain a photograph of the fingerprints of any object in a very short space of time.' Poirot, we glean through Agatha's books, was in the Belgian police force before he became a private detective, and it's interesting that he's using the term 'finger-mark' which is exactly what modern fingerprint specialists do today, despite the fact they're more generally known as fingerprints by laymen (Agatha is spot-on here). In the above he's describing the most common use of powder and a brush to make a fingerprint — or fingermark if we're to be technical — visible in order to photograph it. It's the most familiar trope which springs to mind when considering fingerprints: the crime scene examiner or CSE 'dusting for prints' with a large, powdery brush and transferring them onto what looks like sticky tape, a technique used for what are known as **latent prints**.

Latent prints come about from the typical transfer of our skin's secretions and salts, thanks to those extra perspiration pores on finger pads, onto another surface. However, they're not visible to the naked eye and need to be enhanced in some way to make them discernible. There are several ways to go about this depending on which surface the print was left.

One method is the CSE example given above: gently powdering the printed surface with a soft brush made of natural hair or fibreglass. This technique can be used on most non-porous surfaces like window panes, painted or varnished doors and drinking glasses. During Christie's reign as Queen of Crime this is the method which would have commonly been used, albeit with only the option of a natural fibre brush (made from goat, squirrel and even camel hair, or possibly bird feathers). Some investigators still use these natural brushes depending on their preference and what surface the print has been left on. Another possible option is to spray the 'printed' object with ninhydrin, a compound which reacts with the amino acids in the fingerprint secretions to create purple 'dabs' (yet another word for fingerprints used by early crime scene professionals, and indeed mentioned in 1963's *The Clocks*). This ninhydrin compound is often used when the printed surface is porous, such as paper, untreated wood and some fabrics, and the process can show up fingermarks which are up to fifteen years old! Although this sounds like science fiction and might be assumed to be a fairly modern technique, the earliest mention of ninhydrin as a 'valuable reagent for the detection of amino acids' was in 1910 by Siegfried Ruhemann (the shade which ninhydrin turns these latent prints is therefore known as

Ruhemann's Purple), and it was patented for usage on fingerprints in Britain in 1955, with the US and Germany following suit not long after. It's possible Agatha was aware of this technique. In *Mrs McGinty's Dead*, published just three years before ninhydrin was patented, Poirot actually informs a suspect that 'there are new scientific methods of bringing up latent fingerprints'. This may have been a few years before the use of ninhydrin on latent prints was *patented* but it is common with cutting-edge discoveries for news of their development to circulate much earlier, and this innovation is certainly something which we can imagine being discussed at Detection Club meetings.

'Dusting for prints' with powder is a technique Christie refers to in many of her books. Like Poirot, William Henry Blore — who features in *And Then There Were None* — was an ex-police officer. Blore, despite being retired, still carries his fingerprinting kit with him, and powders a suspected murder weapon for fingermarks in the hopes of identifying the murderer who's been whittling down his group one by one. Considering their professional backgrounds, Blore and Poirot would be expected to be familiar with the processes of taking fingerprints.

Perhaps more surprising is that Christie's other famous sleuth — the elderly Miss Marple — seems somewhat of an expert herself, despite never having any criminalistic training. Miss Marple really operates in the opposite way to Poirot, hiding the fact that she has her wits about her rather than lauding her 'little grey cells' at every turn. She has a unique understanding of human nature, and an opinion of people's characters that can often be rather bleak, particularly when contrasted with her gentle demeanour, fluffy white hair, sparkling blue eyes and propensity to knit. But this unintentional disguise is what makes Miss Marple privy to information which may otherwise not be so forthcoming. As she says in the penultimate Marple book, *Nemesis*, 'I'm very ordinary. An ordinary rather scatty old lady. And that of course is very good camouflage.' Miss Marple has always known where her strengths lie, right up to the end of her investigating days.

In an early short story, 'The Tape Measure Murder', published in 1941, a young inspector tells her: 'People don't leave fingerprints and cigarette ash nowadays, Miss Marple.' Maybe this is why, in 'The Case of the Perfect Maid', published a year later, Miss Marple doesn't leave anything to chance when it comes to evidence, and carries out her only forensic investigation. She assumes that a rather suspicious-acting housemaid won't be careless enough to leave her own fingerprints all over a scene for the police to find, and decides to retrieve them herself. She plays on her dithering old lady image and characteristically drops her handbag just as the maid in question is seeing her out of the door. When a half-sucked and unwrapped stick of seaside rock tumbles onto the floor, followed by a pocket mirror, the maid seizes the chance to prove what a wonderful help around the home she is by picking up one, then the other, and handing them to the seemingly grateful old lady. But what she couldn't have guessed is that this sweet rock isn't tacky because a child enjoyed some of it and popped it into Miss Marple's bag, as she apologetically tells the housemaid. It was deliberately placed there by Marple herself, along with the mirror, in the hopes of trapping the maid into depositing sticky prints onto the mirror's shiny surface! Fingermarks that can be deposited in this way are called **patent prints** — i.e. via a substance which makes them apparent and slightly three-dimensional.

The term 'patent' means *lying open*, as in the phrase 'patently obvious', so patent prints are visible to the naked eye, unlike latent prints. The fingermarks many of us may be guilty of leaving visible on stainless steel appliances in the kitchen, however, don't come into this category as those prints are still made of our own natural secretions. Patent prints are clearly visible due to some *additional* substance being transferred by the fingertip such as blood, paint, chocolate, ink, red wine, faeces, or in Miss Marple's case, sticky sweets . . . the list is endless. These can usually be photographed and compared to the known prints without any special retrieval methods being employed.

I wonder if Miss Marple knew them to be called patent prints, or that they could be photographed? Either way, it's no surprise that she is so respected by head of Scotland Yard Sir Henry Clithering, whom she helps catch many a criminal in the twelve books — and numerous short stories — she features in.

The final type of fingerprints — not featured anywhere in Christie's works — are called **plastic or impressed prints**, found where someone has left a 3D imprint of their fingertip in a soft, malleable material like the putty around a window, modelling clay, or candle wax. As with patent prints, they don't need much additional processing in order to make them visible — they can be detected by the naked eye. Fingerprints have even been discovered on chocolate in true crime cases, so be aware that if you pick up the hard toffee from a variety box of chocs and, realising your mistake, put it back in the hopes of swapping it for a softer one — you may get found out if there is a budding CSI in your family. Usually these prints too are captured using photography, with appropriate lighting to make them clearer for the pictures.

All of the above refers to 'prints' and we're using *finger*prints as an example. But of course, this can all apply to palm prints and even heel and toe prints too, although they're not as commonly retrieved from crime scenes. They are just as admissible in court, however, because of their uniqueness, and maybe Agatha Christie predicted this back in 1926? She has Dr Sheppard in *The Murder of Roger Ackroyd* comment, 'If there had been toe marks on the dagger handle, now, that would have been quite a different thing.'

History of Fingerprint Analysis

Historically, the earliest reference to the deliberate, functional use of fingerprints was during the reign of Hammurabi of Babylon, around 1800 BC. Babylonian authors of the time added their prints to cuneiform writing on clay tablets to prevent forgeries, particularly if the writings referred to business transactions like contracts. Babylonia was a state in the historical region of Mesopotamia, an area which Agatha Christie not only visited for archaeological excavations, but also wrote several books about — including, most obviously, *Murder in Mesopotamia*. Whether she knew that her much-loved fingerprints were originally utilised thousands of years previously in a place she frequently called home, I can only speculate, but I do appreciate the surprising connection it creates between her detective fiction and her archaeological interests. In her autobiography, when speaking of how much she enjoys helping her husband Max excavate in Mesopotamia, she says: 'The contract tablets are interesting, throwing light on how you sell yourself into slavery, or the conditions under which you adopt a son,' so there's every chance she saw the very first fingerprints used to identify individuals but perhaps didn't know how this linked to their significance in forensic science. She didn't consider herself to be a 'scientific enough digger' and spent most of her time photographing and cleaning finds, but her husband Max disagreed, saying, 'Don't you realise that at this moment you know more about pre-historic pottery than almost any woman in England.'

Even more relevant than the fingerprint impressions used to sign contract tablets is that the Babylonians also took the fingerprints of *criminals* for identification purposes, illustrating a clear forensic use millennia before various fingerprint bureaux were formed in the Western world. Over the course of the near four thousand years from then to now, the humble fingerprint embarked upon a very interesting journey.

Throughout history, finger- and handprints were predominantly used to represent identity, rather than for the forensic purpose we're familiar with today. In China, from 300 BC, friction ridges of the fingers and palms were used as a form of identification, initially in clay and then as prints in ink. From China, the use of these prints spread to Japan, which had adopted many Chinese practices. When immigrants from China and Japan settled in neighbouring countries the practice of fingerprinting is believed to have travelled with them, reaching as far as India.

It's unsurprising that Agatha Christie makes reference to India in a large proportion of her books, given the country was under controversial British rule from 1858 to 1947. The British Raj is the reason so many of her characters, such as Major Barry in *Evil Under the Sun*, Captain Wyatt in *The Sittaford Mystery* and Sir Henry Angkatell in *The Hollow*, have spent time in India and tend to 'bore people' with accounts of their exploits there. One of these loquacious characters — Major Palgrave from *A Caribbean Mystery* — tells tales of India to anyone who'll listen, including the ever-observant Miss Marple, although she is only partly paying attention on this occasion due to concentrating on her knitting — something she regrets after Palgrave is found dead the next morning. Palgrave says: 'In India, for example, in the bad old days, a young wife who married an old husband. Didn't want to get rid of him, I suppose, because she'd have been burnt on the funeral pyre . . .'

He's describing Suttee — or Sati — a complex and horrifying practice occurring in some parts of India. Suttee dictates that the wife of a deceased male must also die or face disgrace. These women were often immolated, i.e. burned alive on the husband's funeral pyre; sometimes they were buried alive with his corpse. Although it was never a sanctioned funeral custom, it was practised in various places until the mid-nineteenth century and even into the twentieth despite being difficult to comprehend through a Western lens. One aspect of the custom was for these doomed wives to leave a handprint at what is known as a Suttee or Sati gate before they went to their deaths. These gates still remain, covered in handprints, the identities of these women 'writ in stone', a far more harrowing use of prints for purposes of identity. During the contentious British occupation of India, Suttee was often on the rulers' agenda as a 'horrible' and 'cruel' practice, and it was banned by the British in 1829, with the help of Raja Ram Mohan Roy.

Our occupation of India, and the mixture of practices regarding finger- and handprints, brings us to the most pertinent parts of the history of fingerprint usage in the UK. In the 1850s, Sir William James Herschel was working as an Officer in the Indian Civil Service. He may have been using fingerprints to identify individuals but this wasn't exactly his original motivation. On a whim, he had a local businessman impress his palm print onto a contract he'd signed and said the purpose was ' . . . to frighten [him] out of all thought of repudiating his signature'. And it worked on the natives: they were convinced that physical contact with the document made the contract more binding than a signature alone. Eventually Herschel used only the index and middle fingerprints of signatories, but the effect was the same, meaning the first widespread, contemporary use of fingerprints was based on superstition rather than science. That said, the frequency with which Herschel used prints did lead him to examine them more closely. He began to study his own — and others' — fingerprints and documented the results throughout the rest of his lifetime, thereby demonstrating their enduring nature — a significant factor. He is credited with being the first British person to note fingerprints' individuality and, importantly, their permanence.

Concurrently Henry Faulds, a Scottish physician and missionary working in Tokyo, made a fascinating discovery, which set off what would become a twenty-year 'fingerprint feud' in the UK. While visiting an excavation with an American archaeologist friend, Faulds noticed that ancient potters signed their work — after a fashion — by imprinting their finger or thumb marks onto them. After close inspection of the various pottery prints, and then the fingertips of his own hands and those of his friends and even students, he became certain that each pattern was unique and began to study them using a scientific approach. He and his medical students shaved off their finger ridges with razors until no pattern could be traced (please don't try this at home) but the ridges came back. They repeated the experiment, removing the ridges by various different methods, and each time they reappeared in exactly the same pattern.

This happened because Faulds and his students were not causing deep tissue damage to the finger pads during these experiments. Removal of the ridges is a concept that crops up from time to time in fiction. Those of you who've seen the film *Se7en*, in which Kevin Spacey plays a serial killer obsessed with the seven deadly sins, may recall he leaves no fingerprints at his scenes because he shaves them off with a razorblade. It's natural to think at first that this is an ingenious idea and wonder why criminals don't do this in real life. The answer is, *they do* . . . but it's not so ingenious. In *Se7en*, Spacey's character ends up wearing plasters on his constantly bleeding fingertips which begs the question: why not just put plasters over your fingers with the prints intact and save yourself the pain? In real life, razoring off fingerprints was attempted by many criminals during what is known as the public enemy era, in 1930s America. Infamous outlaw and 'public enemy number one' John Dillinger opted to have a German doctor pour hydrochloric acid into cuts in his fingertips in an attempt to erase his prints during what must have been an agonising process. He was eventually shot and killed by Chicago police in 1934, and — despite having had facial surgery to alter his appearance — was immediately identified in the mortuary via his fingerprints! The acid hadn't worked. Interestingly, Dillinger's niece and nephew applied for his body to be exhumed in 2019 for DNA testing, as they believe their uncle was never really killed by the police that day. They cite evidence such as physical attributes of the body in the grave which don't match their uncle's, including ear shape and tooth alignment. As of time of writing, this request for an exhumation has been denied by a judge.

Anyway, back to Henry Faulds and his razor-wielding students. Because he'd amassed so much research on the topic, in 1880 Faulds contacted noted biologist Charles Darwin with the information. Although Darwin declined to work on the topic as he was getting on in years (he died in 1882; eight years before Agatha was born), he passed it on to his half-cousin, the polymath Francis Galton, who would go on to fine-tune Faulds's research. At the same time, Faulds also wrote a letter to the journal *Nature*, entitled 'On the Skin-furrows of the Hand'. In it he documented his discovery of the uniqueness of fingerprints and how they could be classified, how to take fingerprints using printer's ink, and some information on the forensic identification of criminals. He even included a remarkable forecast that fingerprints from mutilated or dismembered corpses might be of forensic significance in identification, and spoke of the necessity of a register or database of criminals and their 'for-ever-unchangeable finger-furrows'.

The very next month, William Herschel inserted himself into the picture when he wrote a response to Faulds's letter in *Nature*, stating that *he'd* been using fingerprints in an official capacity since 1857. He had, of course, but he hadn't mentioned that he began to do so as a way to take advantage of superstitious natives, and he didn't mention their possible forensic use. He now stated he'd been using prints to identify criminals in prison, and he fingerprinted pensioners to avoid pension fraud.

Not one to be deterred, Faulds was heading back to England, in the late 1880s, when he had a brainwave. He contacted Scotland Yard and other major police forces in the UK to persuade them to open a Fingerprint Department using his methods, but he was rejected and it's not clear why. By now Faulds was probably quite tired of being fobbed off and ignored! His comprehensive and informative letter to *Nature* seemed to get little attention apart from that response from Herschel claiming *he* was using fingerprints first, and now this . . . ! He was beginning to feel that fingerprints would never be taken seriously as a form of identification. Ultimately it was the scientific work carried out by Francis Galton, using Faulds's original research, that established some pivotal points about prints which backed up everything Faulds had already claimed. Fingerprints:

1. Persisted indefinitely
2. Were unique to an individual
3. Could easily be classified, stored and matched in large number

But interestingly Galton had his own motivation for working on fingerprints and some may say it was with less altruism in mind than Faulds's proposal. What Galton was trying to do was determine people's ethnicity, heredity and intelligence using fingerprints — a very controversial concept when viewed through modern eyes. He wasn't able to demonstrate that fingerprints could reveal any of those things, but he did note those three important points above. And he was Francis Galton, he was related to Charles Darwin, so it was *his* work which cemented the value of fingerprints for the purpose of criminal identification. In 1892, when Galton published his book *Fingerprints* and began promoting the topic and, for some reason, the work of Herschel as his inspiration, people paid attention. Herschel tried to remedy this by having another letter published in *Nature*, giving full credit to Faulds for his original discovery. This disclaimer went largely unnoticed by readers who by now associated fingerprints with Herschel — and Galton.

Despite all the work Faulds had done on fingerprints, and despite Herschel publicly declaring Faulds had been first, it seemed that the credit would always go to Herschel. Galton also continued on a successful trajectory, publishing two further books on the topic, *Decipherment of Blurred Finger Prints* (1893) and *Fingerprint Directories* (1895).

Soon after, in 1901, a former Inspector-General of Police in Bengal, Edward Henry, returned to England and became Assistant Commissioner at Scotland Yard. He championed the use of fingerprints in a forensic context, explaining that he'd used them in India and had developed a classification system which made their usage much easier. He'd modestly called it 'The

Henry System', and it included the now-familiar set of ten fingerprints on a card, sometimes called a 'ten-print card'. This time the idea of using fingerprints in the criminal justice system was taken very seriously, no doubt aided by the fact that Edward Henry was a friend of — you guessed it! — Francis Galton. The Fingerprint Bureau at Scotland Yard was formed the very same year, and soon after the US and Canada followed suit.

In most historical accounts, credit for the discovery of the forensic use of fingerprints is given to three men: Herschel, Galton and Henry, leaving out Faulds's contribution altogether. He spent many years writing letters to relevant publications explaining he discovered the value of fingerprints first, and that he'd tried to persuade Scotland Yard to open a fingerprint bureau twenty years earlier, but it made no difference. It's no wonder he was embittered by the lack of recognition for his work when he died in March 1930.

* * *

There is always opposition to adopting novel forensic techniques — fingerprinting being no exception — and often this hesitancy comes from a fear of the unknown. However, it can also be based on previous failures: methods which were perhaps used and deemed to be 'infallible' which then fell out of favour or were discredited very publicly. In *The Murder on the Links*, Hercule Poirot refers to 'the publicity the Bertillon system has been given in the press', alluding to an identification system that was overtaken by the accuracy of fingerprinting. It's not the only time that

Christie mentions the previous method, proving once again that she knew her forensic history.

Alphonse Bertillon, the pioneer of this earlier identification system, was a Parisian officer who began working at the Prefecture of Police in 1879. He is known for developing a way to identify individuals using various measurements of the human body. Named after him, it came to be known as Bertillonage, or the Bertillon system, and, most scholars argue, it was the beginning of what we now call biometrics. It was a form of anthropometry — literally meaning 'human measuring' — a term which encompasses other sciences such as auxology, which is the study of human growth, and various pseudo sciences. (One eighteenth-century pseudoscience that many are familiar with, and which comes under this banner, is phrenology, in which specialists claimed to be able to 'read' an individual's personality via the bumps on their head. That fell out of favour in the early nineteenth century, but of course has left a fabulous legacy in the form of those ornamental ceramic heads with a cranial map on the surface.) Bertillon was building on the experimentation and hypotheses of a slightly earlier Italian criminologist called Cesare Lombroso, who believed that a criminal could be identified by their physical characteristics alone. He thought they looked more savage, and had heavier brows and a sloping forehead, amongst many other traits — a theory known as 'atavism'. His work quickly fell out of favour but Agatha was well aware of him and his initial contribution to criminalistics, stating in the short story 'Sing a Song of Sixpence' that a retired Scotland Yard detective was reading Lombroso while sipping excellent black coffee: 'Such ingenious theories,' he thinks to himself, 'but so completely out of date.'

Bertillon, instead, surmised that all people could be differentiated and therefore simply identified by systematically measuring a set of specific body parts and recording the results. *Of course* he thought this was the case: his father was a statistician and his brother, Jacques, also became a famous statistician and demographer — numbers were clearly in the Bertillon blood. It just so happened that the Victorians, who loved to label and categorise, had passed the Prevention of Crimes Act in 1871 which required all criminals in the UK to be kept in some form of register. Also at that time — in the wake of the invention of photography — pictures of offenders were kept at police stations in haphazard 'rogues galleries' all over Europe, pinned up on boards or tossed in drawers. But Alphonse Bertillon was an orderly man who wasn't satisfied with the chaotic methods used to identify the increasing number of captured criminals and he realised there was a need for a more streamlined system. (The description 'orderly' makes me wonder whether Agatha knew this and based a small part of her character Hercule Poirot on Bertillon. He was also described as 'eccentric', as was Poirot.) His solution was to catalogue individuals for identification purposes by focusing on aspects of the human physique which wouldn't particularly change over time, like the distance between the eyes. His system took five large measurements from the body:

1. Head length
2. Head breadth
3. Length of the middle finger
4. Foot length

5. Length of the 'cubit' (the forearm from the elbow to the end of the middle finger)

These were stored, along with a photograph of the person and a note of their eye colour on a document.

As complicated as it was to cross-reference all these details, the Bertillon system was unbelievably beneficial to police agencies. Interestingly, one of the features recorded in the system was ear shape, and it makes me wonder about the previously mentioned John Dillinger: an aspect of the corpse catalogued by his niece and nephew as being inconsistent with 'the real John Dillinger' was the shape of the ear. The reason they had information on the shape of his ear in the first place could have been thanks to Bertillon.

With his system, Bertillon was the first person in history to attempt to collate data which could identify people in an organised way — specifically recidivists. It wasn't until this point in the nineteenth century that any systematic, reliable method of identifying criminals was needed — owing to the population increase — and for a while the Bertillon method addressed that need. But the incredible American case of William West and Will West eventually cast a shadow over the system entirely.

In Kansas, in 1903, a man called Will West was convicted of a minor crime and sent to Leavenworth Penitentiary. However, when he arrived there, he was informed that he was *already imprisoned there*, having been convicted of manslaughter and incarcerated two years previously. 'But I didn't do that!' exclaimed Will West, to which the records clerk probably thought 'Like I haven't heard that one before . . . ' Of course, the clerk then realised that if Will West was already in prison, serving a life sentence, he couldn't be standing in front of him being readmitted to jail. On closer inspection, it was discovered that there *was* already a William West in prison there, and it wasn't just the name that was strikingly similar — all of the Bertillon measurements were identical and the faces were like those of identical twins — and yet the men were not known to be related:

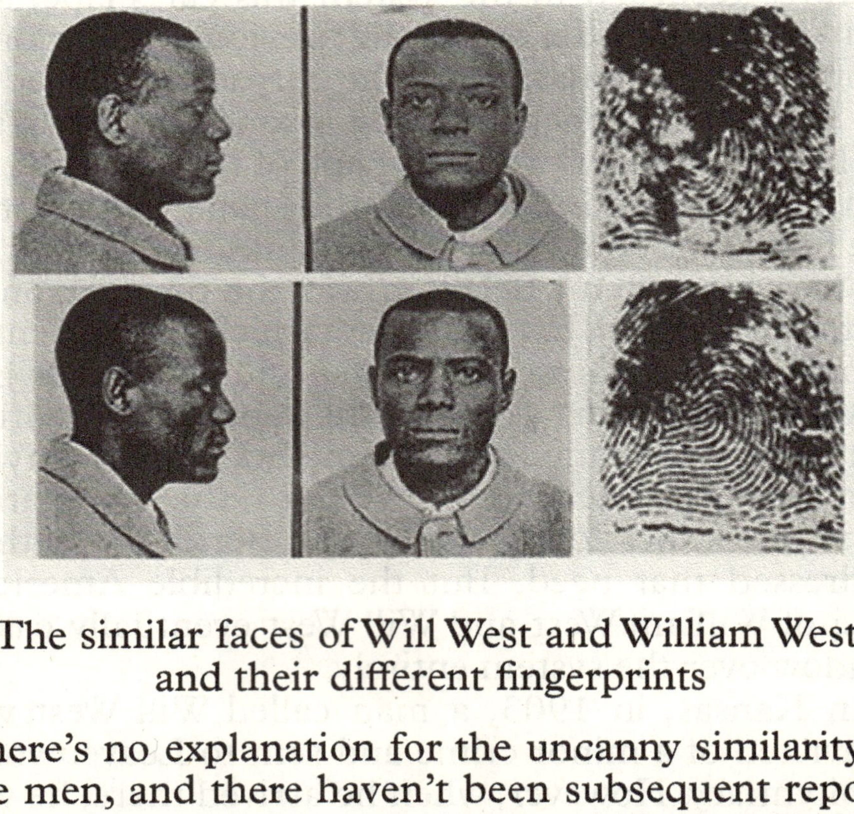

The similar faces of Will West and William West, and their different fingerprints

There's no explanation for the uncanny similarity of the men, and there haven't been subsequent reports of similar cases, although they would be less likely to be recorded after this date because the Bertillon System very quickly stopped being used in its entirety. However, Bertillon had been using fingerprints in newer versions of his system, working in fact with the forensic pioneer Edmond Locard, so the two 'Will'

Wests in Kansas had their prints taken and these were shown to be different. From that point on there was no real need to use the complicated Bertillon system of measurements, when fingerprints alone would suffice, and the rest of the system of measuring and recording was dropped (and I'm sure the police were thankful for the streamlining).

Despite the system proving fallible, Bertillon deserves an honourable mention and still enters the Forensic Science Hall of Fame. His other notable criminalistic work included handwriting analysis, footprint preservation and ballistics. His pioneering use of photography at crime scenes led to a forensic specialism in itself: that of Crime Scene Photography. Finally, the particular format he chose for the photographs in his Bertillon System documents involved two pictures of the head: one face on and one side on, as illustrated by the image of Will and William West. This was, as we now know it, the mug shot, and it too is still very much in use today.

* * *

It often takes just one sensational or extraordinary murder story to propel a forensic science into the mainstream and grease the wheels of acceptance by the judicial system and the public at large, particularly if there has initially been some scepticism about the technique. This would have been how Agatha Christie frequently learned of the various developments in criminalistics. In the case of fingerprints, this honour goes to the Farrow Murders, also known as the Deptford Murders, in 1905.

Early on a Monday — 27 March — sixteen-year-old William Jones headed to his work at a paint shop on Deptford High Street, London. Chapman's Oil and Colour Shop was managed by Thomas Farrow and his wife Ann — who lived in the flat above — and usually opened around 7.30 a.m., although William didn't need to start work until 8.30 a.m. On his arrival that particular morning he was quite surprised to see that the store's shutters were still closed. He knocked and received no response. Given that William's boss and his wife were seventy-one and sixty-five respectively, William worried that perhaps one or both of them had been taken ill. Unable to gain access he peered through the window to see that furniture inside had been tipped over and, feeling increasingly uneasy, he called a friend to help him break down the door. Together they discovered Thomas's body lying beneath an overturned chair, his head smashed open. Blood had seeped into the carpet and over the ashes in the fire, and the boys were fairly certain he was dead. At this horrific tableau they called the police, correctly assuming that they shouldn't wander through the house in case it was a crime scene. It was the first policeman to respond who then found Thomas's wife Ann upstairs in bed, also brutally beaten, and clinging on to life by a thread.

The motive for these vicious attacks appeared to be gaining access to a moneybox that was lying empty on the floor, which William Jones informed the police usually contained around £10 (the equivalent in modern money is £1,200), the shop's weekly takings, which should have been deposited in the bank by Thomas Farrow that morning.

Head of CID Melville Macnaghten was put in charge of the case and he was determined to solve it. After picking up the moneybox with his handkerchief — remember, crime scene kits containing gloves did not yet exist — Macnaghten noticed what appeared to be a fingerprint on the bottom of the coin tray. He wrapped the whole thing in paper and took it to the fledgling Fingerprint Bureau at Scotland Yard, which had recently been set up by Edward Henry. (At this point it really hits you that a fledgling fingerprint bureau had been established a few years previously, yet the idea of providing investigators with gloves — so they wouldn't deposit their *own* prints at a crime scene — wouldn't come for another twenty years!) Despite the fact that a burglary had been solved using prints three years before, there was still some suspicion about them, and their usage had, as Val McDermid notes in her excellent book *Forensics: The Anatomy of Crime*, 'the taint of palmistry about it'. In this case, the bloody print turned out to be an intact thumb print . . . What luck! A complete print which matched neither the boys who'd discovered the bodies, nor the Farrows, nor the police at the scene. So whose was it . . . ?

With the criminal fingerprint databases the police have built up over the last century it's difficult for us to imagine a time when that wasn't the norm. But in 1905, when the use of fingerprints was just gaining momentum, the selection the police had on file was sparse by today's standards — though it did already contain those of around 90,000 individuals, a huge number considering they existed as physical tenprint cards which would have to be manually searched and compared, using a magnifying glass. However, collecting a print from a crime scene is of no use unless there is a suspect to collect an *exemplar* print from in order to compare it — something Agatha knew only too well. To quote Detective Inspector Hardcastle in *The Clocks*, 'We sent up his fingerprints to see if he's got a record of any kind. If he has, it'll be a big step on the way.'

Unfortunately, in the Deptford case, Ann Farrow was unable to give the police a description of who had attacked her because she died of her brutal injuries without regaining consciousness. However, there were witnesses who came forward to identify possible perpetrators of this horrendous crime. Onlookers described two men either in the vicinity of, or actually exiting, the Farrows' paint shop: one in a brown suit and cap, the other wearing a blue suit and bowler hat and sporting a moustache.

In all cases, the descriptions pointed the police in the particular direction of two brothers, Alfred and Albert Stratton.

The Stratton brothers were swiftly tracked down and fingerprinted as the main suspects in the murders, and the print on the moneybox was found to match that of Alfred Stratton's right thumb. This was novel evidence to present to a jury of laymen and could have seemed confusing or too scientific, but the prosecution adopted the approach of using blown-up photographs of the prints from the crime scene, of the sort we previously saw Inspector Raglan studying in *The Murder of Roger Ackroyd*. The technique when used in the courtroom of the Stratton case was similarly successful; perhaps this innovative and highly publicised judicial demonstration is what inspired Agatha to include enlarged photographs in her book. The jury could see for themselves the uniqueness of all the prints, and also see the twelve points of similarity between the print retrieved from the moneybox and the exemplar from Alfred Stratton. It mesmerised them. Just nineteen days later, on 23 May 1905, both Stratton brothers were simultaneously swinging from the gallows at Wandsworth Prison in south London.

The Murder of Roger Ackroyd was Agatha's third Hercule Poirot novel, and was published in 1926, by which time the notion of collecting fingerprints at a crime scene was fully established — particularly among those who were well read. In a humorous passage at the scene of Ackroyd's death, Inspector Davis attempts to impress Dr Sheppard with what he believes is a bombshell of forensic knowledge, telling Sheppard that he can clearly see fingerprints on the murder weapon despite them not being apparent to the layman.

Dr Sheppard responds to the Inspector's patronising manner with a scathing inner monologue: 'I do not see why I should be supposed to be totally devoid of intelligence. After all, I read detective stories and the newspapers, and am a man of quite average ability.' Dr Sheppard knows that fingerprints on a dagger handle at the scene of a stabbing are to be expected, and anyone with a rudimentary understanding of crime investigation would know it, even — as Poirot muses in *Mrs McGinty's Dead* — a 'moron'.

With fingerprints now such a well-known tool in the detective's arsenal, Christie's characters in *The Murder of Roger Ackroyd* 'take matters into their own hands' as it were, and empower themselves by fingerprinting themselves or other people. The cheeky-chappy secretary of the deceased Roger Ackroyd, Geoffrey Raymond, adopts a do-it-yourself approach to being fingerprinted. Knowing it is inevitable that he will be asked to provide his prints, ostensibly for 'exclusionary reasons', he speeds up the process by taking them himself. He says, 'Shall we oblige Inspector Davis with a set of our fingerprints also?' and we are told:

> He took two cards from the card tray, wiped them with his silk handkerchief, then handed one to me and took the other himself. Then, with a grin, he handed them to the police inspector.

Although the cards aren't described, I could hazard a guess that they perhaps had a shiny surface, for several reasons. Firstly, he wiped them with a silk handkerchief which would imply the surface is wipeable to start with, and that there were other possible prints to wipe off. We know that to take prints like this without the aid of ink or any other substance will provide us with *latent* exemplars, which criminalists at the time couldn't process very well on a porous surface as the use of ninhydrin to develop them was still in its infancy in 1926.

Raymond isn't the only character in a Christie book to take it upon themselves to carry out latent fingerprint retrieval, and there's a very similar example from 'The Jewel Robbery at the Grand Metropolitan' published just a few years before *The Murder of Roger Ackroyd.* In this short story, it's Poirot himself who carries out the ruse when he hands a card to a possible jewel thief under false pretences. The suspect — a maid — falls into the trap, taking the highly glazed card as Poirot asks innocently if she has ever seen it before among the effects of her employer, Mr Opalsen. She says she hasn't, and hands it back to Poirot.

He then repeats the process on a second suspect, and after Hastings enquires about it, he admits:

'*Une blague!* The card was one with a specially prepared surface — for finger-prints. I went straight to Scotland Yard . . . As I had suspected the finger-prints turned out to be those of two well-known jewel thieves who have been 'wanted' for some time.'

It makes absolute sense that Poirot would take these fingerprints to Scotland Yard from our point of view in the twenty-first century (although I'm told by current fingerprint examiners he would be in a lot of trouble for obtaining them this way!), but at this stage the fingerprint department at the Yard, which Poirot mentions, had only been in existence for two decades. Poirot *could* wait for the criminals to be found and fingerprinted in the usual manner, but this way he gets to be one step ahead — which is very much where he always is, much to Hastings's frustration.

This is an example of Hercule Poirot being rather crafty in his detection methods, and it's interesting to witness this sneaky behaviour. After all, he often prides himself on his openness, telling Hastings that he conceals nothing from him, 'You have all the facts. Everything I know, *you* know.' But there are times when the original, functional ex-police aspect of Poirot comes to the fore instead, and his approach is 'no-nonsense'.

He searches for fingerprints in a more overt way in *Murder on the Orient Express*, for example, which has a darker and more serious tone than *The Murder of Roger Ackroyd*. After the titular murder of the American passenger Mr Ratchett, we're told that Poirot examined the frame of a window on the train carefully. He then took a small case of fingerprinting powder from his pocket and blew it over the frame, noting there were no fingerprints at all. He surmises that the frame has been wiped.

Then he repeats this trick, or a variation of it, while on holiday again in *Appointment with Death*. Although this time I'm not going to tell you whose prints, or where he sends them, as it will give away the ending! In these 1930s novels, we see more of Hercule Poirot 'criminalist' rather than Hercule Poirot 'criminologist', as he retrieves forensic evidence *himself* — something he seems to look on with derision in later novels. In these earlier examples, it could simply be that Christie was paying far more homage to Arthur Conan Doyle before developing Poirot as a character unto himself: she acknowledges this in her autobiography, talking about how steeped she was in that world at the time. Or perhaps Poirot's memories of being in the police force are rather fresher in the earlier books, and therefore his instinct to look for typical forensic evidence slightly harder to shake. Otherwise why on earth is he carrying fingerprinting powder with him on his holidays? Either way, it's important to note that the development of Poirot is not linear and he often contradicts himself as we go through Agatha's canon. Sometimes he relies on the physical evidence, sometimes on what he calls 'the psychology', and sometimes a mixture of both.

* * *

Fingerprints are important at crime scenes, and we've seen that Agatha's detectives — both professional and amateur — knew that. But does that mean that a lack of fingerprints at a scene is something every investigator dreads? *Not necessarily*. Agatha Christie was aware of an important principle of forensic science that we perhaps take for granted: the absence of certain evidence — such as fingerprints — can tell us just as much as their presence. Often, a lack of fingerprints simply means an object has been wiped — which in many circumstances makes sense. It's something that we're rather more used to as an idea now, but given that the use of fingerprinting was still in its infancy Agatha made vast leaps in understanding their importance very quickly, and she uses this absence of fingerprints in many of her novels to indicate a killer with more knowledge than your average homicidal maniac. In *The ABC Murders*, Hercule Poirot is certainly *not* dealing with your average homicidal maniac, but a rather complex set-up in which someone is trying to appear as one. (Interestingly, it was fellow Detection Club Member and writer of the Father Brown whodunnits, G. K. Chesterton, who gave Agatha the seed of an idea for the ABC murders). The types of evidence expected in serial killer cases — 'calling cards', organisation and consistency in method, for example — are all evident in the book. Poirot ends a conversation with Hastings by discussing some physical evidence left at a murder scene which had also been left at several others, indicating some significance: the ABC train timetable. Hastings wonders if it has been dropped, but Poirot points out the lack of fingerprints.

> 'What was yesterday evening? A warm June night. Does a man stroll about on such an evening in *gloves*? Such a man would certainly have attracted attention. Therefore since there

are no fingerprints on the ABC, it must have been carefully wiped.'

There are many ways to avoid fingerprint detection. Yes, you can wipe them off, but in truth it's better to wear gloves to avoid adding your own prints to any existing ones. Agatha doesn't shy away from giving quite specific reasons as to when a murderer would have been wearing gloves, and several of her murderers boast of this themselves: 'I'd got gloves on, so I knew I hadn't left any fingerprints' in *Mrs McGinty's Dead*, for example. But a keen investigator who can think outside the box may see something important in these absences.

Crooked House is a novel Agatha usually cites as her favourite. With well-drawn characters, misdirection aplenty and a shocking conclusion it's not surprising Agatha described it as 'pure pleasure' to write.

The patriarch of the titular 'crooked' house, Aristide Leonides, is killed when his eye drops — which contain the toxic substance eserine — are injected into his bloodstream instead of his insulin. Given that his eyesight is clearly bad, which is why he needs eye drops, there's a chance he may have done it himself by mistake — I once squirted ibuprofen gel into a bolognese sauce thinking it was tomato puree, because the tubes were similar and I carelessly kept them both in the same fridge drawer! Or perhaps someone else did it erroneously because they weren't paying attention? Accidents do happen, after all. But the murderer makes an error in choosing to wipe *all* the fingerprints off the bottle, rather than wear gloves:

'We have found the eye drop bottle, empty — in the dustbin, with no fingerprints on it. That in itself is curious. In the normal way there should have been fingerprints.'

Now the investigators know the switch between the insulin and the eye drops was done deliberately, because accidental handling would cause any prints to remain. A murderer tried to avoid detection, and made a very basic mistake in doing so. This illustrates that it doesn't always pay to wipe an item completely clean of fingerprints when committing a crime, as that draws attention to their absence: something Agatha repeated time and again in her books.

But what if the lack of fingerprints is a double-bluff? In some of Agatha's books she goes so far as to trick us — and Poirot — using this method. In the novella 'Murder in the Mews', Poirot is faced with the case of a woman who was found dead by her roommate, Miss Jane Plenderleith, on her return from some time in the country. The case is more complicated than perhaps it first seems: a suicide which could have been a murder staged to look like a suicide, but could just as easily have been a suicide someone staged to look like a murder. (I know, it's very complicated!)

'What about fingerprints, by the way?'

'Well, it's murder all right. No prints whatever on the pistol. Wiped clean before being placed in her hand. She could hardly fire off a pistol without hanging on to it and she couldn't wipe it after she was dead . . . '

A character would need to be clever, and very familiar with forensic evidence, to manufacture a murder from a suicide. They'd be one step ahead of the investigators, knowing what they would be looking for at both types of scene and subverting the evidence available.

As Poirot points out in this short story, a person couldn't wipe their fingerprints off a pistol if they were dead. But could someone else? Is there someone clever enough to outwit Poirot's little grey cells in 'Murder on the Mews'? You'll have to read for yourself and find out.

But fingerprints at a scene aren't always a gift horse to investigators either. If there *are* fingerprints but they're *too* obvious they may be suspicious, and send detectives on a different investigative path. This is the case in *Towards Zero*, and it seems the examining doctor is a little wary of evidence which is too obvious, becoming rather satisfyingly sarcastic:

> 'Lovely set of prints on that club,' he said. 'Clear as anything. Left the weapon — left his fingerprints on it — a wonder he didn't leave his visiting card!'

Or perhaps, sometimes, it's the placement of the prints which makes them a little suspect, such as those on a beer bottle in *Five Little Pigs*:

> And what she must have done was to wipe the bottle and glass and then press his fingers on them Well, that didn't work . . . proved quite definitely by demonstration in court that a man couldn't hold a bottle with his fingers in that position!'

All of these different uses of fingerprints show that Agatha's understanding of their analysis is developing over time and she is becoming more creative with the way she deploys them.

In *The Murder on the Links* Poirot says, ' . . . it interests me very much that there were no fingerprints. It is so amazingly simple to leave the fingerprints of someone else.' But is it so amazingly simple? Perhaps in certain circumstances. In one of Agatha's books from the 1940s, which I'm not going to name so as to avoid spoilers, a completely uninvolved party's fingerprints were placed on an item in a rather ingenious way, which led investigators on a wild goose chase. Poirot discusses this with the culprit towards the end as he's not quite sure how it was done: 'But the fingerprints — how did you manage the fingerprints?' he asks, and the answer? 'An old blind man who sells matches in the street '

But in the absence of a convenient local blind man, is it possible to 'plant' someone's fingerprints; can you take a print off someone with tape, say, and use it elsewhere? Or can you use a lifted print to open, for example, a mobile phone with fingerprint access? The answer is *yes* — and *no*: in the case of using a print to fool a scanner, it depends on the type of scanner. There are two main models and the earlier ones — the optical scanners — simply used sensors to measure the change in light between the ridges and furrows. Because they're simply 'looking and recording' they can even be fooled with photographs of prints and are easily hacked. The more modern types, however, work on electrical conductance, which means they recognise the pattern of the fingerprints via the minuscule amounts of electricity given off as the ridges make contact with the sensors — the ridges being the part which protrude from the finger pads. Without this electricity which all living creatures possess, it won't work. So, a print lifted with a piece of tape, or the finger of the deceased (whether at this point it's attached to the corpse or is some sort of 'skin thimble') lacks this electricity, and the sensor won't register it. If you're thinking of breaking into a high security facility which has a sensitive fingerprint recognition system, think again . . . !

Perhaps it's much easier just to lie about the presence of fingerprints, and plant imaginary ones as bait. In *Death in the Clouds*, Poirot is rewarded with a dramatic slip of the tongue from the murderer when, after a long and heated exchange, he manipulatively suggests carelessness on the suspect's part by suggesting fingerprints were left on a bottle of poisonous prussic acid. The murderer can't help but exclaim that it can't be possible as gloves had been worn.

Poirot's suspicions are therefore confirmed because the murderer is so conceited, they couldn't bear to be told they'd made a mistake.

Poirot uses the same risky method in *The ABC Murders* a year later, presumably because it was so successful the last time! He tells a suspect they'd left a print on a typewriter which had been used to write some goading letters about the ABC killings, containing details only the ABC killer would know. Faced with this 'evidence' the suspect breaks down and confesses, despite the fact they don't really have any memory of carrying the murders out. But surely they *must* have done, especially if they're being told they left a fingerprint on the typewriter in question . . . When they believe the case is solved, Hastings naively — and gratefully — says, 'That fingerprint clinched things, Poirot!' to which Poirot evasively replies, 'Yes, they are useful fingerprints . . . '

They certainly are, whether they're there or not!

The misuse of fingerprints and the fact they can be planted, moved or removed entirely makes their placement at a crime scene far more complicated than might initially be assumed. In only her second book, *The Murder on the Links*, Agatha writes the following exchange:

> 'A fingerprint has led sometimes to the arrest and conviction of a murderer,' said Hastings.
>
> 'And has, without doubt, hanged more than one innocent man,' remarked Poirot dryly.

This demonstrates that Agatha is already familiar enough with the use of fingerprints to understand their fallibility. Let's not forget that at the time of Agatha's writing, the punishment for murder was frequently hanging, and this continued up until 1965, only about a decade before Agatha's death. A fingerprint alone at a crime scene shouldn't really be used to convict someone without other evidence, because the chances of fingerprint evidence proving erroneous are too great, and in the days of the death penalty a wrongful conviction for murder had an irreversible consequence. In *The ABC Murders* one character was nearly hanged for this very reason. I won't explain how this was came about as it will spoil the story, but let's just say it's a very good job that Hercule Poirot was on the case.

* * *

Christie *knows* fingerprints. She illustrates her understanding of their value at crime scenes, keeps up to date with scientific developments and shares that knowledge via crafty characters in her books, even creating fingerprints which aren't there, to coerce suspects into confessing. When they *are* there, they can incriminate the guilty . . . but Agatha also uses them to incriminate the innocent; their mere presence pointing the finger — literally — at the wrong person. She knows enough about fingerprint evidence to reclassify it as a weapon in certain circumstances.

But fingerprints are just one weapon in the forensic arsenal. Another is perhaps not something we leave behind at a scene from direct contact; something we have some control over by wiping items or wearing gloves. Instead, it's traces of ourselves which we may leave behind entirely without our knowledge.

2

Trace Evidence

> Hastings: 'I meant *little* things — traces that may lead us infallibly to the murderers.'
> Poirot: 'Mon ami, a clue of two feet long is every bit as valuable as one measuring two millimetres! But it is the romantic idea that all important clues must be infinitesimal'
>
> —*The Murder on the Links*

In the above quote from 1923, Hercule Poirot is typically perceptive — and melodramatic! — when lamenting the desire that most laymen have for crimes to be solved via minuscule clues. Whether within fact or fiction, it can be thrilling and satisfying to the audience to learn about an offence which would have gone unsolved if not for an unusually astute investigator happening upon a hair from an exotic animal, or a specific brand of cigarette, or a tiny piece of sand from a particular beach. Much of this reader expectation comes from earlier detectives like Sherlock Holmes, who we know inspired Christie, and in her autobiography she mentions this when discussing *The Murder on the Links*. She says, 'I was still writing in the Sherlock Holmes tradition — eccentric detective, stooge assistant, with a Lestrade-type Scotland Yard detective, Inspector

Japp,' so we can assume much of her knowledge of trace evidence came from Conan Doyle. The first mention of Sherlock's expertise on the subject of tobacco ash is in Conan Doyle's first full novel, *A Study in Scarlet* from 1887, and this knowledge is referred to several times elsewhere in the canon. In the short story 'The Boscombe Valley Mystery', Sherlock says, 'I have, as you know, devoted some attention to this, and written a little monograph on the ashes of 140 different varieties of pipe, cigar, and cigarette tobacco.' The suggestion is that this particular minute clue is often the one which helps him solve the cases. *The Hound of the Baskervilles*, *The Valley of Fear* and 'The Adventure of the Resident Patient' all contain crucial tobacco evidence as well.

Christie was initially inspired by Conan Doyle's fiction, and Conan Doyle was in turn influenced by a real Scottish doctor called Joseph Bell, so Agatha was indeed learning about the science of trace evidence that was burgeoning at the time. She was later inspired further by Conan Doyle's real-life methods, such as the formation of a members' only club to discuss crimes of the day, so it's fair to say she paid homage to both Conan Doyle and Bell, and to both fact and fiction, when she amassed the forensic knowledge she would go on to use in her work.

It is not only Christie whose characters and stories have been influenced by Sherlock Holmes: more recently we see this kind of impressive encyclopaedic knowledge of seemingly unimportant minutiae in Gil Grissom from the TV show *CSI*, the implication being that any detective worth his salt can tell you off-hand what a perpetrator smoked, where he walked, what pets he had, where he bought his carpets and much,

much more. Frequently this is how a case *is* solved in detective fiction — because it's exciting! Usually within the plot there are clues and red herrings, and it's the reader's job to try and pick out those tiny details which are relevant to solving the whole puzzle. Often the smaller, the better. Perhaps that's because it suggests we need to look harder and pay closer attention. Or perhaps it's because those minuscule clues are more likely to adhere to scenes and suspects without anyone noticing . . . except the very best detectives, and the most astute reader.

Of course, Hercule Poirot really *is* the best, certainly in his own mind, and also in Agatha Christie's world if his track record is anything to go by. Hastings says in 'The Adventure of the Italian Nobleman': 'Poirot *was* right. He always is, confound him!' and Poirot is indeed constantly, quietly, getting the better of his often confused sidekick Hastings.

What is it that makes Poirot such a fantastic detective? He attributes it to his astonishing brain power — his 'little grey cells' — and prides himself on approaching every case using order and method: 'Method and order, they are everything.' When describing a lecture given by Angela Warren in Christie's book *Five Little Pigs*, Poirot lauds her intelligent deduction from the facts. According to Christie, 'The soul of Hercule Poirot approved. Here, he considered, was an orderly mind.' Poirot is very particular and perhaps a little obsessive about his surroundings: he straightens pictures which are hanging crooked, prefers angular 'modern' furniture as it's more streamlined, and is offended by the fact that chickens don't lay their eggs in exactly the same sizes: he'd actually prefer them to be square. In fact, in *Hickory Dickory Dock*, the final book of Agatha's loosely based 'nursery rhyme' series, we are told he lunches on square crumpets and a square cake, which are presumably hard to come by! Doubtless his equally orderly and efficient secretary, Miss Lemon, made them or sourced them for her rather fastidious employer. He's described as excessively neat, and his senses are assaulted by anything seemingly out of place: an 'imaginary' speck of dust on his suit or a hair in his moustache which is imperceptibly longer than the others — imperceptible, that is, to anyone but him. Presumably, then, this means he has a good eye and appreciation for trace evidence? We may well be wrong to presume. Poirot ostensibly takes a very superior attitude towards trace and what he might call 'typical' evidence. In *Lord Edgware Dies*, a 1930s mystery, he explains to Hastings: 'You wish me to measure footprints, to analyse cigarette ash, to prostrate myself on my stomach for the examination of detail. You never realise that by lying back in an armchair with the eyes closed one can come nearer to the solution of any problem. One sees then with the eyes of the mind.' This is Poirot the criminologist talking rather than Poirot the criminalist — but he does tend to flip between one and the other at will, as we shall see . . .

* * *

We've already met early criminalist Edmond Locard and his basic tenet of forensic science — 'every contact leaves a trace' — and there is certainly no more relevant subject than trace evidence to illustrate the principle, particularly because he was referring to small, fragmentary clues. A passage from a 1953 book by Paul Leland Kirk expresses the importance of this evidence beautifully:

> Wherever he steps, whatever he touches, whatever he leaves, even unconsciously, will serve as a silent witness against him. Not only his fingerprints or his footprints, but his hair, the fibres from his clothes, the glass he breaks, the tool mark he leaves, the paint he scratches, the blood or semen he deposits or collects . . . It is factual evidence.

Kirk does, however, go on to explain that physical evidence is seldom wrong, it's in fact human failure which can diminish its value.

It does seem as though Hastings, in general, is particularly preoccupied with this factual trace evidence, whereas Poirot — rather surprisingly, given his personality — is not. In *The ABC Murders* when Hastings complains of the killer, 'If only he had left some clue!' Poirot is quick to criticise this train of thought:

> 'Yes, the clue — it is always the clue that attracts you. Alas that he did not smoke the cigarette and leave the ash, and then step in it with a shoe that has nails of a curious pattern! No — he is not so obliging.'

Trace evidence links suspects, places and things. It may be much to Poirot's chagrin, but often in real-life forensic cases it is the only evidence that legal teams have at first. Because of that, I'm going to legitimately satisfy poor Hastings and his desire for physical clues by delving into the fascinating world of the *little* things which help to solve murders — and on this occasion I don't mean Poirot's little grey cells.

What is Trace Evidence Analysis?

When we hear Locard's principle 'every contact leaves a trace', it is more than likely *trace evidence* that we think of specifically. The phrase puts us in mind of specialists squinting over powerful microscopes to analyse minute fibres, delicate hairs, powdery glass fragments or flecks of paint. This type of evidence can be defined as that which is 'usually too small to be seen with the naked eye' and can include hair, fibres, glass, paint chips, dirt, plant material such as pollen — basically any *very small* physical material which can be transferred from person to person, or between a person and a crime scene. It's perhaps the 'smallness' of these clues which gives them more credence. In *Lord Edgware Dies*, Poirot bemoans the desire people often have for this very small physical evidence, at the same time referencing the *Murder on the Links* case from ten years earlier. He says, 'I found a clue once, but since it was four feet long instead of four centimetres no-one would believe it.'

The term 'very small' is relative, and here it depends on the era or decade in question. For our purposes, a trace examiner in a Christie story (as opposed to a modern-day investigator employed to collect or examine trace) could simply use a hand-lens or magnifying glass, which can enlarge an object to x10 — a favourite tactic of Miss Marple. However, the invention and subsequent commercial availability of the Scanning Electron Microscope (SEM), from 1965 onwards, changed the face of *all* sciences, not just those of a forensic nature. Owing to a completely different mechanism from that of the microscopes used during Christie's time the SEM can magnify objects to a whopping x500,000, effectively redefining trace evidence. As ultra-modern as that sort of magnification sounds, trace evidence analysis can be — ahem — *traced* back to a time when medicolegal specialists had to work with slightly more substantial detritus, and during Christie's literary golden era less powerful microscopes would have been used for examination. Because of this I'll describe trace evidence — 'trace' for short — as that which can be *seen* by the naked eye, but perhaps not adequately examined; and in addition doesn't really fit into other categories. Examples might be hair; carpet or rug fibres; cigarette ash; fragments of fabric; fingernails; pieces of glass; paint chips; and soil, dirt or vegetation. They're items which generally don't need to be highly magnified to have some significance in these stories, or the crimes in Agatha's contemporary newspapers. Some interesting examples from research at the time even include earwax as trace! Longshoremen who'd been unloading coals the previous year had their earwax studied and it was found to contain coal particles despite the amount of time that had passed. The same was found to be true of other workers: coffee-roasters had coffee particles in their earwax despite leaving their occupation some time before, and more gruesomely the earwax of barbers contained small traces of other people's hair.

Conveniently, in the Christie books these clues are also frequently grouped together when referred to by the characters. 'Don't policemen look for clues? Cigarette ash, footprints, burnt matches?' asks Henrietta in *The Hollow*. (Earwax isn't mentioned in any of Agatha's books as it was relatively specialised knowledge, so we can happily leave that out!)

In a way trace evidence can still be generalised like this. Now, just as in Christie's era, many types of trace are initially examined in the same way: via the naked eye and with a magnifying glass under appropriate lighting. The lighting can be angled around the specimen to bring out details by creating depth and shadow. It's a bit like using the 'contrast' Instagram filter on a picture of yourself: slide the control one way and those under-eye bags look more like suitcases; but slide it the other way and — behold! — they disappear. Once this inspection has taken place, the specimen, and any particular areas of interest which have been identified with this cursory examination, is studied in detail under further magnification.

There are several types of microscopes currently used, and most are based on the one we're probably all familiar with: the optical microscope. It has a lens which magnifies the specimen after it's placed on a focal plate, and an attached light will usually help the examiner see the item better.

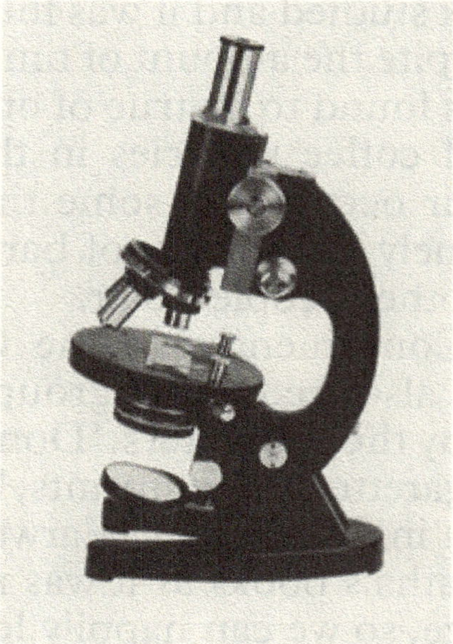

A photograph of a basic microscope as used in Christie's era

This microscope type is what Christie-era criminalists would have used to examine trace evidence, but we will come briefly across other kinds — such as the SEM mentioned above, and comparison microscopes — as we discuss the sciences.

Collection methods too have moved on since the golden era. Back then, many types of trace evidence might have been lifted using sticky tape, in the same way that fingerprints were, but this isn't the case now. As our modern analytical tests have become more refined and able to detect negligible amounts of chemicals — which can help to identify the origin of the trace in question — preferred practice is to use manual collection methods such as tweezers and forceps (which are very finely pointed tweezers), or even special vacuums dedicated to the task. The sticky residue from adhesive tape can contaminate present-day trace evidence so the only type of lift used now is a 'static lift', in which static electricity rather than adhesive attracts the trace material to a piece of acetate. It's just as effective — we've all seen the detritus that can collect on an inflated balloon due to static, after it's been floating around a room for a while!

So, what is trace evidence analysis and how does it appear in Agatha's stories?

Hair

In *The Mystery of the Blue Train*, Poirot confides in his travelling companion, Katherine Grey, while showing her an item he'd collected:

'Do you remember, Mademoiselle? You saw me take these hairs from the rug in the railway carriage.'

Katherine leant forward, scrutinising the hairs keenly.

Poirot nodded his head slowly several times.

'They suggest nothing to you, I see that, Mademoiselle. And yet — I think somehow that you see a good deal.'

Neither Katherine nor Poirot reveal what they are 'seeing' and we move on to the next chapter, but Poirot is right that hair evidence is incredibly useful and there certainly is a lot to see when you know what to look for.

Hairs are found absolutely everywhere and if you're anything like me and have dyed your hair unusual colours, you're a trace examiner's dream. (Conversely, I'm my husband's *nightmare!* He hates pulling clumps of red, or peach, or orange hair out of the plughole in the shower, and it's not as though I can pretend they're not mine.)

Bearing in mind that animal hair differs from that of a human; and that human hair itself differs on any individual according to where it's come from on the body, there are particular characteristics which experts look for when trying to identify the origin of a hair or determine a match. These physical characteristics derive from the structure of hair, which is loosely like that of a pencil: each hair has a central *medulla* which would be the graphite lead of the pencil; a *cortex* which would be the wood of the pencil's main body, and an outer *cuticle* which is like the paint layer. There are aspects of each feature which are used by experts to identify a hair and/or match it to an unknown exemplar:

Medulla — The medulla, the core of a hair, has a couple of important features for forensic purposes. First, the medullary index — the medulla's width as a proportion of the total width of the hair — in most mammals is around 0.5. (This may sound complicated but all it means is that the medulla makes up half the thickness of the hair:
0.5 is 50 per cent.) In humans, however, the medulla is particularly narrow, with an index of around 0.3 — that is, about one third of the overall thickness of the hair — which allows human hair to be distinguished quite easily from that of an animal. This thin component of the hair is what resembles a pencil's lead.
Second, the medulla contains cells, the distribution and fragmentation of which also help to determine which species the hair came from.

Cortex — This layer, surrounding the medulla, is the largest part of the hair (in terms of mass) and is like the wood of a pencil surrounding the lead. It contains the pigment which gives hair its colour. You might picture it in cross-section as the coloured iris of an eye surrounding the pupil. Pigment particles are incredibly varied, which is why we and other mammals have so many hair colours, and their variety — shape, hue, distribution — is what enables examiners to use them for identification purposes.

Cuticle — The cuticle is likely to be the part of the hair most people are familiar with, as it's often referred to in commercials for hair products. 'Reduces frizz by smoothing the cuticle layer' is a typical claim. In reality the cuticle is a layer of cells which protect the rest of the hair by covering the entire hair shaft like fish scales, pointing away from the root down to the tip (hence blow-drying hair in that direction flattens them, to give an exquisite shine, something I never seem to be able to replicate in the absence of a professional). Helpfully, the shape of these cuticle cells or 'scales' varies again according to species:

- Coronal or 'crown-like' scales are often found on rodent and bat hairs. They make the hair strand look like a stack of crowns.
- Spinous 'triangular' scales are like petals and are usually found on the hair of cats and rabbits, and the triangles protrude slightly from the hair.
- Imbricate 'flattened' scales are the ones which appear on human hairs, and also on the hair of dogs and many large animals — they are flat and smooth against the hair shaft.

Taking all these features into consideration, a trace examiner can identify a hair at a scene or on a victim who may be unknown, and perhaps compare it to a known sample: let's say a victim's hair was found in a suspect's underwear, or a suspect's hair found in a victim's bedroom despite the fact they were apparently unknown to each other. Agatha refers to this quite simplistically in *Towards Zero* after a suspect's jacket is examined:

> 'The red hairs were on the cuff, blonde hairs on the inside of the collar and the right shoulder . . . Mr Neville Strange does seem to be a bit of a bluebeard. His arm around one wife and the other's head on his shoulder.'

This 'evidence' wouldn't stand up in court of course, because it's reliant on simple observation of colour rather than examination of DNA, which didn't exist in Christie's time (not until the 1980s in fact), but it's an easy way for the investigators to try to reconstruct people's actions using hair evidence in a closed circle, while awaiting more conclusive results from a lab.

The other notable thing about hair is that it's fairly stable under adverse natural conditions, even extreme decomposition: while the hair may slough off the skull as the skin decays, as long as the body isn't out in the elements it will be present for a couple of centuries and can still be examined. Notably any drugs or poisons a person has ingested which have been deposited in their hair can still be detected long after death.

Soil

Clumps of earth on a piece of furniture help solve the murder of Aristide Leonides in Agatha's favourite book, *Crooked House*. The narrator, Charles Hayward, and Chief Inspector Taverner of Scotland Yard observe that on the seat of a chair are a few fragments of earth. 'Curious,' says Taverner. 'Someone stood on that chair with muddy feet. Now why was that?' Hayward comes back to this extremely significant evidence later, even using the word trace: 'Yet there had been a clue there — the traces of earth on the seat of the old chair in the washhouse.' Suddenly, because of this soil evidence, the identity of the murderer living in the 'Crooked House' becomes shockingly clear. Soil isn't simply 'dirt' — it's a complex mixture of substances which come from animal, vegetable and mineral, as well as microscopic inclusions from man-made sources like glass, paint and concrete. The composition of soil varies hugely, and it's this variety of components which helps to identify what type of locale it's likely to have come from, and perhaps even narrow it down to a specific location. Some examples might include:

Animal hair — If soil contains particles of animal manure or perhaps animal hair, there's a likelihood it's from the region of a farm (depending on the animal type). Yet man-made substances such as glass and paint in a soil with animal inclusions could point in the direction of an inner-city zoo.

Sand — Sandy inclusions might indicate a beach location, and be particularly notable if discovered inland.

Plants and seeds — Plant materials can be found in all soils and using these particles to help identify a soil in a forensic context is a science in itself, often called forensic botany. Detritus like pine needles or seeds can indicate what types of flora are in the area the soil came from. More recently, hardy pollen grains have proved to be pivotal in high-profile forensic investigations and this particular branch of trace examination is known as forensic palynology. I prefer to call all of this 'planted evidence . . . '

Glass

The short story 'Dead Man's Mirror' introduces us to glass as trace evidence, when a character observes, 'Funny the way that mirror was smashed by the shot.'

Knowledge of how glass breaks can be incredibly useful in helping experts to determine the direction in which glass was broken, even from microscopic particles. This could have been the case in *Five Little Pigs* which is, in my opinion, one of Agatha's best books. Twenty years after temperamental yet handsome painter Amyas Crale is poisoned with coniine (a hemlock derivative), Poirot is called in to review the evidence. He does so in reference to five particular suspects; the 'Five Little Pigs' of Agatha's title. During one of the character's recollections we're told a glass pipette had been found crushed to splinters on the path up to the house, and it becomes a clue in this fantastic, character-driven yarn.

Glass has applications in corroborating a story, for example to determine if a break-in is genuine: was the glass window broken from the outside in, or did someone stage it and break the glass from the inside? (This is something Jessica Fletcher frequently notes in the ever-popular mystery series *Murder She Wrote*. It's never really been explained why the police don't seem to notice the ruse as quickly as she does!)

Sometimes the glass itself is a clue: the composition of glass from car headlights can be so specific it will lead investigators to a particular make of car. If broken fragments of spectacles are found at a crime scene, a good analyst may be able to work out the prescription of the glasses they came from, which could point to an individual.

If glass is found in two different locations, the expert will be able to compare the two samples and perhaps find a match because the fractured edges allow 'edge matching'. This is alluded to in 'Dead Man's Mirror', in reference to the mirror being 'smashed by the shot'. But Poirot notices something more, a tiny sliver of mirror in a rather unexpected place — on the base of a bronze statue.

> 'I asked myself, how does a sliver of broken looking-glass come to be there? — and an answer suggested itself to me. The mirror had been broken, not by a bullet, but by being struck with the heavy bronze figure. The mirror had been broken deliberately.'

Here, Poirot falls short of 'edge matching' the mirror fragments, but the underlying principle of noticing glass in two different locations and realising they originated in one place is a more rudimentary version, and certainly something which Poirot could achieve without the aid of a microscope.

Fibres

Fabric as evidence is mentioned in several of Christie's books, beginning with her first, *The Mysterious Affair at*

Styles. We're told Poirot discovers a 'fragment of some dark green fabric — only a thread or two, but recognizable' in the bedroom of the murder victim. Later on, he tries to find out where it came from. After learning one of the ladies in the house has a green dress he asks what shade it is. On being told it's a light green chiffon, he replies: 'Ah, that is not what I want'.

In a very rudimentary sense, Poirot is trying to 'place' a suspect at the murder scene by finding out who — in the household — owns an item of dark green fabric (since this is what he found). Pale green chiffon is not the same as the 'dark green fabric' described in the book, so Poirot discounts that particular garment and keeps on questioning the suspects.

Poirot's fragment was mere threads, but, as with glass, larger pieces of fabric (retrieved from a scene with tweezers or forceps) can sometimes be 'edge matched'. Moving down in scale: all fabrics, whether natural or synthetic, shed fibres.

Fibres barely visible to the naked eye can be collected carefully and, alongside a visual examination, be subjected to an alternate light source — such as an ultra-violet light — which might reveal chemicals coating the fabric: perhaps an applied dye, stain resistor or fire retardant. This type of trace isn't limited to clothing; it also encompasses soft furnishings in houses, car upholstery and more.

History of Trace Evidence Detection

Although microscopes have been around since the seventeenth century, their use in criminalistics is relatively recent, and examination of trace evidence did not become routine until the early twentieth century, in the wake of several cases where it played a crucial part. By the time of Christie's writing, investigators in the nascent field of forensic science had managed to progress beyond illuminating their microscope slides with the aid of a small mirror positioned to maximise the available light: criminalists were now using light microscopes, which utilise an electric light source and magnify up to x1500 (a huge improvement on the x10 traditional optical microscopes, though still far removed from the x500,000 of the Scanning Electron Microscopes which would come into use in the 1960s).

Of the cases that brought trace evidence to the fore, there's one in particular, from the USA, which stands out as encompassing some pivotal trace investigation, and which caused an international sensation in the press at the time, which is why I'm confident Agatha would have known about it.

In 1930s New York, 33-year-old Nancy Titterton appeared to have it all. She resided in an upscale apartment within an area of the city popular with artists and intellectuals; she lived with her devoted husband of seven years, British-born Lewis Titterton — an NBC executive; and she was considered to be a promising author, whose fiction had appeared in *Scribner's Magazine*. At this point, Nancy was working on a novel and, not unlike Christie herself, she was described as 'pathologically shy, timid and soft spoken'. She considered the cocktail parties and candlelit dinners hosted in their apartment as quite intrusive, although she politely held court, upholding her wifely duty (as it was in those times) to her popular husband. Because she was fairly well known in literary circles and lived in 'posh' Beekman Place, Manhattan, her violent murder caused media fascination — as did the way in which the murder was solved.

On the morning of 10 April 1936 two men from a local upholsterer were returning a loveseat to the Tittertons' fourth-floor residence, having re-padded and reupholstered it for the couple. Upon arrival, the two men — Theodore Kruger and his assistant John Fiorenza — were surprised to find the apartment door ajar. Tentatively peering into the flat and announcing their presence, they became aware of the sound of the shower running . . . but could see that the bathroom door was open and any amount of hollering received no reply. They realised something was wrong, so they put down the loveseat and went to investigate. On their way to the bathroom they passed the bedroom which, through the open doorway, looked as though it had seen a struggle. Ripped undergarments were strewn across the floor along with a torn grey skirt, and the bedding and furniture were in disarray. Upon finally entering the bathroom they discovered Nancy Titterton's dead body in the empty bath. She was lying on her front in the bathtub, naked except for some stockings which were pulled down to her ankles, and some pink and red pyjamas which were wound around her neck: they had been used to strangle her. Her wrists bore the red, raw marks of ligatures though the bindings that had been used to tie her up weren't immediately evident. Finally, although the shower was on, the bathtub wasn't filling up as the plug hadn't been pushed in. She had been, according to later medical reports, 'subjected to the full rigors of the killer's lust' either before or after her face had been beaten, a rather euphemistic way of recording what must have been a brutal sexual assault. A newspaper of the time describes the appearance of her 'ravished' body, but really a more appropriate word is 'ravaged'.

Shocked and appalled by this unexpected scene the men called the police and, as the Tittertons were well known and highly respected, a huge team of fifty officers was assembled to investigate the murder, under the supervision of Assistant Chief Inspector John Lyons. This eventually increased to sixty-five due to media pressure, making it, *to this day*, the biggest single homicide investigation in New York history. That, and the fact that every scientific twist and turn received front page coverage from a fascinated press makes me firmly believe that Christie would have been aware of the case.

Several items of trace evidence became apparent to the investigators: green paint had been smeared on the bedspread, there was mud on the carpet in the hallway, and crucially some hair was discovered within the dishevelled bedsheets. Even more significantly, when Nancy's body was finally moved and taken to the Bellevue mortuary, she offered up a secret in the form of a 13-inch length of cord — very similar to Venetian blind cord — hidden beneath her. None of the blinds in the apartment were missing their cords so this was a breakthrough find, as it must have been brought to the scene of the attack and, until this key discovery, had been presumed to have been taken away. The perpetrator had tried to remove evidence of the ligatures which had been around Nancy's wrists, in an attempt to leave as little evidence as possible . . . but he hadn't seen the piece hidden *beneath* her body. This desire to remove items linking the attacker to the scene illustrated their awareness of forensic techniques and perhaps explained why the shower had been left on:

to wash away evidence.

As time raced on, the scant amount of trace was examined at the Police Research Lab and Alexander Gettler of the New York Office of the Chief Medical Examiner (OCME) gave information on the findings.

They found that the green paint on the bedspread was probably not as significant as perhaps first thought. Nancy's building was being painted this colour, but all the painters' whereabouts could be accounted for at the time of the attack. Plus, there was every possibility that Nancy had brushed up against the paint and transferred it to the bed herself. The only story the paint told was that someone had been in the building and had then gone into Nancy's bedroom — that much was known already.

Similarly, the mud on the hallway carpet contained traces of the type of lint typically found in upholstery premises, so this had very likely come from the delivery men, Kruger and Fiorenza, rather than some unknown intruder.

However, the bedsheets proved interesting. Besides the fact that a fountain pen had broken and leaked over them, sad symbolism for the demise of an aspiring writer, there were the hairs to consider, one of which was white and quite stiff. On closer inspection with a microscope, Gettler identified it as a horsehair of the type used to pad out furniture, just like the loveseat the upholsterers had brought to the Tittertons' apartment. It was compared to a known horsehair from that piece of furniture and they were considered to be microscopically indistinguishable, which is as close to saying 'a match' as most scientists will get! This may not seem to be particularly significant to those of us who aren't trace experts, but in relative terms horsehair is *heavy*.

Although it was certainly likely that some horsehair from the delivery men might have been at the scene in the hallway (just like the mud was) or even in the bathroom which the upholsterers entered together, it's too heavy to have simply blown into the bedroom — and yet those men apparently hadn't entered the bedroom. It had to have been *carried* in by someone else: Every Contact Leaves a Trace.

Suddenly a whole new avenue of investigation opened up to the team — how did this horsehair get there?

In addition to the hair evidence, the cord found beneath Nancy's body had been identified as what the trade called a '60 size, 5-ply cord' made up of jute and low-grade hemp. Once this was established, investigators visited cord manufacturers in the area and beyond, in an attempt to find out where it was manufactured and perhaps who it was delivered to. Eventually they hit pay dirt. The twine was made by The Hanover Cordage Company in York, Pennsylvania and a check of their sales records showed that a single roll had been sent to Theodore Kruger's Manhattan upholstery business just a day before the murder.

These results painted an unexpected picture.

The investigators had gone full circle and the upholsterers the Tittertons had employed were now the focus, not simply witnesses. Although Theodore Kruger had an alibi for the time of day before he had delivered the loveseat to the Beekman Place apartment, his assistant, John Fiorenza, did not. Confronted with this seemingly 'futuristic' and irrefutable evidence, Fiorenza confessed to the rape and murder of Nancy Titterton. He'd apparently become infatuated with her when he and Kruger originally picked up the loveseat for repair. On the day of the attack he was counting on the fact that he'd 'discover' her body *with a witness* to exonerate him from any kind of suspicion. A double-bluff of the type we'd see in a Christie book, but of course I can't tell you which ones or it would give the game away!

It was just ten days after the crime that Fiorenza was arrested, and yet the man hours which had gone into the investigation were more consistent with a month of work. The scientific techniques used were so novel that details were in the headlines every day, and the public were kept up to date with the remarkable forensics. Fiorenza went to the electric chair in January 1937, but the event itself made fewer headlines than did the spectacular forensic investigation which put him there.

A photograph of Nancy Titterton

In the early days of the social network Facebook, users had a variety of options to choose from in order to describe their relationship status on their profiles. They could be single, married, and other such common labels, or they could instead state — rather enigmatically — 'It's complicated.' When I began to research Hercule Poirot's relationship with forensic evidence, particularly *trace* evidence, I realised 'it's complicated'.

In Agatha's second Poirot book, *The Murder on the Links*, we are told via Hastings's narration that Poirot 'had a certain disdain for tangible evidence such as footprints and cigarette ash', and believed that these sorts of clues alone would never enable a detective to solve a case. (This seems odd given that he had what appeared to be his own crime scene kit in the first book!) When Hastings queries this opinion out loud, suggesting these are of vital importance, Poirot elaborates in a way that will initially appease the forensics experts out there: 'But certainly! I have never said otherwise! The trained observer, the expert, without doubt he is useful.' However, with typical endearing egotism he continues to explain, 'But the others, the Hercule Poirots, they are *above* the experts!' In a hilarious conversation during which Poirot uses the analogy of fox-hunting as detective work, he explains to Hastings that during the process it is hounds which track the foxes' scent, not humans. He makes his point by saying,

> 'You did not descend from your horse and run along the ground, smelling with your nose and uttering loud Ow Ows?'

causing Hastings to laugh in spite of himself. Poirot continues, 'So. You leave the work of the hounds to the hounds', asking why he should be made 'ridiculous' by closely examining the ground looking for imagined clues.

Oddly, though, in other books and stories Poirot does describe himself as a hound! In *Three Act Tragedy* he says, 'Like the *chien de chasse*, I follow the scent, and I get excited, and once on the scent I cannot be called off it.' In fact, he uses the analogy time and time again, even calling himself 'a very good dog' in one instance.

These are metaphorical statements, of course, so let's consider his behaviour in *Death on the Nile*, published in 1937, three years after *Three Act Tragedy*. When examining the cabin of the murdered young heiress Linnet Doyle, we are specifically told, 'Quietly, deftly, Poirot went about his search. He went down on his knees and scrutinised the floor inch by inch' — which is certainly not metaphorical, and sounds very much like the behaviour he often derides. It's a strange contradiction that Poirot expresses more than once in the span of books where we're fortunate to follow his exploits.

Unlike his predecessor Sherlock Holmes — or indeed his Christie-canon rival Miss Marple — Poirot doesn't carry a magnifying glass around with him. In fact, he seems to get far more use out of his 'large turnip of a watch' according to Hastings. Poirot sees the physical evidence as only *part* of the puzzle, and the rest is assembled via 'the psychology'. Perhaps this is because Christie was such a self-confessed people-watcher, aware of the passions and emotions which drove people to carry out extreme acts like murder, more so than the technical aspects of solving cases.

But when trace examination is absolutely essential to the story, she has Poirot change his tune slightly, and despite his seeming 'disdain for tangible evidence' it does feature in many of the Poirot books, illustrating that he is aware of the old adage the devil's in the details. Christie wrote a phenomenal sixty-six detective novels and kept things fresh and interesting over a career which spanned fifty years. Perhaps, then, it's understandable that the methods by which her most prolific detective solved his cases varied. Poirot appears in thirty-three books, two plays and over fifty short stories whereas Miss Marple is in only twelve books and around twenty stories. Marple doesn't have as much time to vary her methods, and she was never a professional investigator, unlike Poirot, so it makes sense that Poirot would use numerous techniques and continually grow as a detective.

In *Murder on the Orient Express*, Hercule Poirot is a passenger on the famous cross-continental train, taking him all the way from Istanbul in Turkey to his home in London. It's winter, and the train travels through snowy regions in the Balkans as part of its route. It's bad luck that the train gets caught in a huge snowdrift and is forced to remain stationary, and it's *extremely* bad luck that someone is murdered while they're all trapped on board. This book once again shows Poirot's contradictory nature where physical evidence is concerned. For example, he examines two spent matches in the ashtray while searching the compartment of the murdered Samuel Ratchett and says significantly, 'Those two matches are of a different shape . . . One is flatter than the other. You see?' At the time no-one does see, but that's typical Hercule, noticing the little things others don't. He examines several types of physical evidence in this way, storing the details in his little grey cells. Later on, in the same book, he does elaborate, 'It is the psychology I seek, not the fingerprint or the cigarette ash. But in this case I would welcome a little scientific assistance' and I think there is a specific reason for this. In this book in particular, Poirot and the rest of the characters are cut off from the world; stranded in a train carriage which has been buried in the snow, unable to communicate with the outside. This means he has no 'hounds' to sniff out trace evidence for him and it's probably the reason that this is the book where we see Poirot carrying out his one and only forensic experiment. (It's something rather exciting involving burned documents, which we'll come on to later.)

But that very distinct type of isolation can't be used as an excuse in other stories. The very first time we meet Poirot in *The Mysterious Affair at Styles*, he's more like a crime scene investigator than in later books, and I've already mentioned Christie equipping him with something akin to a CSI case, long before they were available for real criminal investigations. He inspects the room where elderly Emily Inglethorp has died:

> Suddenly something in the bolt itself seemed to rivet his attention. He examined it carefully, and then, nimbly whipping out a pair of small forceps from his case, he drew out some minute particle which he carefully sealed up in a tiny envelope . . .

Forceps and tiny envelopes! Surely these are the tools of the trace trade? We'd be forgiven for thinking that actually Poirot is a connoisseur of this tiny physical evidence, but bear in mind that *The Mysterious Affair at Styles* was Christie's first book. In this narrative more than in others the influence of Conan Doyle's 'Sherlock' permeates the text, and we can also assume she hasn't yet developed Hercule Poirot's personality to her satisfaction. Perhaps because it's her first detective novel she relies more on Conan Doyle's knowledge of forensics than her own.

That said, Poirot still focuses on some trace evidence in the next book, *The Murder on the Links*, in the form of hair . . . maybe because it stood out and offended his need for neatness:

> Poirot remarked casually, 'It was here that Monsieur Renauld received his guest last night, eh?'
>
> 'It was — but how did you know?'
>
> 'By *this*. I found it on the back of the leather chair.'

And he produced a long black hair.

Later on in the book, Monsieur Giraud of the Sûreté — Poirot's intellectual rival — also finds a hair from the same, and apparently rapidly shedding, woman.

Further on in the story Giraud holds the hair up to the head of a female suspect and says, 'You permit that I see whether it matches?' We know this isn't correct forensic technique, given that important features like the medulla can't be seen by the naked eye, but it was 1923 and cases like the Nancy Titterton murder had yet to hit the headlines. It would be 1931 before the seminal textbook on the microscopic analysis of hair would be published. In it the author, Scottish forensic expert John Glaister, advised:

> The avenue of medico-legal investigation demands an exhaustive study of animal and human hairs . . . For the purpose of identification, it is essential that the examiner should have at hand a comprehensive collection of known hairs for comparison.

It's certainly very likely that Gettler, the scientific pioneer in the Titterton case, read this book during his investigation of that pivotal horsehair (if not before).

In *The Mystery of the Blue Train*, Poirot carries out a similar hair comparison. When searching the compartment of the unfortunate murder victim, Ruth Kettering, he takes a rug (probably a blanket) over to the window to have a look in the light, and notices four auburn hairs which he believes are from the victim.

Again it's a simple comparison with the naked eye, but the basic premise of trace evidence collection is there: he discovers the auburn hairs and compares them to the hair on the victim's head. However, what we're not told at this point is that he is also considering the location of the hairs he discovered, and why this sheds a different light on the case.

Towards Zero, published a decade and a half later, illustrates that Agatha has become much more au fait with hair as used in a forensic context, and it appears that in the absence of Poirot as a character she really goes to town with all sorts of trace evidence in this book. The discovery of some strands of hair becomes a key part of the plot from the start. Something which appears to be the weapon used to murder the white-haired Lady Tressilian, a 'heavy niblick' (golf club), is not only bloodstained, it also has white hairs sticking to it. The examining doctor tells us, 'I'll analyse the blood on it, make sure that it's the same blood group — also the hairs.' 'Analysis' sounds rather more scientific than simply holding hairs to up to a head in order to ascertain a match! Although we can't be sure of exactly what the 'analysis' entails in the story, it's likely to be comparison with a light microscope, and it indicates a progression of Agatha's forensic knowledge. Of course, a Scanning Electron Microscope wouldn't have been used in 1944 when this book was written. However, the advancement of the science in real life and in Agatha's fiction is there. But at this point in the twentieth century, scientific knowledge of hair analysis was still quite specialised, even to the police. Superintendent Battle muses, 'She was hit with something heavy — that's heavy. It has blood and hair on it, therefore presumably her blood and hair. Ergo — that was the weapon used.' Yet we know it's not quite as simple as that. Later on, there is some suggestion that the niblick wasn't the weapon used at all and that perhaps the hairs were planted. Trace evidence can only take you so far when dealing with a canny murderer.

If the Superintendent doesn't understand the microscopic potential of hair, then the layman *certainly* doesn't. When one of the suspects in *Towards Zero* is presented with some different and incriminating hair evidence he has no idea exactly what can be determined just by examining it:

> 'That dark blue coat you wore at dinner the night of the murder, it's got fair hairs inside the collar and on the shoulders. Do you know how they got there?'

'I suppose they're my hairs.'

'Oh no, they're not yours, sir. They're a lady's hairs, and there's a red hair on the sleeves.'

'I suppose that's my wife's — Kay's. The others you are suggesting are Audrey's. I caught my cuff button in her hair one night . . . '

'In that case . . . the fair hair would be on the cuff.'

Things don't look good for this suspect . . . . Perhaps he should have read John Glaister's book. There is an important point to be made from the above. When Battle says that the hair is from a lady he won't have come to this conclusion from the science of the time. We can't tell whether a hair has come from a female using scientific analysis on a microscopic level, but macroscopically the likelihood is that Superintendent Battle used the hairs' length and perhaps colour and scent to ascertain a higher likelihood of them being from a female.

The main concept behind the phrase 'every contact leaves a trace' is that the finding of trace evidence can possibly place a person at a scene (just as a fingerprint can), or indicate that they have been in contact with someone, and therefore corroborate or refute their claims. What it can't do is prove that a person is guilty. In the case of *Mrs McGinty's Dead*, it's an important distinction for the main protagonist and murder suspect James Bentley. Accused of the brutal slaying of his landlady, the titular Mrs McGinty, he looks more and more guilty as the forensic evidence against him begins to mount up. We're told that blood and hair have been found on Bentley's clothing, the hair being a match to Mrs McGinty's (incidentally the blood is also the same blood type as Mrs McGinty's, something we'll discuss in a further chapter). It seems very incriminating but ever-alert Poirot is capable of making an important distinction. The evidence suggests Bentley had contact with the body, but it doesn't necessarily prove he *killed* her. Trace evidence is an important tool in the arsenal of an investigator, but it has to be taken alongside other factors. For example, where was Mrs McGinty found dead? The answer is her *home,* which is also the home of the suspect James Bentley, as he is her lodger. So perhaps he ended up with her blood and hair on him because the killer tracked it all over the house and Bentley inadvertently rubbed against it? Or simply because he found the body and his sleeve made contact as he checked to see if she was alive? This finding might be more significant if — for example — James Bentley lived two towns away and told police he'd never even met Mrs McGinty before her death.

Trace evidence also happens to be fairly easy to inadvertently plant. More importantly, a recent study from Northumbria University showed that textile fibres can be transferred between clothing without contact. We're not talking from miles away, but standing in the same lift, say, it's possible for microscopic fibres to be transferred from one person to another through the air. This means that if you stood in a lift or a small room with a murderer there's a minute chance the detritus from their clothing could end up on you. This kind of novel research is far removed from the science of Christie's time, but it illustrates that as scientific methods become more sensitive the need for them to be used correctly increases. This is why, in 'The Disappearance of Mr Davenheim', when Inspector Japp asks Poirot if he's going to play down the importance of trace evidence as a clue, Poirot's — or should that be Agatha's? — answer is perfect:

> 'By no means. These things are all good in their way. The danger is they may assume undue importance. Most details are insignificant; one or two are vital. It is the brain, the little grey cells' — he tapped his forehead — 'on which one must rely.'

As Paul Leland Kirk reiterated in his quote, trace evidence has to be considered in conjunction with common sense.

* * *

Luckily, things remain fairly simplistic in Christie's stories, such as her use of substances like soil, sand and soot as clues to push investigators in the right direction. For the most part, her sleuths are content with merely identifying the presence of the material at a scene and on a suspect, and trying to reconstruct the ways in which it's likely to have ended up there, rather than breaking it down into its molecular constituents.

In 'Dead Man's Mirror', Poirot pays close attention to the footwear of one of the suspects. He picks up a small piece of earth which had fallen from the shoe of Ruth Chevenix-Gore, considers it for a moment, and then characteristically tidies up by throwing it in the bin.

'You have an explanation for everything, for the mould on your shoes, for your footprints in the flowerbed . . . '

On this occasion Poirot actually determines Ruth's innocence of the murder by listening to this 'explanation' and reconstructing when and why she was in the flowerbed, but part of me does wonder if that was even why he was looking at her foot in the first place. Throughout the Christie canon, Poirot's personality develops in various ways and perhaps one of the more surprising is his unrestrained admiration for women's feet, shoes and stockings! In this story, and many others, the shoes solve the case. There are other, more significant stocking and slipper moments in *One, Two, Buckle My Shoe*, *Cards on the Table* and *The ABC Murders*, but I won't focus on them here.

However, just as with fingerprints, the *lack* of this trace evidence can be as important in some instances for corroborating a story. In the short story 'King of Clubs', Poirot tells Hastings he is suspicious of a particular woman's shoes. The story told to him, that she had run across the grass of a garden in terror, doesn't fit with the trace evidence Poirot can see with his own eyes: the shoes are clean.

Moving away from shoes, trace can be found anywhere, and appears in *Murder Is Easy*, one of Christie's few books to feature an out-and-out homicidal maniac. During the course of the book there are around ten deaths, both on and off the page, most of which are deemed 'accidents'. But given the small population of the village — the delightfully named Wychwood — it becomes clear to the book's narrator and ad-hoc investigator, Luke Fitzwilliam, that there is a murdering genius lurking amongst the thatched cottages and rose bushes.

In the book, trace evidence clinging to a wound tells a different story from the one everyone is supposed to believe about an accidental head injury: 'Do you know what I felt on the back of his head — in with the stickiness and mess — grains of sand. There's no sand about here . . . ' So where did it come from? The insinuation is that this was actually a murder, and the weapon was a sandbag. (Sandbags seem to be a relatively common weapon in Christie's books, featuring for instance in *The Sittaford Mystery* and *Cat Among the Pigeons*, and were presumably in use during her era more than they are in ours, possibly because of the war — as they are often employed for military fortification — or perhaps simply because they're more common in rural communities and many of her books are based in small villages.) Christie is using this tenet of 'every contact leaves a trace' to inform not only the story's investigator, but also the reader, that something doesn't fit here, and for this clue to be noticed by the average person, it can't be so small that it needs specialist equipment to see it: examining the wound in a lab for minute particles of pollen just wouldn't push the story forward quickly enough.

Christie uses finer powders than sand as trace evidence too, as another visible aid to reconstructing crimes. In the short story collection *Poirot Investigates*, Poirot tells Hastings, 'See you, a little white powder has clung to it . . . French chalk.' The astute Superintendent Battle in *Towards Zero* even uses the word 'trace', when discussing the coat of Neville Strange; a coat which offers up a cornucopia of forensic evidence what with this and the previously mentioned hair:

> 'There's a trace of powder, too, inside the coat collar. Primavera Naturelle No. 1.'

Battle knows that, of course, Neville Strange doesn't use face powder and he's aware that the darker-skinned Kaye Strange uses 'Orchid Sun Kiss' so he believes Audrey Strange wore the coat for some purpose.

Of course, the word Battle uses can simply mean 'trace', but it would be rather brilliant if Christie had been referring explicitly to trace evidence, especially since we know she didn't use it in her first novel; only later, after further research on the topic.

It's solid detective work. However, an explanation of why Superintendent Battle is such an expert on female face powder isn't forthcoming — perhaps he wrote a monograph on the topic, rather like Sherlock favours tobacco ash?

* * *

One rather unusual form of trace evidence that Agatha uses is 'traces' of scent left in the air at murder scenes. In *Lord Edgware Dies* Poirot lumps this in with his description of other forms of typical evidence: 'Alas! Not the cigarette ash — nor the footprint — nor a lady's glove — nor even a lingering perfume! Nothing that the detective of fiction so conveniently finds . . .'

Smell isn't scientifically quantifiable, even now (although there are groups of researchers working on ways to detect the volatile compounds left behind by a dead body using sophisticated equipment like Gas Chromatography-Mass Spectrometry, or GC-MS as it's more commonly known). On a rudimentary level, though, many scientists and CSIs are guided by their nose: the scent of a decomposing body, for example, is unmistakable, and can lead investigators in the right direction to find one. In mortuaries, we don't allow people present at an autopsy to smear menthol beneath their noses as they often do in crime fiction. This is because the dead emit olfactory clues as to *how* they died and it's important that investigators can smell them. The scent from alcohol-related deaths can be very sweet due to the high sugar content of alcohol and how it's metabolised by the body. More famously, perhaps, cyanide can be smelled by some of the population in the form of bitter almonds, but 1 in 10 people doesn't inherit this particular quirk and therefore can't smell it. When it comes to autopsies, then, we need all noses on deck. And of course, specialist dogs are trained to detect the scent of dead bodies, flammable liquids and drugs depending on what branch of law enforcement they act for. Though they may not be detectable by the human nose, scents are certainly in the atmosphere of a crime scene.

Perfume can indicate the presence of someone under suspicion, as it does for the 'beautiful brunette' Mrs Vanderlyn in 'The Incredible Theft'. We're told 'Phew, that woman uses a lot of scent' but it appears she is over-scented for a reason in this story, rather than just to insult her gratuitously. The question this leads to is whether she had been in the room when some important papers went missing. 'You'd soon smell if she had. That scent of hers.' So perhaps that's conclusive enough for now. Scent as evidence also appears in *Evil Under the Sun* and *The Hollow*, and the scent of mothballs is combined with a piece of fabric — another type of trace evidence — in *The Man in the Brown Suit*.

Can any sleuth worth their salt consider this form of scent genuine evidence? Agatha begins to expand on this idea in later books such as *Mrs McGinty's Dead*. Poirot and his mystery-writing companion Ariadne Oliver work together to find out who is responsible for the death of poor Mrs McGinty and another new victim. At this recent crime scene, which just happens to be where Ariadne is staying, she smells a particular kind of perfume. Poirot attributes this to a particular female suspect who shouts, 'Anyone could go splashing my scent about!' And perhaps 'anyone' did. Taken with the fact the same woman's lipstick was left on a cup at the murder scene, she's either very careless or someone is trying a little heavy-handed framing . . . And lipstick is another form of trace. (How unfortunate that cheiloscopy, the taking of lip prints, wasn't in use in 1952 — perhaps Poirot and Mrs Oliver would have found out the truth rather more quickly.)

Finally, as with much of the evidence Agatha refers to in her books, there is an absence of scent to be noted too. In the novella 'Murder in the Mews', as soon as Poirot enters the crime scene we're told: 'Delicately, Hercule Poirot sniffed the air.' In typical fashion, the obtuse Inspector Japp is in the dark as to why Poirot did this, leading to a humorous exchange:

> 'Smell — eh? Was *that* why you were sniffing so when we first examined the body? I saw you — *and*

heard you! Sniff — sniff — sniff. Thought you had a cold in your head.'

'You were entirely in error.'

Japp sighed. 'I always thought it was the little grey cells of the brain. Don't tell me the cells of your nose are equally superior to anyone else's?'

'No, no, calm yourself. I assure you my nose does not enter into the matter. My nose registered nothing.'

'But the brain cells registered a lot?'

As for what Poirot did or didn't register, you'll have to read the story to find out!

* * *

Poirot's personality is paradoxical, but this probably comes from the fact that his 'genius' is just so very complete. In The Life and Crimes of Agatha Christie, Charles Osborne addresses this paradox:

> Nevertheless, when it suits him Poirot is not at all averse to snooping about, gathering up the cigarette-end and the fallen match. He has sufficient confidence and vanity to contradict himself whenever he feels like it.

As much as he adores precision and would be more than capable of painstaking forensic analysis, it's not enough for him to simply peer down a microscope and state the facts. He enjoys psychology too much. Legendary criminalist Hans Gross once said of his field,

> A large part of a criminalist's work is nothing more than a battle against lies. He has to discover the truth and must fight the lie. He meets the lie at every step.

Likewise, I think this describes Poirot as he moves through most Agatha Christie stories, particularly the ones in which he has no physical evidence. In *Five Little Pigs* he says, 'The tangible things are gone: the cigarette-end and the footprints and the bent blades of grass. You can't look for those anymore;' in *Cards on the Table* he tells us, 'There was nothing to go upon. There were no tangible clues; no fingerprints, no incriminating papers or documents;' and in *Death on the Nile*,

> 'My friend, we have not been fortunate. The murderer has not been obliging. He has not dropped for us the cuff link, the cigarette end, the cigar ash — or, in the case of the woman, the handkerchief, the lipstick or the hair slide.'

Without physical evidence to examine, an alternative mode of investigation has to be carried out. This is good for Poirot as he likes to talk to the suspects, he likes to work his little grey cells and he wants very much to see the complete picture — not just the part focused beneath a microscope lens.

⋆ ⋆ ⋆

The word 'trace' has so many meanings in the English language it's not surprising that it was used by Agatha from very early on in her career. Whether referring to traces or small amounts of a product such as a face powder, or talking of police trying to discover or 'trace' a person witnessed at a scene, its use in forensics is well established. But the phrase 'trace evidence' is more specialised and is certainly something which came from Edmond Locard's Exchange Principle. Agatha specifically states in her autobiography that 'as a result of writing crime books one gets interested in criminology' and I have no doubt that she read Locard's works and understood the concept of trace evidence exchange incredibly well, in the same way she had researched Bertillon and Lombroso, who came before him. Locard was her contemporary, after all, as he died in 1966, only ten years before Agatha herself passed away. However, despite her references to traces of scent, hair, soil, sand and more, there is one aspect of trace evidence she does seem to omit: gunshot residue or GSR. In the next chapter we'll explore why.

3

Forensic Ballistics (Firearms)

> 'It was Colonel Luttrell who fired the shot. There were ways of deciding what weapon a bullet had been fired from; the marks on the bullet must agree with the rifling on the barrel.'
>
> — *Curtain: Poirot's Last Case*

The word 'revolver' as opposed to 'gun' sounds deliciously nostalgic: the type of weapon made for murder mystery and film noir. Its vintage charm, perhaps, lies in the fact that it's also one of the weapons featured in the quintessential detective game Cluedo, which came on the market in 1949. For those who, like me, are fans of both Cluedo and Agatha Christie, it will probably please you to know that Cluedo was partially inspired by Agatha's 'impossible crime' masterpiece *And Then There Were None*, set in a large, isolated house on Soldier Island. When Anthony E. Pratt devised the game in 1943 it originally had ten guest characters, the same number as the unfortunate inhabitants of the island. It also had more weapons than the final edition, many of them weapons that also feature in *And Then There Were None*. A bottle of poison, an axe and a hypodermic syringe were all included in the original game and were all causes of death in Agatha's book. It's just as pleasing to note that in 'Agatha Christie's Complete Secret Notebooks', painstakingly researched and transcribed by John Curran, Agatha even jotted down an idea for a Cluedo-themed murder mystery story! It's a shame she never wrote it.

Agatha's comprehensive knowledge of poisons meant that her most prolific weapon of choice in a given book was often of a pharmacological nature. Perhaps she believed, as her Inspector Curry did in *They Do It with Mirrors*, 'Poison has a certain appeal . . . it has not the crudeness of the revolver bullet . . . ' Or perhaps her childhood nightmares of a character she called 'The Gunman' — mentioned in her autobiography — gave her a fear of guns. She describes this recurring nightmare saying, 'His pale blue eyes would meet mine, and I would wake up shrieking: The Gunman! The Gunman!' Nevertheless, she certainly didn't shy away from such 'crude' arms. It seems that her knowledge of them progressed throughout her stories, echoing the development of these weapons and trends of the time. Although Agatha was apparently reluctant to use guns in her stories and — according to Kathryn Harkup in *A is For Arsenic: The Poisons of Agatha Christie* — 'freely admitted to knowing nothing about ballistics', she did have a working knowledge of firearms and undertook extensive research on the topic to try to increase her expertise. In fact, though her first book *The Mysterious Affair at Styles* didn't include a gun, her second — *The Secret Adversary* — featured a revolver. But it is *The Murder at the Vicarage*, written in 1930, which really demonstrates that Agatha had absorbed the information she may have read about firearms casually, if not actively researched the topic for literary accuracy. Taking into account some short stories from the 1920s and 1930s it's easy to see that despite being 'reluctant' to use firearms to carry out murder she certainly began shooting people early in her writing career. According to Harkup, who includes causes of death both on and off the page in her final total, Agatha racks up 42 deaths by shooting. This is a lot considering Agatha is usually associated with arsenic, for example, and yet she only dispatches 13 people that way throughout her entire canon.

What's interesting is that unlike other aspects of forensics, we can see that Christie is *trying* but sometimes not quite getting it right when it comes to guns. Often her understanding of the mechanics of guns and how they worked was correct. She had a working knowledge of trajectory too, which is evident in 'Dead Man's Mirror' and *The Murder at the Vicarage*. But sometimes her terminology was incorrect, as we'll go on to see, and she confused the names of guns — yet this was common colloquially. Her knowledge does vastly improve, the further we get through her body of work. *In The Secret Adversary*, the brash American character Julius P. Hersheimer carries what's described as a 'murderous looking automatic' which he has nicknamed — perhaps in a rather Freudian manner — 'Little Willie'. Much later in the book, Willie is incorrectly described by Agatha as a revolver — a completely different type of gun. Even so, it makes for a rather comical moment when he's desperate to shoot someone and exclaims that his 'Little Willie is just hopping to go off!'

Forensic ballistics is a complicated but fascinating topic, and Agatha would have had to research the basics, then delve much deeper to manipulate firearm use for her plots.

What is forensic ballistics?

Forensic ballistics is a catch-all term used to describe the examination of evidence relating to firearms at a crime scene, although the 'ballistics' aspect itself really only refers to the study of the flight path of projectiles. When a gun is fired, evidence explodes in all directions. In the case of a crime scene, the first — and most lethal — piece of useful evidence is the projectile or 'bullet'. The second is the spent cartridge case or casing (sometimes called a 'shell') which is usually ejected from the weapon. Thirdly, partially-burned gunpowder may spray from the gun via the barrel or perhaps the casing, subsequently peppering the shooter or protective clothing with an easily detectable substance. Each of these components can help investigators, so their work at the scene of a shooting is to collect as many of them as possible. A ballistics or firearms expert may then be able to:

- Analyse bullets and cartridge casings found at a crime scene to determine what type of weapon fired them.
- Match a bullet or cartridge casing to a particular weapon or to a sample from a different crime scene to link the two.
- Help to reconstruct the crime scene by estimating the distance a gun was fired from, or calculating the trajectory of the bullets.

In order to comprehend the field of forensic ballistics, it's helpful to first examine the different types of firearms and learn a little about how they work to understand how they can be used for investigation purposes. What follows here is the sort of research Agatha would have done.

Guns

All modern firearms work in a similar way: pulling the trigger causes a firing pin to strike a tiny shock-sensitive charge at the rear of the cartridge. This, in turn, detonates the explosive powder in the projectile, forcing it out of the breech (a hole in the 'body') of the gun, and down the barrel towards the target. Broadly speaking there are three different classifications of gun: Handguns, Rifles and Shotguns.

Handguns

This category, as the name implies, consists of weapons designed to be held and fired using one hand (also called 'pistols'). They fall into three sub-categories: the revolver, beloved of Westerns and, of course, murder mysteries; the semi-automatic pistol; and the machine pistol. Revolvers and semi-automatic pistols are short-barrelled weapons and the difference between them is the method of presenting a bullet to the breech.

Revolvers have a cylinder with multiple chambers each filled manually with a projectile — most commonly 5 or 6 of them, although some models can hold as many as 12. To fire a shot, the cylinder is revolved to place a cartridge in front of the gun's firing hammer — hence the name 'revolver'. The cylinder rotates as the hammer is cocked, either by the shooter's thumb (in a 'single action' revolver) or by being connected to the trigger (in a 'double action'). The spent casing will remain in the chamber until it's manually removed. The revolver fires one projectile at a time until all the chambers in the cylinder are emptied. This is what makes the terrifying 'game' of Russian Roulette possible. As the cylinder turns, no one knows whether the chamber is empty or contains a bullet . . . Revolvers are plentiful in Christie's work, particularly the 1920s and 1930s whodunnits and thrillers, like *Lord Edgware Dies*, *Death on the Nile* and *The Secret of Chimneys*. I think that's why they have such vintage connotations.

Semi-automatic pistols (sometimes incorrectly called 'automatic pistols' or 'automatics') differ from revolvers in that they are loaded via a magazine full of bullets rather than a revolving cylinder, and the empty shell casings of the bullets are ejected from the gun automatically. Like revolvers they fire one at a time — so, one bullet each time the trigger is pressed — but the magazine is provided already full of bullets so a pistol would be no good for Russian Roulette as there wouldn't be any mystery about whether or not you'd get shot! Christie knew about magazine-loaded weapons. In The Hollow the eccentric Lady Angkatell tells us, 'One might have had a few shots at the target and left one shot in the magazine — careless, of course.'

Machine pistols are truly automatic weapons. They possess a magazine and eject their cartridge casings in similar fashion to semi-automatic pistols, but the major difference is that they will keep firing as long as the trigger is depressed and there is available ammunition — you don't have to repeatedly press the trigger as you do with a semi-automatic. I don't think I need to discuss the outcome of a game of Russian Roulette with a machine pistol here . . . !

Rifles

These are long-barrelled guns designed to be fired with two hands. A spent casing is ejected and a fresh cartridge loaded for the next shot, either manually (as in a lever or bolt-action rifle) or by means of a semi-automatic or automatic mechanism. Poirot seems to consider rifles with some derision. In 'The Kidnapped Prime Minister', first published in 1923, he says, 'One can hardly take it seriously. To fire with the rifle — never does it succeed. It is a device of the past!' This is a curious view in light of the superior accuracy and power of the rifle over other types of firearm. There is a reason that the rifle has been the standard infantry weapon since the middle of the nineteenth century! Perhaps Christie was thinking of the rapid-fire nature of the then recently developed semi-automatic pistol as opposed to the cumbersome and slow-firing bolt-action rifle. Certainly, different guns are better for different purposes. A classic example is a shotgun, below, which fires its ammunition in a completely different way to a rifle, and therefore is used for a totally different purpose.

Shotguns

Unlike the guns above, shotguns don't commonly fire single units, i.e. bullets. Instead, the projectiles they're loaded with are called shotgun shells, or cartridges, which are cylinders — usually made from plastic (paper in Christie's day) with a brass or steel head — filled with many small balls of lead or steel called pellets or 'shot'. This means that rather than going in one direction on firing, the projectiles escape into different trajectories in a large cloud. In the context of Agatha's books any shotguns would have likely been loaded with tiny 'birdshot' pellets for use in hunting or clay shooting so would be relatively ineffective for murdering a human being, as we'll go on to see. Shotguns can fire a range of different ammunition types including devastating 'buckshot', and 'slugs' which are effectively like taking all the pellets in a usual shotgun shell and smushing them into one big, solid blob.

A photograph of a typical vintage revolver

All modern ammunition (other than that for antique or reproduction 'black powder' guns), regardless of the type of firearm, comes in the form of a cartridge. The cartridge has its roots in a simple twist of paper containing a charge of gunpowder used with early muzzle-loading firearms. To this was often added the projectile(s), leaving just the ignition source to be accounted for. Until the cartridge era this was part of the gun, for example a piece of flint. The final breakthrough in developing the cartridge was a casing that could expand to seal the chamber, and brass was very suitable due to its malleability. This created the modern 'self-contained' cartridge, containing propellant, projectile(s) and an igniting primer, all stored in a weatherproof case designed to easily fit the gun's mechanism. A cartridge can contain either a single projectile (the bullet fired by a handgun or rifle) or shot (the multiple balls fired by a shotgun):

Shot — Shotgun cartridges or shells contain hundreds of balls of shot — which is why it's a 'shot' gun, as well as propellant and a primer. If you shake a cartridge, it may rattle. As the cartridge is fired, the end is forcibly opened and the shot spreads out in an increasing circular pattern, meaning the user's aim doesn't need to be as precise as with bullets. That's why shotguns are used to shoot birds out of the sky, for example.

Bullets — The first bullets were simple lead spheres, and the word 'bullet' has its roots in the French *boulet*, or 'small ball'. More aerodynamic elongated and pointed bullets were invented in the nineteenth century, and as guns became capable of projecting these at higher velocities, a harder metal coating or 'jacket' became necessary. The lead was still needed to keep the bullet's weight up (bullets that are too light can stray off course and/or do less damage) but now this jacket was also needed to keep the lead in shape, otherwise heat and pressure would deform or even destroy it. The jacket may cover the projectile partially or completely, which is why you may have heard of the phrase 'full metal jacket'. Ammunition that fires at a lower pressure, like shotgun shot or .22 calibre bullets, can still do without a jacket.

A photograph of bullets of various calibres

Slugs — These are effectively bullets for use in shotguns. They are large, solid projectiless ually made of lead or copper. They can be homemade and quite crude, but can also be purchased from a manufacturer, and are for shooting very large game and similar heavy-duty jobs, like stopping cars by shooting their engine blocks! A shotgun loaded with slug is like a modern musket; more accurate thanks to contemporary engineering, but still not as accurate as a rifle.

* * *

Guns that fire the ammunition that we call 'bullets' have spiral grooves cut into the inside surface of their barrels. This is called 'rifling' and it gives the bullet a gyroscopic spin which causes it to shoot out of the gun on a much steadier and straighter trajectory. Shotguns don't require this stabilisation, so shotgun barrels are smooth. However, the muzzles of shotguns are commonly slightly narrower and this is called the 'choke'. The 'choking' effect can help to keep the shot together for longer, which you may want to do depending on what you're trying to shoot, smaller or larger birds, for example.

Looking at the types of shootings which occur in Agatha's books, you'll see different guns are mentioned. There are so many types of guns because they all have different uses. If I wanted to fatally shoot a person from very far away, I'd choose a gun with rifling which steadies the bullet and keeps it on the correct course over a longer distance. A sniper rifle is the perfect example of this. However, we're not likely to come across snipers in Agatha's books, and it's true that rifles weren't frequently used as murder weapons during Agatha's period. If, on the other hand, I wanted to shoot at something which was small — like a rabbit or a bird — and a fatal shot didn't require as much force, I'd choose a shotgun. The pellets would spread out and hit my target with less velocity than a single bullet, but it would do the job and wouldn't require me to be quite so precise. There aren't really any murders with shotguns in Agatha's books, but of course the type of characters which feature heavily in them — the country-dwelling landed gentry — would likely use shotguns as sporting equipment for hunting parties.

The most prevalent guns mentioned in Christie's books are revolvers and semi-automatic pistols because these are the guns commonly used to fatally shoot human beings at fairly close range, which are the shooting deaths we see frequently in her stories.

Calibre vs Bore

In the world of firearms, there are two ways to measure the internal size of a gun's barrel and therefore the size or amount of ammunition that it can fire. You may already be familiar with these. They are: **calibre** and **bore** ('gauge' in the US). By the twentieth century, 'gauge' had fallen out of use in the UK for everything other than sporting guns like shotguns and big game rifles, and calibre was used for most rifles and handguns.

Calibre is the only one Christie mentions. It's the measure of the interior of the barrel — the 'bore' — in hundredths of an inch. This relates directly to the diameter of the ammunition fired from the barrel. For example, a .45 calibre handgun bore (known as a 'forty-five') is $^{45}/_{100}$ of an inch in diameter and takes 0.45-inch ammunition, usually given as '.45'. It stands to reason that the smaller the number, the smaller the calibre and ammunition, so a .22, which is $^{22}/_{100}$ of an inch, is smaller than a .45. This is illustrated in The Murder at the Vicarage when the examining doctor, Dr Haydock, comments, 'I should say in all probability the bullet was fired from a pistol of small calibre — say a Mauser .25,' an assertion he makes by simply looking at the size of the wound. What's interesting in this quote is that there's no indication of how '.25' is pronounced. The convention is — and always has been — to drop the decimal, so that this should be read as a Mauser 'twenty-five' or 'two-five' in British parlance. Yet when Dr Haydock gives the bullet to Colonel Melchett, the Colonel asks 'point two five?' in reference to it. We wouldn't expect a military man to say 'point two five'. In *Death on the Nile* seven years later, Christie writes, 'It was a pistol of very small calibre — as I say, probably a twenty-two,' then again later, ''Twenty-two,' murmured Race. He took out the clip. 'Two bullets fired . . .''

This shows a clear correction of her earlier mistake and we can assume her knowledge of guns has increased. It would indicate to me that her earlier quotes including the word 'point' are perhaps due to her reading some small titbit about guns, but her correct pronunciation later may be because she actually *spoke* to someone about guns and she heard the correct terminology out loud.

Bore is an older system, and once applied to all firearms.

Today, for traditional reasons, it is used only for shotguns and some big game rifles. Effectively, it uses weight to define the diameter of the bore. A 12-gauge shotgun is theoretically equivalent to a solid lead slug weighing one twelfth of a pound ($^1/_{12}$). However a10-gauge shotgun is equated to one tenth of a pound ($^1/_{10}$). This means that, rather confusingly in contrast to calibre, the smaller the gauge number, the heavier the load, because we are dividing a pound into smaller and smaller pieces. So a 16-gauge shotgun fires a lighter load than the most commonly used 12-gauge shotgun. The simplest way to understand it is to think '12 gauge' means 'twelfth of' and '10 gauge' means 'tenth of' and 16 gauge means 'sixteenth of '. By applying simple fractions we know that a sixteenth of something is smaller than a tenth of some thing. Luckily, we needn't worry about this too much, since, as I've established, shotguns weren't common in Agatha's books!

Though quite technical, this information serves to establish the most common types of guns at crime scenes, and their associated ammunition, and is necessary grounding before we delve into the basic tenets of forensic ballistics. How all those components interact is one of the most important aspects of the discipline, and is why we get quotes like 'The bullet had been extracted and was proved to have been fired from a revolver identical with the one held by the police' from Agatha's short story 'The Mystery of Hunter's Lodge'. Loading and firing a gun engraves its ammunition with a wealth of unique marks, and several different parts of the weapon mark the projectile's casing: the magazine may scratch it; the impact of the firing pin may put a distinctive dent in the metal cover that retains the primer; and the explosion that follows stamps the cartridge case with a mirror image of the marks on the breech. Finally, the mechanism that ejects the spent cartridge case also scratches it. Marks on the bullet will come from the rifling inside the barrel of the firearm, and scratches on the bullet duplicate the spacing, size, angle and direction of the grooves — that is, if they are clockwise or anti-clockwise. Many of you will have seen a detective on a TV show pick up a suspicious gun by pushing a pencil or pen down the barrel and lifting it that way, ostensibly to not leave any fingerprints on the handle. But this is a forensic faux pas which could cause damage to the inside of the barrel, something that was known even in Christie's time. In the 1935 book *Modern Criminal Investigation*, author Harry Soderman refers to a gun on a scene as the 'arm' and writes, 'When handling the arm, do not put a pencil or similar through the barrel to pick it up, which is sometimes recommended. By such handling, important clues may be destroyed.' Granted this isn't something Christie specifically mentioned in her books, but it puts into perspective the archaic forensic practices sometimes seen even on modern television. By comparison, Christie's works can actually be considered positively progressive!

In combination with the size and shape of the bullet all of the above information allows someone examining that bullet to identify the type of weapon that fired it, and even match a recovered bullet to a specific gun. This is a mixture of individual and class characteristics which we get in other forensic sciences: the class characteristics are more general, like being able to tell a bullet was fired from a .30 calibre rifle. The individual characteristics tell us the bullet was fired from John Smith's .30 calibre rifle, because a mark on the bullet fired from his gun is repeated every time a bullet is fired from that particular gun. A professional firearms investigator can read all these features as easily as we would read a newspaper article and, in most cases, match the items retrieved from a crime scene to a particular weapon. Agatha illustrates this perfectly in 'Dead Man's Mirror' when Major Riddle, investigating the shooting of Gervaise Chevenix-Gore, asks the examining doctor if he has the bullet. The doctor says he does, so Major Riddle explains, 'Good. We'll keep it for comparison with the pistol.'

History of Forensic Ballistics

In the sixteenth and seventeenth centuries, long before guns became the efficient killing machines we have today, they had rather clunky beginnings and were cumbersome to use. Military firearms sometimes used paper cartridges, but ammunition was typically made up of separate components: gunpowder was poured down the barrel, the projectile went next in the form of a lead ball forced in using a ramrod, and then some kind of 'wadding' (paper, plant fibres, or even a hastily grabbed handful of grass!) was added to keep the spherical bullet in place. If this last part wasn't used the bullet would roll out of the barrel — there are actual accounts of this happening, which sounds rather stressful to say the least. Rifle bullets would typically be loaded with a greased patch of cloth behind the bullet instead of a wad, in order to allow the bullet to be spun by the rifling grooves. To prime the weapon, more gunpowder was placed into a container called a 'pan' at the back of the barrel, and there was a tiny hole between this pan and the barrel, called a 'vent' or 'touch-hole'. Igniting the priming powder in the pan created a cloud of smoke and powerful flame. Channelled into the touch-hole, this created a hot, focused jet of flame that ignited the main charge, rapidly generating a tremendous amount of hot gas and therefore pressure to shoot the lead ball down the barrel of the gun and out of the muzzle. Sometimes, if the touch-hole was clogged or the flash was too weak, only the priming charge would go off. This is where we get the phrase 'a flash in the pan', meaning something briefly impressive but ultimately disappointing.

Before mass manufacturing of guns began, guns and accessories including, crucially, barrels and bullet moulds, were handmade. The bullets fired, therefore, always bore some exclusive impressions which were unique to a specific firearm. This prompted the first instances of the careful examination of individual projectiles in order to trace them back to the gun which fired them. But it's not just the lead ball, barrel and more permanent components of the gun which could be examined for their unique characteristics; sometimes it was the more disposable elements, which were easily overlooked.

The murder inquiry to make history as the first *ever* to be solved by ballistic comparison is said to be a case in England in 1784, about a century before Christie was born. A house carpenter called Edward Culshaw was shot through the head by a thief who was following him as he travelled along the road from Liverpool. The local surgeon performed Culshaw's autopsy. During his examination of the skull, the surgeon discovered not only the ball which had been fired from the muzzle-loading pistol but the remains of a small quantity of paper which had been used as wadding and had been fired from the gun at the same time — that's why it was present in the wound. The paper turned out to be a small section of a song sheet.

After several local inquiries from the constabulary, an informant put forward eighteen-year-old John Toms as a possible suspect. Toms was arrested and immediately searched, and a ripped song sheet was discovered in his pocket. The wad of paper removed from Culshaw's head perfectly matched the remains of this paper, and when this irrefutable evidence was put to Toms, he confessed. Newspapers from the time state, 'On 26 March 1784, before Judge Willes at the Assizes at Lancaster, John Toms was tried and found guilty of the wilful murder of Edward Culshaw of Prescot. He was executed the Monday following.'

The Culshaw case matched wadding to wound, but the first case to feature bullet to bullet comparison was in 1835, led by detective Henry Goddard of the Bow Street Runners, generally recognised to be the UK's first professional police force, founded in

London in 1749.

Seemingly the case was an attempted burglary of a manor house, and Joseph Randall, the household's brave butler, had been shot at while defending the property from these armed intruders. As well as being shot *at* (although the bullet missed him), he had also fired at the burglars and managed to scare them away, so no one was hurt. Detective Goddard carefully inspected all the bullets at the scene and found that those fired from Randall's gun to protect the premises and himself all had a specific defect — 'a very small, round pimple' — but so did the other bullets at the scene. How could those bullets supposedly fired from the intruders' guns have had an identical defect in common with Randall's? On inspection of these defects Goddard came to the conclusion they were acquired during their manufacture, and he set about trying to recover the original bullet mould. He already knew that all of the bullets must have come from the same manufacturer — a person rather than a machine at this point in history — and Goddard had an inkling who that person could be. He realised that recovering the bullet mould would give him solid evidence against his main suspect, and of course the suspect knew nothing about the advances being made in ballistics at this time, so he didn't hide his mould. That person was Randall, the butler. All the bullets had the same defect, which meant they'd all come from one source.

Yep — the butler did it.

On being confronted with this scientific evidence Randall confessed that he'd organised this fake robbery not because he was greedy but because he was hoping to 'find favour' with the mistress of the house,

Mrs Maxwell, for his bravery in protecting her property.

It wasn't until the second half of the nineteenth century that ammunition became more recognisable in the form of cartridges that combined the gunpowder and bullet with some form of ignition in one compact case, or 'jacket'. This was instrumental for mass manufacture, and paved the way for the invention of more modern repeating arms which were much quicker to load and more efficient to use. These were the guns and ammunition being used in Agatha's stories: rifles, revolvers and pistols which were being mass-produced and either bought legitimately in stores or brought back from one or other of the World Wars.

By this time, mass production had brought down the cost of rifling: the spiral pattern cut into the metal of the bore that gives a spin to the bullet and increases the accuracy of its trajectory. The pattern is made of 'lands' and grooves, with the lands being the raised areas of the barrel's interior (just as the ridges of a fingerprint are the raised parts of skin) and the grooves being the indentations of the barrel (the equivalent of the furrows of a fingerprint). Rifling and trajectory might sound unfamiliar and confusing, but in truth we've probably all seen the rifling within a gun barrel: it's the spiral pattern in the circular silhouette aimed at various incarnations of James Bond in the opening credits of the 007 films.

The idea of 'rifling' barrels of guns to improve the bullets' accuracy actually dates back to the mid-fifteenth century, but this feature of firearms manufacture wouldn't have forensic significance until a few hundred years later. Alexandre Lacassagne, a French criminalist who died around the time

Agatha began writing, understood that the rifling of gun barrels, and any other imperfections in there for that matter, left marks on the casing of bullets: marks which could be used to identify the gun they'd been fired from. In 1899 he became the first person to compare the striations on a bullet found in the body of a murder victim with the rifling in the handguns of several different suspects; because of his pioneering evidence, the killer was arrested and finally convicted. Incidentally, Lacassagne was Cesare Lombroso's main rival in the world of criminology, debunking many of Lombroso's atavistic theories, and our friend Edmond Locard was mentored by Lacassagne.

Over in the USA, during the 1920s, the comparison microscope — in which two areas of interest or two specimens can be looked at closely and compared — was improved by US criminalists Calvin Goddard and Philip Gravelle. This binocular device was ideal for comparing bullets and cartridge cases side by side, and I always envisage it as an extremely close-up 'spot the difference'. The comparison microscope revolutionised forensics in general, and Goddard in particular became known as one of the 'godfathers' of forensic ballistics, saying in a published paper:

> Every pistol barrel . . . contains minute irregularities which are peculiar to it alone, and which will never be reproduced in any other. These irregularities leave their marks on every bullet fired from this barrel, and they constitute to all intents and purposes, a fingerprint of that particular barrel.

It's therefore significant that only around ten years later, when Christie's *Death on the Nile* was published, she had incorporated this relatively new method of bullet comparison into the story. When discussing what gun on board was actually fired, Dr Bessner says: 'The bullet has got to be extracted, of course, before we can say definitely.' Perhaps Christie had read Goddard's paper, and if not the paper specifically then certainly some form of report of its findings. We all still do this when we read the newspaper today, with headlines such as 'New Study Shows . . . ' Also, the Detection Club had been going for nearly a decade by then — it would have been interesting news for the whole club.

Goddard and Gravelle went on to form New York's legendary Bureau of Forensic Ballistics in 1925. The reason the Bureau became legendary is because it was pivotal in the investigation of one of the world's most notorious gang slayings.

On Valentine's Day 1929, six men were lined up against the wall of a Chicago garage and shot, in an attack that would come to be known as the St Valentine's Day Massacre. Most of the victims died at the scene — unsurprising since they suffered on average around twenty bullet wounds each — while a couple lasted until hospital before succumbing to their injuries. The six men were reportedly members of the 'Bugs' Moran gang, shot by four men with Thompson sub-machine guns, better known as 'tommy-guns', a weapon Christie was surprisingly familiar with. In a discussion of the phrase 'bumped off', in *Sparkling Cyanide* (published in 1944), we're told by Lucilla Drake, 'That dreadful expression refers, I believe, to gangsters executing each other with tommy-guns. I'm so thankful that we have nothing of that kind in England!'

The criminal code is binding in many forms of gang warfare and the St Valentine's Day Massacre remains officially unsolved because of it. Initially, when police turned up to the bloody garage that day and found one man alive, they asked him to name the perpetrators. The dying man replied, 'I'm not going to talk — nobody shot me!' although the seven bullets found inside his body at autopsy didn't corroborate his story . . .

A year later, two tommy-guns were retrieved from the house of a known hit man called Frank Burke, in connection with a different investigation in Michigan. On a hunch, Calvin Goddard compared the bullets from the Chicago massacre with these tommy-guns and they matched. These were the guns used to execute Bugs Moran's men in the St Valentine's Day Massacre a year previously, and that indicated it had been a mob hit, likely organised by Moran's arch rival, the notorious Al Capone. That said, Burke and his gang were never charged with the crime — theories state that it's due to the corruption that was rife at the time. So, while it is 'officially' unsolved, it was Goddard's forensic ballistic work which gave us scientific closure.

I do find it odd that the adorable 1970s musical comedy *Bugsy Malone*, which starred child actors as 'gangsters' who shoot at each other with whipped cream, was inspired by rather a dark and bloody period of American history.

Agatha Christie isn't usually associated with gangsters, but she writes about them more frequently than you may think. In *Poirot Investigates* there is a mention of 'The Mafia, or the Camorra', and in *Murder on the Orient Express* we get the quote ' . . . not like those nasty murdering Italians one reads about'. It's suggested that the villain in this book, 'Mr Ratchett', has a pseudonym because he has mob connections (and incidentally a 'ratchet' is part of a revolver. I wonder if Agatha knew this?). *Lord Edgware Dies* provides a humorous exchange when the American actress Jane Wilkinson laments the lack of gangsters in London when musing about having her husband killed, 'Of course, if we were only in Chicago I could get him bumped off quite easily, but you don't seem to run to gunmen over here.' To which Poirot adds dryly, 'Over here, we consider that every human being has the right to live.' As Agatha is often associated with 'cosy crime' it seems unusual that she would reference gang activity, but there was a dark side to her voracious news consumption which began when she was a girl. In her autobiography she tells us she read the news to Grannie every day: ' . . . the horrors of infanticide, rape, secret vice and all the things that cheer the lives of the old'. And perhaps as Agatha aged she became very much like her Grannie, and her gentle old lady sleuth Miss Marple — interested in the dark side of human nature.

* * *

In the UK, at around the same time as the St Valentine's Day Massacre, a very unusual and brutal shooting occurred in Essex. At approximately 4 a.m. one September morning in 1927 Police Constable George Gutteridge left his partner, Constable Sydney Taylor, to start his mile-long walk home at the end of their shift. He never made it back. It was around six in the morning when a local postman noticed a large item on the side of the road, and on moving closer to inspect it, realised it was a man. PC Gutteridge was slumped in a semi-sitting position against a grass bank, with his pencil in one hand, notebook in the other and his legs extending into the road. It was clear that a shooting had been the cause of his death as there were two bullet entry wounds beneath his left ear and two corresponding exit wounds in the right side of his neck. But, horrifically, he had been shot point blank in each eye. This desecration was taken to be a malicious gesture, and the barbarity of the shooting shocked the nation. In fact, this action on the part of the killer is believed to be due to a rather archaic superstition that the last thing a person sees before they die is 'printed' in some way on the retinas, and that a photograph could be taken of the image — a process known as optography. In order to destroy any such image, PC Gutteridge had been shot through the eyes by his half-witted attacker who had likely been in a car and had driven away after the killing. Two bullets were prised out of the surface of the road by investigators at the crime scene, and two more were removed from his body at the subsequent autopsy.

At the same time a car which had been stolen ten miles from the murder scene was found abandoned in Brixton, London, covered in blood. (Interestingly, the car was a Morris Cowley, the exact make of Agatha Christie's first car and her favourite purchased item. She had sold the serial rights to *The Man in the Brown Suit*, in 1924, for £500 — a substantial amount in 1924, equating to about £30,000 in modern money! — and bought the car with the proceeds.) The pieces were starting to come together: it appeared that this stolen car would have taken in PC Gutteridge's beat on its way from Essex to London. The bloodstains would need to be tested, of course, but an unusual cartridge case in the car was also an important clue as it had a unique defect which was likely to have been caused by a gun which had been damaged by a cleaning rod or ram rod. This gun must have recently been fired for this empty cartridge case to have been found in the car.

At this time, Robert Churchill, nephew of gun maker and Scotland Yard consultant Edwin Churchill (but no relation to Winston!), was an established firearms expert in the UK, having been working on cases since 1911 with his uncle. He examined the bullets from the Gutteridge crime scene and because of their class characteristics — such as their rifling marks — he concluded that the murder weapon was a Webley revolver. This gave investigators a starting point, and numerous Webleys were seized and analysed over several months, but all were excluded as the murder weapon. They didn't create the particular defect on the cartridge cases of the bullets they fired, i.e. they didn't possess the individual characteristic consistent with the cartridge case in the stolen car. An appeal for information and a reward of £2,000 — another huge amount in 1927, about £127,000! Who knew there was so much money being bandied about in the 1920s? — led to the police eventually arresting known car thieves Frederick Browne and Patrick Kennedy for the crime. The pioneering forensics then clinched it. Browne and Kennedy admitted shooting PC Gutteridge because he'd stopped them in the stolen car. After the two were executed in May 1928, one newspaper headline read 'Hanged by a Microscope', referencing the novel scientific investigative methods which had caught the two killers.

Agatha would have been well aware of this case given the sensation it caused; in view of that, it does surprise me that she never mentioned optography in any of her stories despite frequently referring to other elements which were similarly esoteric: seances, table turning, ectoplasm and more. It seems to me like a wonderful plot for a writer who enjoyed misdirection with the 'supernatural'.

Interestingly, Robert Churchill toured America the year that Goddard — the 'Father of Forensics' — was gaining press for his successful use of the comparison microscope in ballistics cases. When he returned to the UK, Churchill had his own instrument made in London and it became known as 'The Silent Detective'. Just like the images in a comparison microscope, forensic ballistics developed in the UK and the US side by side.

Robert Churchill and the comparison microscope

There's a surprising amount of forensic ballistic material from very early on in Agatha's writings. Perhaps she wasn't as afraid of guns as everyone seems to think, or perhaps she overcame that fear knowing that guns would be particularly dramatic weapons in her fiction.

Agatha's most prolifically scientific mystery, in terms of ballistics, is *Death on the Nile*; perhaps one of her most well-known books. It was the fifteenth to feature Hercule Poirot and was considered by crime writer Robert Barnard to be 'one of the top ten' mystery novels of all time. The story revolves (no pun intended) around several different shootings which occur on a Nile cruiser called the SS *Karnak*, as it slowly drifts along the famous river in Egypt. Among the passengers are the beautiful and incredibly rich American heiress Linnet Doyle, her new husband Simon Doyle, and Simon's bitter, jealous ex Jacqueline de Bellefort, who appears to believe Linnet stole Simon from her. She's been following them on their honeymoon, stalking and taunting them ever since. Two of the shootings are fatal but are carried out with different guns, and the first victim — perhaps unsurprisingly given Jacqueline's very evident anger — is Linnet Doyle, who we're told was 'shot through the head; shot at close quarters'. Other victims are apparently collateral damage. To complicate matters, it seems that nearly everyone on this ostensibly sophisticated and glamorous vessel is 'packing heat'. Several of the ladies are armed with what are described as small-calibre, pearl-handled pistols which look like dainty, feminine toys. One, which seems to belong specifically to Jacqueline de Bellefort, is described by Poirot: 'There is the ornamental work on it — and the initials J.B. It is an *article de luxe*, a very feminine production, but it is nonetheless a lethal weapon.' It's all enough to cause one of the exasperated investigators, Colonel Race, to exclaim, 'Does every girl on this blinking boat carry around pearl-handled toy pistols?' Well it's very probable! Guns were certainly far easier to get hold of and more prevalent before the Firearms Act of 1937 — the year in which *Death on the Nile* was published — and females did seem to have a predilection for dainty and ornate weapons that might fit in a handbag and not look out of place next to a powder compact. In fact, from the 1920s, some cosmetic companies like the Weidlich Bros actually created make-up compacts in the shape of pistols, with the powder in the handle and the lipstick — *shaped like bullets!* — in the barrel. In *The Seven Dials Mystery*, published eight years previously, we're told that Lorraine Wade:

> . . . opened the drawer of her dressing table and took out a small, ivory-handled pistol — almost a toy in appearance. She had bought it the day before at Harrods, and was very pleased with it.

It might be hard to believe for those of us in the UK, but Harrods — the famous, luxury department store — indeed used to sell guns (and probably gun-shaped cosmetic compacts). In the 1920s and 1930s, in London's Oxford Street, Selfridges even had its own all-girl gun-club, on the roof of its department store!

But it's not just the ladies on the Nile cruiser carrying guns; another passenger, Mr Pennington, is travelling with a rather larger firearm, which we're told is 'a big Colt revolver' — a gun which is subsequently stolen and used to shoot another victim. When Poirot tries to find out how this could have happened by asking the guests, we're told Pennington was carelessly bragging about carrying a revolver when he travels.

What an odd conversation for a group of wealthy socialites to spontaneously burst into! With all this gun-toting and firearm chatter you'd be forgiven for thinking it was actually an NRA meeting rather than a pleasure cruise. However, the Firearms Act, which would lead to the British having some of the strictest gun control measures in the world, had only just been passed, and that's evident in the writing of this book.

Clunky as this exposition is, the ingenious nature of the actual whodunnit does rely on sound science and knowledge of ballistics. First, despite how much the jilted Jacqueline de Bellefort talks about wanting to murder her ex-best friend Linnet Doyle, it's not taken for granted that *her* gun was the murder weapon: 'That her pistol was used is not absolutely certain' we're told, as the investigators seemingly reserve coming to any conclusions until more information is available after the post-mortem. This is a progressive approach when it comes to golden-age murder mysteries. Agatha's characters are acting like logical investigators rather than making an assumption based on circumstances, encouraging the reader to do the same.

Also, the wound which Linnet Doyle suffers after being shot in the head is described very realistically:

> 'See — here just above the ear — that is where the bullet entered. A very little bullet — I should say a twenty-two. The pistol, it was held close

against her head, see, there is blackening here, the skin is scorched.'

When a gun is fired, it's not only the projectile which exits the barrel; smoke and gases are also forced out along with different proportions of unburnt, burnt or burning propellant. If the muzzle is in contact with the surface it's shooting at, or exceedingly close, this sooty mixture will be transferred onto it. In the case of skin, it will be seen as the 'blackening' referred to in the quote above, and if particles of the soot actually penetrate the skin it's forensically known as 'tattooing'. One of the reasons it's called this is because the result is actually quite similar to cosmetic tattooing with a needle, not in terms of its appearance but because particles of charcoal are deposited in the epidermis of the skin, the same way ink is in a commercial tattoo. The extent of blackening and/or tattooing allows ballistics experts to determine the distance the shot was fired from. When a gun is fired, this residue also explodes backwards onto the hands of the person shooting, whether it's their skin or the fabric of their gloves. Interestingly, Christie never mentions tests for this gunshot residue (GSR), because it wasn't until the 1970s that such analysis became standard practice. Although tests did exist in Agatha's time, they were very long-winded and rudimentary.

She does refer to small blackened bullet holes in several other books, for example *One, Two, Buckle My Shoe*, to give the story realism. But in *Death on the Nile* Christie doesn't just describe this wound to give us a clearer mental picture of the injury suffered by Linnet; it's a pivotal clue for us to solve this puzzle when taken with other discoveries, as this exchange between Hercule Poirot and Colonel Race suggests:

> Poirot said gently: 'All the same . . . it is odd. Cette pauvre Madame Doyle. Lying there so peacefully . . . with the little hole in her head. You remember how she looked?'

Colonel Race is certain that Poirot is trying to tell him something with this comment . . . but he's not quite sure what.

Another one of these discoveries is a wet velvet stole, or scarf, used to wrap up the offending small pistol which has several small holes and some scorching. But the shawl served an additional purpose, as Poirot points out. He illustrates to the Colonel that it's likely been used to deaden the sound of a gunshot. Poirot alone is astute enough to understand the significance of this and elaborates later:

> 'You, Dr Bessner, examined Linnet Doyle's body. You will remember that the wound showed signs of scorching — that is to say that the pistol had been placed close against the head before being fired.'

Dr Bessner confirms that this is so, and Poirot explains the paradox: if the pistol was wrapped in a velvet stole to deaden the sound of it being fired, there wouldn't have been any scorch marks on Linnet's wound.

Poirot is spot on. Although Dr Bessner's pathology is exactly right, he hasn't understood the significance of the makeshift silencer and linked the two, as Poirot has: if the shot that killed Linnet Doyle had been fired through a velvet stole, her wound wouldn't have displayed this scorching effect. So what was shot through the velvet stole, if not Linnet Doyle? I won't give away any more about this story — it's one of my favourites and if you've not read it yet I don't want to spoil it! But it's perhaps one of the occasions in which a little technical knowledge of forensic pathology, and an understanding of how ammunition is introduced into guns, are huge bonuses to solving this particularly clever mystery.

* * *

Agatha didn't just dive straight into writing a fantastically technical whodunnit about forensic ballistics without a little practice, and firearms feature in varying degrees from her very earliest work. *In Peril at End House*, from 1932, a bullet is the item that begins the story. This is the sixth novel featuring Poirot, written at the start of a particularly prolific period of Agatha Christie's life, as she was beginning to accept that writing was her full-time profession, and was no doubt becoming more confident in her skill. The book opens with Poirot and Hastings on holiday in Cornwall, meeting young, carefree Magdala 'Nick' Buckley and her friends. After a series of events, including a falling boulder missing Nick by inches, an oil painting falling and almost crushing her, and a bullet hole found in her hat-brim (she initially thinks the bullet was just a wasp shooting past her head), Poirot decides the girl needs protection. The method of divining which gun caused this aperture is not mentioned in the book but Poirot finds the spent bullet and from that, along with the appearance of the bullet hole, asserts that a

Mauser pistol was used. The opening, situated in the brim of the hat, is described as 'a small, neat hole. Quite round' by Hastings, but no more detail is given. However, Poirot will have seen a lot of bullet holes in his time as a police officer and private detective, so we can assume this increased the accuracy of his estimations. Because the hole in Nick Buckley's hat was described as 'small' and the typical calibre of a Mauser C96 was .30, this could have also helped in determining the model of gun which was fired. It's also likely Poirot surmised this from the fact that the Mauser C96 was a very popular commercial pistol at the time, and was made more so by Winston Churchill who called it the 'best thing in the world'. We are told something about the missing Mauser later on: 'It was Dad's. He brought it back from The War,' which insinuates that it was likely that most men of a certain age at that time owned this type of pistol. The Mauser C96, or 'Broomhandle' as it was often called, is now known as one of the world's most iconic firearms, and was even the basis for Han Solo's blaster in the *Star Wars* films.

The Mauser is mentioned frequently in Agatha Christie's books, including *The Murder at the Vicarage*, *The Hollow* and *Death on the Nile*. In *A Murder Is Announced*, and the play *The Unexpected Guest*, we can conclude a Mauser is being referred to on several occasions: 'Foreign make — fairly common on the continent;' 'There's the revolver to work on. It's a German make;' 'But this country's absolutely full of continental makes of guns' and finally 'The gun is a 'war souvenir'.' I don't think this frequency is because the Mauser was a favourite of Christie's — since she admitted she wasn't keen on firearms I can't imagine she'd have a particular preference. I'd surmise it's just an indication of how common they were.

To return to *Peril at End House*: if the bullet hole had been created at close range — let's say someone held a gun to Miss Buckley's hat and fired through the fabric to her head — then, just as with the shot that killed Linnet Doyle in *Death on the Nile*, the muzzle would almost certainly leave a pattern on the hat which could be traced back to a Mauser pistol by a ballistics expert. Guns leave their mark on fabrics and other materials, just as they do on skin. The phenomenon isn't mentioned in *Peril at End House* in reference to the fabric, but Christie was already aware of the process, as it is alluded to in a much earlier thriller, *The Secret of Chimneys* (1925). I believe that in *Peril at End House* Christie is making us well aware that the shot to Miss Buckley's head was seemingly from far away; an important aspect of the plot. Had we been lucky enough for the shot to have been in contact with the hat, the muzzle mark left on the fabric would have helped Poirot identify the gun but it also wouldn't fit the narrative.

Images of the various marks left by contact wounds from muzzles started to be compiled in a database in the early twentieth century and nowadays the information available is prolific. In the 1930s, however, these databases weren't anything like as large as they are now and they weren't common knowledge, so the issue of what gun was used to shoot at Nick in *Peril at End House* is resolved in typical fashion for golden-era detective fiction. When it's discovered that a character's Mauser pistol has been stolen, this is considered enough evidence to conclude that Poirot was right about the type of gun aimed at Miss Buckley.

That is often the case in Christie's earlier stories: a shooting will be linked to a particular weapon circumstantially if the weapon is found nearby or discovered to be missing from somewhere else. We see it in the short story 'The Mystery of Hunter's Lodge', when Hastings heads off on his own to solve a murder, with Poirot following his progress from his sickbed.

> 'Now, as to the weapon?' [Hastings] asked.
> 'Well I can guess at it, Captain Hastings. A pair of revolvers of my husband's were mounted upon the wall. One of them is missing. I pointed this out to the police, and they took the other one away with them.'

Later in the story we are told that the bullet had been extracted and was proved to have been fired from a revolver identical with the one held by the police. This is important because she's not saying the bullet was fired from *that* gun but rather the same *sort* of gun.

This indicates Agatha's knowledge is gradually accumulating, possibly after many years with the Detection Club and carrying out independent research. As we progress through Christie's canon, it's clear that she's becoming aware of further developments in the science of forensic ballistics and moving away from more circumstantial evidence.

* * *

The forensics of *Death on the Nile* predominantly focuses on gunshot wounds, whereas in The Hollow — published nine years later — the science associated with the identification of firearms is the main feature, and there's a feeling that Christie is deliberately informing the readers of these extraordinary techniques after discovering them herself. After the shooting of the adulterous Dr John Christow at the country house called The Hollow, confusion ensues when the revolver at the scene is tossed into the pool by a careless family member. It's retrieved as evidence because 'identification of the revolver is the next thing' on the investigation agenda, according to Inspector Grange. However, it subsequently transpires that, unlike in earlier Christie stories, the firearm found at the scene was *not* the one used in the crime. In this book, we have a deliberate shift from the circumstantial evidence found in earlier murder mysteries to a much more scientific evidence-based approach, and the first mention of 'ballistics'. Furthermore, when discussing the possible murderer, it's suggested they 'mightn't know about our being able to identify the gun used from the marks on the rifling'. Poirot muses, 'How many people do know that, I wonder?' and the conversation concludes, 'quite a lot of people would know — on account of all the detective stories that are written'.

Crucially here, Christie uses the technical term 'rifling', referring to that spiral pattern cut into the inside of the barrels of some guns, and even has a character mention the 'ballistics report', showing a clear development in her knowledge of firearms investigation; knowledge which she is imparting to her readers by 1946. Whether her readers already share her knowledge, or whether this is new information to them, is something we can only speculate on, but she wouldn't be the first writer to introduce factual science through their fiction. We've already discussed Arthur Conan Doyle's tendency to do this via his Sherlock Holmes stories. This too is important to point out because in *The Hollow* there is a meta-loop in which we discover that the murderer very nearly gets away with the real-life crime because of something they had recently read in fiction:

> 'I'd read in that detective story about the police being able to tell which gun a bullet has been fired from. Sir Henry had shown me how to load and fire a revolver that afternoon. I'd take two revolvers. I'd shoot John with one and then hide it . . . '

Just prior to this, in the early 1940s, Christie had written *Curtain*, which was to be the last book to feature Poirot and Hastings. (Fearing that the war might put an end to her and her writing career, she wanted to give Poirot fans closure, so she wrote this final chapter in their adventures — along with her 'final' Miss Marple book, written for the same reason — and both were sealed in a bank vault until publication in 1975 and 1976 respectively. In the interim she produced many more books featuring both Miss Marple and Hercule Poirot, but was always safe in the knowledge that should something happen to her their endings were already recorded.)

Again, in *Curtain*, we have mention of rifling, this time from Captain Hastings when musing about a man who accidentally shot his wife:

> 'It was Colonel Luttrell who fired the shot. There were ways of deciding what weapon a bullet had been fired from; the marks on the bullet must agree with the rifling on the barrel.'

Though the book was published in 1975 just before Christie's death, we know she wrote it in the 1940s and was therefore aware of rifling in that decade. In keeping with this timeline, *A Murder Is Announced*, from 1950, has an accurate description of forensic ballistics after an intruder is shot at twice during a blackout. In the days following the crime, we're told: 'The two bullet holes showed plainly. The bullets themselves had been extracted and had been sent for comparison with the revolver.' The revolver was found on the floor after the incident, and again it's no longer taken for granted that it was the gun used in the shooting. Christie drives this point home in *At Bertram's Hotel*, published in 1965, one of the last books of hers published to feature contemporary gunshots: 'The ballistics experts have examined it. You know enough of firearms to be aware that their evidence is reliable.' As Christie progresses through the decades, she realises there now has to be a scientific comparison for her mystery stories to be believable.

* * *

Returning to the pre-Firearms Act days of the 1930s: *The Murder at the Vicarage* is the full-length novel which introduces us to the complex character of my favourite fictional sleuth of all time, Miss Marple. Described as an old Victorian lady with snowy white hair and piercing blue eyes, Miss Jane Marple appears to be a very unlikely nemesis of criminals with her mild manners, propensity for knitting and darkly cynical mind; perhaps a tad far-fetched. But little did Christie know that one of her most famous creations would manifest in real life as a bespectacled mature American woman called Frances Glessner Lee. Ms Glessner Lee — born in the Victorian era, just like Jane Marple — was heiress to a vast agricultural fortune, and was discouraged from her interest in forensic pathology by her family. Her brother was allowed to attend Harvard, yet she was not, so she satisfied her fascination with crime by reading the Sherlock Holmes stories, just as Agatha Christie had done. After her brother's death in 1930, aged fifty-two, she finally took steps towards a career in forensics. Having inherited the family fortune, she possessed the money to fund her interests, and she is most famous for using it to create the Nutshell Studies of Unexplained Death. Whereas some old ladies are said to be rather clichéd in their charitable interests, and are often depicted as giving their money to donkey sanctuaries and cats' homes, Frances Glessner Lee spent her cash creating doll's-house depictions of actual murders to train investigators at the new Department for Legal Medicine at Harvard University (a department she endowed and helped to create). These intricate dioramas are tiny crime scenes she made between 1944 and 1948 and are so called because she wanted to train homicide investigators to 'convict the guilty, clear the innocent, and find the truth in a nutshell'. They are all so realistic they contain working lights, bullet holes at various angles, functioning mousetraps and accurately discoloured corpses. At the time, each one cost between $3,000 and $4,500 to create — around $40,000 in modern money! While the dioramas do draw on real cases, Glessner Lee imagined and designed each setting to resemble but not replicate the original scenes, embellishing them with elements from her imagination and the world she inhabited. They are still in use today for training by the Harvard Associates in Police Science.

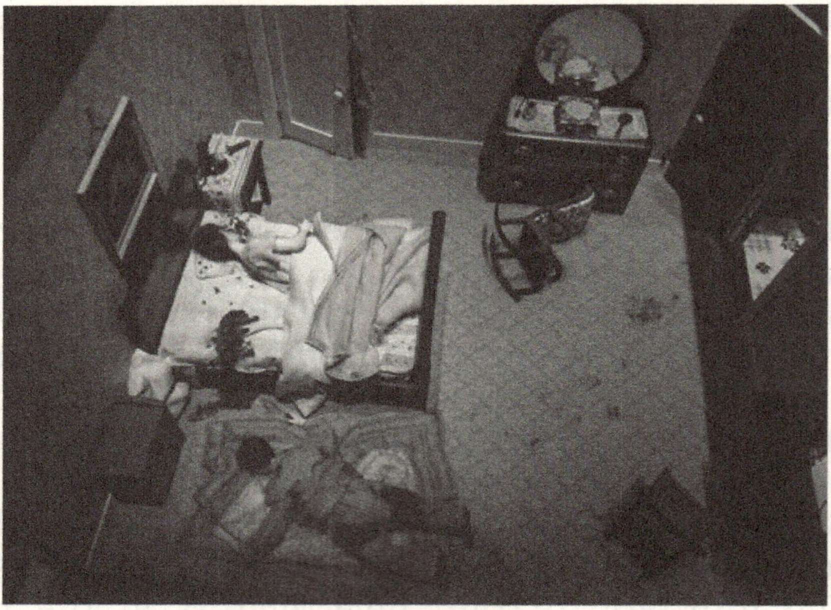

One of the Nutshell Studies of Unexplained Death created by 'real-life Miss Marple' Frances Glessner Lee

I find the notion of miniature crime scenes utterly fitting for a book on Agatha Christie, given that she had a passion for real houses as an adult which she attributed to her childhood love of toy houses. She says in her autobiography that she absolutely loved her doll's house as a child, and goes on to explain that when it came to spending her pocket money, apart from boiled sweets — and a penny in the 'waifs and strays' box — 'The rest went towards the furnishing and equipping of my dolls house.'

I should add that Glessner Lee wasn't the first person to use miniature simulacra to help convict the guilty and clear the innocent. Tiny crime scene dioramas were used in the British legal system and are known as 'English crime-scene miniatures'. One notable example was in the 1920s, when the Crumbles Murder, mentioned in the introduction, was attended by pathologist Bernard Spilsbury. The entire scene was reconstructed in Lilliputian scale to place before a jury, to try to ascertain whether or not the story of the defendant, Patrick Mahon, was credible.

But Glessner Lee didn't just create the Nutshell Studies. She also commissioned a series of ceramic chest plates which illustrate the typical wound patterns caused by gunshots fired from a variety of weapons at different distances. The plates, made in 1940 and depicting both entry and exit wounds, are still used as teaching aids and for reference. Because of her contribution to the advancement of forensic science, Lee became the first honorary female police captain in the US, and is considered the 'godmother of forensic science'. It's clear that with a quick mind, the will to seek justice and the time or means to do so, the most unlikely people can become super sleuths, just like Miss Marple!

Frances Glessner Lee, the real-life Miss Marple

That said, it does seem in *The Murder at the Vicarage* that perhaps Miss Marple's knowledge of firearms is a little too implausible: among various devices used to distract and befuddle witnesses, Christie's murderers cleverly employ a silencer to disguise the actual time of the shooting. (A silencer is a piece of equipment manufactured to decrease the sound of a gunshot, but the word 'silencer' is really a misnomer as a gunshot can never be completely silenced. For this reason, professionals tend to call the contraption a *moderator* or a *suppressor* nowadays, although they wouldn't have done in the 1930s.) What doesn't quite make sense is why the one who figures out the discrepancy between what seemed to be a shot heard by the villagers and the actual time of death is the old dear with the snowy white hair — stating, 'There is, I believe, an invention called a Maxim Silencer' — when there is an army colonel and several police officers on the case! Miss Marple, and by extension Agatha Christie, is right in some respects: the Maxim Silencer was the first commercially successful sound suppressor, patented in 1909 — but she did unfortunately get some details wrong. This type of silencer was designed for fixed-barrelled rifles, not pistols, but we know the weapon used in this particular case was a pistol because the suspect 'Went right in, threw down the pistol on the table, and 'I did it,' he says, just like that.' The original advertising for the Maxim Silencer states: 'revolvers and automatic pistols are not adapted to be silenced and therefore cannot be fitted.'

Miss Marple explains that she knows about Maxim Silencers from reading fictional detective stories and, in a strange self-referential way, Christie is drawing attention to the fact that these stories aren't always 100 per cent accurate — often there needs to be some artistic licence. Perhaps, as her knowledge of guns increased, she realised her earlier mistakes.

After all she has Poirot comment, in *Death on the Nile*: 'A man — certainly a man who had had much handling of firearms — would know that. But a woman — a woman would not know . . . No. She would have read the detective stories where they are not always exact as to details.'

For our purposes here, though, her details are exact enough. Agatha Christie may have considered the revolver bullet crude and she may have favoured methods such as poison, but that's not the case in real life. In fact, in the modern world, more people are killed by handguns than by any other method of murder. Our current ballistics experts have to keep altering their methods and improving their knowledge to keep up with advances in gun manufacture and usage, and Christie did the same by keeping her ballistic knowledge up to date.

* * *

Christie apparently didn't like guns, and yet in her stories she dispatched dozens of people using firearms, both on and off the page. Her knowledge was initially limited, but as time passes her vocabulary improves, her science becomes more complex and we even see her correcting a mistake from an early book with a comment in a later one! Remember how in *The Secret Adversary* from 1922 Julius P. Hersheimer's 'Little Willie' was referred to as both an automatic and a revolver, two different types of gun? I can only assume that Christie thought the words revolver and automatic were simply synonyms for 'gun' and didn't understand the complex mechanisms which make them completely different. However, in *The Hollow*, twenty-four years later, where we get those mentions of the ballistics report and the specific term 'rifling', we also have this exchange between Inspector Grange and the butler, Gudgeon:

> Grange said, 'That's an automatic pistol, not a revolver.'
>
> Gudgeon coughed, 'I may have used the term *revolver* rather loosely, Sir.'

Is this an admission that Agatha did the same in earlier days? Agatha used guns for mayhem and misdirection, as well as suicide and murder. In various stories the sounds of the gun are disguised among the noises of fireworks or muffied in some way, and the guns themselves are used to distract and confuse. When it comes to firearms, Christie certainly wasn't afraid to put her finger on the trigger.

4

Documents and Handwriting

Suddenly he saw faint indications of letters.
Words formed themselves slowly — words of fire.

— *Murder on the Orient Express*

The forensic sciences have as objects of study such ostensibly compelling elements as bones, bullets and burnt bodies; I'm therefore under no illusion that you picked up this book because you're looking forward to this — the forensic documentation chapter — most of all. Paper? Ink? Handwriting? Compared to the other forensic disciplines it sounds potentially dry and uninteresting, and often books on criminal investigations opt to leave out the subject altogether, maybe because they see it as too specialist, maybe because they see it as too banal. But questioned documents and related evidence are incredibly exciting. 'Poison pen letters', for example, are a common feature in murder mysteries; both Agatha and her fellow Detection Club member Dorothy L. Sayers used them as plot devices. Ransom notes may be some of the most terrifying pieces of evidence available, needing immediate specialist attention to save the most precious lives. And some of the biggest cases in criminal history have been solved using the sciences applied to questioned documents and modes of communication, rather than from analysing savage scenes of blood spatter and broken glass. Famously, gangster Al Capone was imprisoned for eleven years not for his Prohibition rackets or violent mob hits like the St Valentine's Day Massacre, but for tax evasion, requiring the examination of comparatively boring written ledgers and fake tax returns. The terrifying BTK Killer — initials standing for 'Bind Torture Kill' — active in 1970s Kansas, who was caught in the 1990s via a floppy disk which he sent to a local TV station to boast of his crimes, stated after his arrest, 'The floppy did me in.' Closer to home, notorious poisoner Dr Harold Shipman, responsible for more than 250 deaths over 23 years, using diamorphine or sedatives, was only caught because he tried to forge the will of his last victim, Kathleen Grundy: the very first time he had tried to do something like that, as financial gain had never been a part of his MO.

Similarly, some of the world's most famous *unsolved* murders and their perpetrators have become the stuff of legend because of associated documents. Jack the Ripper and the Zodiac Killer gained increased notoriety through the correspondence the police received, supposedly from them, though both killers remain unidentified to this day. The Zodiac Killer was active in Northern California during the 1960s and 1970s, and named himself 'Zodiac' in a series of letters and cryptograms which he tauntingly sent to Bay Area police. During the height of the Ripper frenzy in 1888, Scotland Yard received many missives purporting to be from Jack the Ripper himself. Though none was ever proved to actually come from him, and some indeed were traced to mentally unstable people who were claiming to have committed his crimes, these letters are responsible for giving him the name 'Jack the Ripper' and have become synonymous with his reign of terror over London's Whitechapel slums.

These are just a few, most well-known examples: it is quite common for killers to want to draw attention to themselves or taunt the police, and in especially high-profile cases there may be many individuals who claim they committed the crime just for some publicity of their own. Agatha herself references this phenomenon in *Sparkling Cyanide* when Colonel Race says, 'You'd be surprised how many lying spiteful letters get written after any event that's been given any sort of publicity in the press.'

Jack the Ripper, along with many real-life murderers, played a role in inspiring Agatha to write The *ABC Murders*, and he's mentioned in the book by name several times: 'Remember the long continued successes of Jack the Ripper,' Poirot says as the alphabetical killings begin, and later on a character laments that she doesn't want to read the newspaper headlines because, 'It's like Jack the Ripper all over again.'

Agatha was — as so many are — aware of the infamous Ripper murders and seized on the idea of provocative letters to the authorities to fuel the rampage of 'The ABC Killer'. (Whether any of the historical Ripper letters were actually penned by the serial killer himself is irrelevant in this context.) Her ABC Killer is on the face of it a serial killer, despite the fact that specific term isn't mentioned in the book. We're told one of the characters, Dr Thompson, is very interested in the '*chain* or *series* type of murder' instead. That's because, in Agatha Christie's aforementioned clairvoyant style, she wrote the book at least twenty-five years before the term 'serial killer' was even coined, which was in the 1960s at the earliest. And it wasn't just Agatha Christie who touched upon this topic. Despite the comfortable, predictable and safe reputation golden-age detective fiction now has, Martin Edwards insists that these books in the 1930s 'explored miscarriages of justice, forensic pathology and serial killings long before these topics became fashionable (and before the term 'serial killer' was invented).'

It is therefore typical of Agatha not to shy away from such harrowing subject matter. Despite the commonly held belief that she only wrote about 'cosy killings', in reality she frequently touched upon some of the darkest aspects of human nature. In the introduction to the 2014 edition of *After the Funeral*, Sophie Hannah says that Agatha Christie,

> . . . understands the depravity, ruthlessness and dangerous weakness of human beings. She knows all about warped minds, long grudges, agonising need; in each of her novels, a familiarity with the darkest parts of the human psyche underpins the narrative.

I therefore find her use of questioned documents, typewriters, handwritten notes and threatening missives just as exciting as the other forensic aspects of her stories, and they feature as key evidence in some of her most *outstanding* books. Forged letters and communications are pivotal in gathering the ten island guests in the seminal *And Then There Were None*. Without these summons we would never have read about how the victims were all ingeniously dispatched, one by one, on secluded Soldier Island. In *The Murder of Roger Ackroyd*, which specifically launched Agatha into the upper echelons of detective writers, the whole plot is dependent on a letter sent to the titular Roger by a woman who later commits suicide — a letter which the murderer feels they have to kill for. And in *Murder on the Orient Express* it is a tiny, burnt fragment of a letter — expertly recovered by Hercule Poirot with some improvised forensics — which gives him the single clue that enables him to solve the *whole case*. He says of the fragment, 'The letter was burnt by the murderer. Why? Because it mentioned the word 'Armstrong' which is the clue to the mystery.'

What is Forensic Document Analysis?

Also known as questioned document examination (QDE), this forensic discipline encompasses many aspects, including:

- Distinguishing forged documents from genuine ones
- The identification and interpretation of alterations, deletions and additions to documents
- Restoring or detecting erased or obliterated writing
- Analysing inks, papers, machines or chemicals involved in document creation
- Attributing handwriting, signatures, printing and other writing to individuals, either for exclusion or comparison

The current guidelines for forensic document

examiners (FDEs) indicate there are four components to the discipline. They state that an examiner 'makes scientific examinations, comparisons, and analyses of documents' to:

1. Establish genuineness or non-genuineness, or to expose forgery, or to reveal alterations, additions or deletions
2. Identify or eliminate persons as the source of handwriting
3. Identify or eliminate the source of typewriting or other impression, marks, or relative evidence
4. Write reports or give testimony, when needed, to aid the users of the examiner's services in understanding the examiner's findings

The list of items to which all of the above can be applied is hugely varied and might include determining whether a lottery ticket has been altered, whether an autograph on a piece of memorabilia is genuine or fake, who wrote a ransom note, what year an apparently ancient text was written, or if a piece of note paper was torn off a particular note pad. FDEs use the term 'document' incredibly broadly. It can mean any material which has been written on or marked in some way, be it graffiti on a wall or a message written in blood at a murder scene or, in more pedestrian cases, a signed guitar or football. It could even be the manufacturer's stamp on a product like meat or eggs. In Agatha's books, unexpected items which come under the umbrella term of 'questioned documents' include a monogrammed handkerchief, clothing tags, bridge scores, an altered passport, receipts for costumes and the fragment of a drug vial label.

Agatha included some basic document examination tropes in her stories from the very first: burnt fragments which have their meanings misinterpreted in *The Mysterious Affair at Styles* and edge-matching pieces of paper in the Tommy and Tuppence short story 'The Gentleman Dressed in Newspaper' (from the 1929 collection *Partners in Crime*). In this story Lady Merivale is seemingly murdered by Captain Hale — the Gentleman of the title — at a costume ball, and Christie gets the forensic process spot-on:

> 'Do you know what we found clasped in the dead lady's hand? A fragment torn from a newspaper. My men have orders to take Captain Hale's costume away with them . . . If there's a tear in it corresponding to the missing piece — well, it'll be the end of the case.'

However, I want to focus mainly on the first three components of the above numbered list, and will start with number one, the issue of genuineness.

Forensic examiners can establish the provenance of a questioned document as a whole by confirming whether it's made up of the correct constituents: does the paper seem consistent with the year the document is purported to be from? Is the ink a type that was available then? Are any folds, creases and tears present consistent with the document's age?

Many forgeries are much more straightforward than the creation of a whole new document and may simply consist of making small alterations to an existing one — as for instance occurs in Agatha's quintessentially English *The Murder at the Vicarage*, the first full-length novel to feature Miss Marple. In the book, the inhabitants of the idyllic village of St Mary Mead — home of Miss Marple — are going about their usual summer activities such as playing tennis and having tea with the local vicar, when a brutal murder rocks the small community. Inspector Slack thinks he's incredibly lucky that the victim of a point-blank shooting was writing a note to the vicar at the time of his murder, and had helpfully added the time of writing to it:

> It was a piece of vicarage notepaper, and it was headed at the top 6:20. 'Dear Clement' — it began — 'Sorry I cannot wait any longer, but I must . . . '

The note abruptly ends here, punctuated by a bullet in the head rather than a full-stop for the unfortunate scribe and victim, Colonel Protheroe. The assumption is that after writing the time down he began the note which ended almost immediately afterwards — meaning he was killed at 6:20. But this seems too good to be true, as these types of 'clues' often are and it's lucky for Inspector Slack that a suspicious Miss Marple is on the scene to help investigate this complex crime . . .

When examining handwriting, the second task FDEs may carry out is to identify or eliminate a particular person as the writer. The genuine forensic expert is concerned only with the physical characteristics of the writing, in an attempt to match the unknown exemplar with perhaps a known suspect. They don't try to determine someone's personality from their writing style; their job doesn't lie in trying to equate an anonymous writer's large, swirly lettering with a confident or egotistical personality. This type of speculative analysis is something we have recently seen in newspaper headlines, which have stated 'Forensic Handwriting Analyst examined Royal Letters; Compares Meghan to Kate and Diana!' This isn't 'forensic' and it's not handwriting analysis — it's known as *graphology*, and it is not an accepted forensic science — it's more of a pseudoscience, like the previously mentioned phrenology.

At its simplest level, this aspect of questioned document examination could be considered a visual comparison of one specimen of handwriting with another, and it's in Christie's works from her very first case. In *The Mysterious Affair at Styles*, Poirot carries out this comparison himself: 'Then I will leave the remarkable similarity of hand-writing between the note, the register and your own to the consideration of the jury.' It may be the first time he compares and contrasts handwriting in this way but it most certainly won't be the last.

In real life, several different features of handwriting are noted by examiners undertaking a forensic analysis, such as construction of character forms — for example, we each have our own way of writing our capital Gs and capital Es. The lines of our letters slope slightly to the left or right, the spaces between them vary, and a particular letter or number may be written entirely differently by two people. Some of us write a '7' with a line across the stem, and some don't. Some people loop the tails on their lowercase 'g', 'j' and 'y' so that they form a complete ellipse, and some don't. Even one individual's handwriting can vary depending on the time of day, the speed at which they're writing, and how long they've been writing for. This is known as 'variation'. A five-point scale of certainty is then used in the UK and USA to record a conclusion, from highest possibility to lowest:

1. Common authorship
2. High probability
3. Could well have been written by the same person
4. Inconclusive
5. No evidence

In Agatha's books, these numbers aren't used directly but the principles of many of the points are there in her works. Yet when she describes handwriting analysis it's clear that she knows it can be done, but stops short of knowing exactly *how* it can be done. Returning to *The Murder at the Vicarage*, and the mysterious note which was ostensibly penned by the victim, Colonel Protheroe, we learn that Miss Marple is right to be suspicious, because it's a forgery. When Colonel Melchett informs the vicar of this fact, the vicar asks, 'Are they certain?' and Melchett replies, 'Well, they're as certain as experts are. You know what an expert is! Oh, but they're sure enough.'

Typewriters are frequently found in Agatha's books, which brings us to component number three. These machines, admittedly not widely used any more, consist of individual metal characters (letters, punctuation, numbers, etc.), each attached to the end of a type-bar which is raised when the corresponding key is depressed; the action presses the character stamp onto an ink-infused ribbon and thus transfers its image to the paper behind. There are so many separate parts to a typewriter, and such a variety of faults which can manifest on those parts, that its combination of individual imperfections may make a machine — and the typed image produced on it — unique. This is true particularly as a typewriter gets older and acquires these identifiable flaws.

In *And Then There Were None*, when looking for clues from the various typed invitations the guests and staff received, Mr Blore studies the typewriter: 'Coronation machine. Quite new — no defects. Ensign paper — the most widely used make. You won't get anything out of that.' A 'Coronation' isn't a model of typewriter, but a Corona is. Perhaps Christie wasn't allowed to mention brands, but either way, it's rather spectacular that Blore is able to identify the exact model of machine which typed the letters, just from looking at the text. There's no explanation as to why this should be the case, except, perhaps, that Blore is an ex-police officer. But it does illustrate Christie's awareness of document examiners' techniques. The typewriter which Blore describes as 'quite new' is no help in providing any clues to the guests stranded on the island. That said, if the typewriter was indeed incredibly new and only used to type out a few letters to these particular guests, it might be productive for an expert to examine the ribbon, as the characters typed would likely still be visible there in impression. (On an older ribbon, that has been frequently rewound in continued use over an extended period of time, these individual letters would become impossible to ascertain as they'd all merge into one splodge.) It's a tedious and laborious process. But the people on Soldier Island aren't experts so we can't expect them to know that, not even Blore. Nowadays, a computerised optical system for transcribing ribbons in this way has been developed but has less cause to be used in our modern era.

* * *

There are some aspects of what we might loosely call 'document examination' which feature more in murder mysteries than in real life. One of the most well-known and perhaps even clichéd forms of this discipline is the process of revealing writing which has been left on underlying sheets of a notepad. In books and in other forms of media, we're often shown someone lightly rubbing a pencil over an apparently empty page only for the depressed writing to be made visible by the pencil's graphite. It's a favourite method of amateur sleuths like Jessica Fletcher in the iconic *Murder, She Wrote*, but Agatha resisted falling into the trap of using it. The closest she gets is in the previously discussed 'Murder in the Mews' when Poirot is evidently looking for *something* of this kind at the scene of what appears to be a suicide. No suicide note is present so he examines the blotter pad. He later reveals, 'The blotting book had on top a clean, untouched piece of blotting paper,' meaning there was no blotted ink on it, but also no indentations. Had there been, I'm sure he would have gently run a pencil over them to reveal them! In real life, this process of impression examination does occur — but not by rubbing a pencil over the page in this clichéd manner — and methods of detection depend on the depth of the impressed handwriting. Deeper etchings can usually be detected using a light directed over the document at a low, oblique angle, and this was the case as early as the 1930s. Fainter impressions can be revealed using a process called Electrostatic Detection or ESDA, which is a sensitive yet complex process, but as it was developed in London in 1979 it isn't relevant to Agatha's writings.

History of Forensic Document Analysis

Document examination is one of the oldest of the forensic disciplines, and in fact is often considered to be the progenitor of forensic science. Historical references show that frauds involving documents, such as forgery, evolved along with the development of writing itself. During the Roman Empire (around the first century AD), expert testimony regarding written documents was accepted in the courts of law, indeed in the *Forum* (*Forum Romanum*), which, as mentioned, gives us the word 'forensic'. At this point document examination for forensic purposes might have involved, for example, a witness examining a signature and declaring whether or not they thought it was genuinely that of the signatory. This is simple visual recognition and a rudimentary method, but document analysis nonetheless.

Despite its use so early on, there was a gap in its development for many centuries — as is also the case for some other forensic sciences like entomology (study of insects), blood spatter analysis and autopsy. Indeed, the first recorded use of document examination in an English-speaking court is usually held to be the *Goodtitle d. Revett v. Braham* case heard in 1792, nearly two thousand years later. The revolutionary aspect of this case was that, rather than witness recognition being used, two documents were compared side by side: the questioned document and the exemplar, in what would become a standard forensic comparison between the known sample and the unknown sample.

The early part of the twentieth century — when Agatha was starting to write and subsequently becoming a household name — was the time when the forensics of document analysis really boomed. In 1901, Daniel T. Ames, a penmanship teacher and early examiner of contested handwriting, published a book titled *Forgery* which illustrated various cases of falsification and fraud. Then Albert S. Osborn, now known as the Father of Questioned Documents, wrote his pivotal book on the subject in 1910, and a second edition was published in 1929. With this book, *Questioned Documents*, he brought a scientific approach to the forensic examination of documentation and expanded the discipline to include the examination of paper, ink and typewriters. Together, Ames and Osborn are responsible for the field of questioned documents as we see it today, by pioneering the use of magnification and oblique lighting in their examinations.

We've met Bernard Spilsbury several times so far, and although he was considered to be the 'real-life Sherlock Holmes' in the UK, he shares that title with a contemporary known as 'American Sherlock'; the criminalist Edward Oscar Heinrich. E. O. Heinrich, as he preferred to be known, was active in 1920s and 1930s California and is described uncannily like Spilsbury: the words 'methodical' and 'commanding' are often used to illustrate his character. In the latter part of his career he worked with Paul Leland

Kirk, whom we met in the Trace Evidence chapter. Heinrich is most commonly associated with the sensational Fatty Arbuckle case, in which the silent-film star was accused of sexually assaulting young model Virginia Rappe and causing her death via ruptured bladder and peritonitis, in 1921. But he really came to prominence when he forensically examined the handwritten ransom note sent to an archbishop after the kidnapping of a priest in Colma, California, in 1924. His opinion differed from that of the other handwriting experts who examined the note and he made an extraordinary statement about the kidnapper: 'Your man is a baker.' He surmised this by noting the form of some of the letters, for example 'the square bottom of the 'U' . That's the style bakers use in writing on cakes.'

Eventually California police found their man and he was indeed a baker.

Ultimately, though, the Questioned Documents Unit (QDU) of the FBI exists because of one of America's most notoriously cruel crimes. It was established after the kidnapping of the Lindbergh baby in 1932, a contemporary case which Agatha used as the starting point in *Murder on the Orient Express*.

In March 1932, the twenty-month-old son of famous American aviator Charles Lindbergh was kidnapped from his bedroom in New Jersey. A ransom note was left demanding $50,000 for his safe return (over $800,000 in today's money — a huge amount, especially for a nation in the midst of the Great Depression). The ransom money was handed over a cemetery wall, as instructed in the note, and the distraught father was assured that his son was safe and alive in a boat off the Massachusetts coast. He anxiously flew back and forth over this coast in an attempt to find the baby himself, with no luck. Eventually, tragically, Charles Jr was found murdered just four miles from where he had been originally taken, and — more distressingly — it was discovered that the infant's death had been caused by a blow to the skull which was received around the time he had been taken; the plan had never been for Charles Jr to be returned to his anxious parents alive.

Investigators turned quickly to one of the main pieces of evidence: the ransom note. Neither the note nor the envelopes revealed any latent fingerprints, so the handwriting was examined instead. Analysts noted poor grammar and unusual linguistic characteristics, which led them to believe the person who had penned it was poorly educated and of German descent. The fact that a homemade ladder had been used in the kidnapping also suggested someone with carpentry skills. The investigation team had some further document information in the banknotes used to pay the ransom, as they were all labelled with recorded serial numbers, exactly as money is today.

The case, however, seemed to stall.

But over the next couple of years some of the numbers on the ransom money occasionally surfaced in a higher concentration in the Bronx, New York. At the same time, novel forensic work was being carried out on the homemade ladder, which had distinctive characteristics — so distinctive that the wood it was fashioned from was traced to a particular lumber company *also* in the Bronx. The net was beginning to tighten.

Later on, yet another note with a serial number from the Lindbergh ransom was used at a petrol station. In this case, the man paying with it was acting suspiciously, so the attendant wrote down his licence-plate details. The vehicle was registered to Bruno Richard Hauptmann, a carpenter of German descent. He was arrested and his house was searched. As well as wood matching that used to fashion the ladder found at the Lindberghs' house, police also discovered the remains of the ransom money.

In 1935, three years after the initial kidnapping of Charles Lindbergh Jr, Bruno Richard Hauptmann was convicted and executed.

The shocking case was described in worldwide press as the 'trial of the century' so it's no wonder Agatha was inspired by it to write *Murder on the Orient Express*. Perhaps, having had a young child of her own, the crime seemed particularly distressing to her, although it's more likely she was intrigued by the characters she could create to 'solve' the crime. Her book was published in 1934, so at the time of her writing it no one had yet been held to account for the baby's murder — that wouldn't happen for another year. Perhaps that's why she found it so necessary to provide her own fictional justice for the crime, and wrote this 'justice' in such a satisfying manner. I'd never want to give away the plot but there is something incredibly gratifying — and original — about the way in which vengeance is meted out to the aforementioned villain Mr Ratchett, which is not only spectacular storytelling but also perhaps Agatha's attempt to provide catharsis or some closure to a crime that hadn't yet been solved — at a point at which nobody knew whether it ever would be.

* * *

Sometimes murders hit the headlines not only because of the identity of the victim, or the brutality of the crime, but because the methods used to solve them involve innovative techniques or combinations of cutting-edge sciences. The following is a fantastic example of novel techniques used to solve a notoriously gruesome crime, and a pivotal case in the development of forensic science because it was the first time certain key new methods were used.

On the morning of 29 September 1935, a young woman called Susan Haines Johnson was enjoying the fresh Scottish air in the town of Moffat, Dumfriesshire. The area was named The Devil's Beef Tub, and as she crossed the corresponding Devil's Bridge something disturbing caught her eye. A package of some kind had become wedged against a rock on the banks of the stream; a package with a human arm poking out.

After Susan had informed the authorities, a thorough search was made of the stream and a multitude of similar parcels were found containing body parts and pieces of flesh which were highly decomposed and infested with maggots. They were carelessly wrapped in various newspapers and women's clothing and — particularly disturbing — a head was wrapped in a child's romper. At least two heads were discovered, and a total of around seventy packages, so investigators knew they were dealing with the remains of more than one individual. The case came to be known as 'The Jigsaw Murders', and I believe Agatha references it in *Dumb Witness* when Hastings remarks, 'Poirot, you don't think she'll turn up in parcels or dismembered in a trunk?' This case would have only just happened at the time she was writing her book (it reached publication in 1937).

It wasn't simply the quantity of mutilated body parts which made this case so disturbing, it was the *way* in which they had been mutilated: the perpetrator had obvious medical knowledge, and even some knowledge of medicolegal (forensic) techniques. In order to obliterate the identity of the victims the macabre killer had peeled flesh from their faces, removed their fingertips and pulled their teeth out. Even birth marks, scars and other identifiable features had been removed — a fact which was discovered later. Despite this careful and systematic mutilation, the perpetrator made one critical error: they wrapped some of the parcels in copies of an English newspaper called the *Sunday Graphic*, yet the bodies were discovered in Scotland. Furthermore this particular issue was what is known as a 'slip edition', published for a specific event in a particular region, in this case the Morecambe Festival in Lancaster. For the investigation this narrowed down the search area dramatically. In a relatively small town of around 90,000 people it took no time at all to identify the victims. (For comparison, at that time my home town of Liverpool had over 850,000 inhabitants.) Police discovered that two women were missing: Isabella Ruxton (who was married to a Dr Buck Ruxton, a medical doctor) and their housemaid, Mary-Jane Rogerson. The hypothesis became that Dr Buxton had murdered his wife Isabella in a fit of rage, and then turned on the housemaid because she had either seen him commit the act or suspected he'd done so. He'd done everything he could to strip these women of their identity, and yet overlooked the fact he'd wrapped them in the local newspaper.

A rhyme repeated by locals at the time went:

Red stains on the carpet, red stains on the knife,
Oh Dr Buck Ruxton you cut up your wife.
The nursemaid she saw you and threatened to tell,
So Dr Buck Ruxton, you killed her as well.

After the doctor was arrested, police searched his home and found human flesh and blood in the drains leading from the bath, as well as bloodstains on the carpets. They had their man, but they still had to positively identify the remains as those of Isabella Ruxton and Mary-Jane Rogerson.

In the absence of DNA testing and without teeth and fingerprints, the new method of structural facial comparison was used to identify the victims. Images of Isabella's decomposed and stripped skull, taken from various angles, were superimposed on photographs of her face and positioned at corresponding angles. The same method was used to identify Mary, and this was even demonstrated in court at Dr Ruxton's trial.

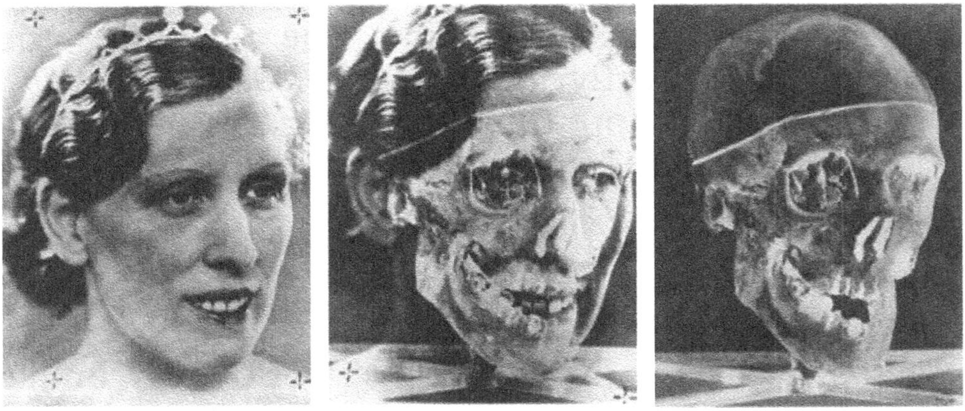

A photograph of Isabella Ruxton's face superimposed over the image of her skull

Taken with other circumstantial evidence such as the fact he asked a cleaning lady to come and clean a huge red stain out of the carpet, a stain which she swore in court was blood, and he was seen burning items of possible evidence in the garden, Ruxton's guilt seemed very clear. It didn't take long for the jury to find him guilty of murder and mutilation, and he was hanged in 1936.

The most interesting aspect of this case is those newspapers. Without that initial clue to point investigators to a small town in the north of England, these murders would have been nearly impossible to solve in the 1930s. The case wasn't only known locally — it made national headlines and a book, *Trial of Buck Ruxton*, appeared in a very significant series called Notable British Trials which the Detection Club referred to frequently. The series had been running since 1905, and covered not just this but many other cases Christie would go on to feature in her canon. She may well have read the Notable British Trials series in its entirety for inspiration for her books, in addition to national newspapers, and certainly would have read the Buxton volume. She references the Ruxton case directly in *One, Two, Buckle My Shoe*, when Inspector Japp wonders if their missing person will be somewhere ' . . . cut up in little pieces like Mrs Ruxton'.

* * *

Agatha lived in a pre-'paperless' world, very unlike the one we live in now. Her characters were called on house phones (if they even had them), and any messages were taken down on notepads; threats were made ransom-note style with an alphabet cut out of magazines and pasted onto sheets of paper; letters were folded into typed envelopes and posted; and people communicated by placing personal ads in newspapers or sending handwritten missives via a 'boy'. This gave her a huge amount of relatable, everyday material to work with.

It also means that she wouldn't have relied on software, USBs and 'the cloud' to store her ideas and help create her works — she wrote ideas in notebooks, some of which she never got around to finishing. In her autobiography she describes how she writes down all her ideas in little notebooks, but that she often loses them. She says, 'I used to make notes in them of ideas that had struck me, or about some poison or drug, or about some clever bit of swindling that I had read about in the paper.' Eventually she realised that all she needed was her typewriter and a steady surface to write on, as she'd begun working straight from the typewriter rather than jotting down entire books or stories with a pencil and paper first. Her typewriter of choice was a Remington Portable, and once she'd switched to this more mobile piece of kit she sometimes even typed in the bath.

Agatha was familiar with the instruments of communication — as everyone else would have been at the time — so it makes sense that she featured paper and typewriter evidence in many of her books, often referencing makes of typewriter or ink. In some ways, she understands that handwriting can be as unique and telling as fingerprints, and that ink patterns can rival those of blood in some instances. Lots of her stories may not seem as though they feature document evidence on first consideration, but it later transpires that such evidence is a pivotal part of the plot — sometimes even initiating the story. In *The ABC Murders*, ominous letters sent to Poirot set him on the trail of a serial killer; at the beginning of *Sad Cypress* Elinor Carlisle is manipulated into visiting her ailing aunt Laura, whom she is subsequently accused of murdering, by an anonymous letter containing a warning; in *The Moving Finger* a spate of poison pen letters appear to lead to the suicide of one recipient and further deaths, and in *A Murder Is Announced*, the first murder only occurs after it was announced in a local newspaper.

In other Christie books, the mystery can be solved only if we pay attention to the document evidence, like Carlotta Adams's letter to her sister in *Lord Edgware Dies*, Josephine's diary in *Crooked House*, the newspaper clipping saved by Mrs McGinty in *Mrs McGinty's Dead* and numerous wills, forged wills and codicils throughout her novels.

* * *

One of the objectives of a questioned document examiner is to expose forgery, and this can be done in different ways, as, of course, can forgery itself. The falsification of a document sometimes involves removal or erasure, of, say, a letter or digit; sometimes it may involve an addition. When modifying a cheque, a forger may add a zero — increasing the amount of money to be paid out tenfold. In the Christie canon, examples of an added letter or number start from her very first book, *The Mysterious Affair at Styles*. Poirot points out, 'You do not see that the letter was not written on the 17th, but on the 7th — the day after Miss

Howard's departure? The '1' was written in before the '7' to turn it into the 17th.'

Returning to *The Murder at the Vicarage*, most confusing is the note found at the death scene of Colonel Protheroe. Although Inspector Slack was grateful for its presence and happily saw it as a very convenient clue, it struck Miss Marple as 'exceedingly peculiar' from the beginning — possibly because it was a little *too* convenient. When the document was duly shown to be falsified it was assumed that the Colonel had written the bulk of the note — which seemed to indicate he'd had enough of waiting and was heading off home — and then it had been added to by a person or persons unknown. But in the end we're told:

> 'You know that unfinished letter that Protheroe was writing when he was killed? We got an expert on it — to say whether the '6:20' was added by a different hand . . . *That letter was never written by Protheroe at all.* It's a forgery. The '6:20' they think is written in a different hand again.'

It's a double-bluff! The letter itself was never written by the Colonel, but planted to make it look as though it was, and later on a second person, in collusion with the first, didn't realise the note was a forgery so added yet another example of handwriting and ink.

Miss Marple manages to catch out another forger during the murder investigation in *A Murder Is Announced*, when she notices that one of her cheques isn't quite right. And, of course, she's Miss Marple, so she knows exactly who is responsible and tells the Chief Constable all about it:

'He altered a cheque, you say?'

'You can see it was for seven pounds and he altered it to seventeen.'

She explains that she was the wrong person to try this technique on, since she's set in her ways:

> 'Seventeen pounds is a sum I *never* write a cheque for. For my personal expenditure, I usually cash seven — it used to be five, but everything has gone up so.'

* * *

Another of the roles of document examiners is to 'identify or eliminate persons as the source of handwriting' and, at the most basic level, Agatha understood handwriting comparison. It's something she knew the value of from the Lindbergh case — as did many of her contemporaries — but she must have learned about it long before that case brought it to the masses, as she features handwriting analysis in *The Mysterious Affair at Styles*, published twelve years earlier. The book's narrator Hastings, discussing what he and Poirot term 'the Cavendish case', tells us: 'The handwriting experts were called upon for their opinion of the signature of 'Alfred Inglethorp' in the chemist's poison register. They all declared unanimously that it certainly was *not* his hand-writing.' Which does have an important bearing on the murder, but rather as a bit of misdirection. That's why in the next Poirot book, *The Murder on the Links*, Poirot reminds Hastings of this form of evidence — 'Remember the handwriting testimony in the Cavendish case?' — although the reason he's mentioning it here is to point out its abject failure!

When there is a need to identify the source of handwriting beyond a shadow of a doubt, most often in Christie books it's in order to determine whether the correct person penned a suicide note. There may be some spoilers coming up, but in Agatha's novels, it's fair to say, there is always likely to be some ambiguity over suicide notes or there would be no 'murder' in the mystery.

In *Cards on the Table*, there is a question as to whether Mrs Lorrimer actually penned a set of suicide notes which she posted out to various recipients. The problem is, no one involved knows what her handwriting actually looked like, so they can't identify the suicide notes as being genuine. That's why in real-life investigations there has to be a verified exemplar of handwriting from the person in question to compare the unknown to.

In several novels there's a question about whether examples of handwriting meant for other purposes were in fact ingeniously repurposed as suicide notes. In *The Moving Finger* Mrs Symmington's suicide note, we're told, is 'I can't go on' on a scrap of paper; and in *Hickory, Dickory, Dock*, Celia's is 'Dear Mrs Hubbard, I really am sorry and this is the best I can do' on a similar scrap. It's their writing and no one can dispute that, but are torn scraps of paper really appropriate suicide notes? No. More often than not, people intending suicide take time to write their final missive properly, and scraps of paper aren't frequently used. They write with care, in their own, legible handwriting, and never repurpose bits from other correspondence — any note in a Christie book which appears to be a part of some other correspondence or doesn't directly reference suicide needs to be treated with caution.

For the most part in Agatha's books, however, the question is not about confirming who wrote something, but more about noticing discrepancies between one scribe and another. Agatha must have had knowledge of this process which is why she has Poirot so frustrated over a letter penned by victim Carlotta Adams in *Lord Edgware Dies*. He exclaims, 'There is no forgery of any kind here — no, it is all written in the same hand. And yet . . . it is impossible!' He knows what he's looking for in terms of a forgery, something he could have feasibly learned during his years as a detective, and he isn't finding it. It's actually something else about the letter which helps him solve the case in the end, making the paper — not the handwriting — the important piece of evidence here.

In *Mrs McGinty's Dead*, Poirot does the work of the forensic document examiner with more success, and asserts,

> 'The name Evelyn Hope, written in the book, is in your handwriting — the same handwriting as the words 'My Mother' on the back of this photograph. Mrs McGinty saw the photograph and the writing on it when she was tidying your things away.'

This is the clue which helps him solve the mystery of why Mrs McGinty was killed, and — importantly — *whodunnit*. But this type of comparison only works if the exemplar is truly from the source it's believed to be. In Miss Marple's final case, *Sleeping*

Murder, the disappearance of Helen Halliday is being investigated: 'You know I've got those specimens of Helen's handwriting? I'm posting them off today. I got the address of a good handwriting expert last week.' When they finally receive 'the report of the handwriting experts', we are told: 'Then those letters *weren't* a fake. They were *genuine*.'

But that's *not* actually what the experts are asserting.

They are saying the two handwriting types submitted for comparison were very likely written by the same person . . . but they have to take it for granted from the person who gave them the exemplar that it came from the person in question! For example, I could murder a friend and tell everyone she was alive and well in the French Riviera, and had been for the last few months. I could then write some letters to myself, pretending they were from that friend to me. But eventually people may start to get suspicious about whether or not that friend really is alive and writing these letters. Provided I am above suspicion, I could 'assist' with the investigation by giving these letters to a handwriting examiner to compare with a diary which belonged to that friend, to see if the handwriting matched . . . but what the investigators don't know is that I also wrote the fake diary. Therefore, the handwriting examples *will match each other*, they just won't be the handwriting of the deceased.

Of course, investigators are aware that malicious scribes may also attempt to disguise their writing in some way, perhaps using their non-dominant hand:

> 'You may have noticed that I made each passenger write either a signature or an address. That is

not conclusive, because some people do certain actions with the right hand and others with the left. Some write right-handed, but play golf left-handed.'

This is from *Murder on the Orient Express*, by which time Poirot is really establishing himself as a handwriting expert.

Another attempt at disguising might be for the writer to use words and phrases they wouldn't normally use, like the anonymous sender of the missive in *Sad Cypress*. Elinor Carlisle tells Poirot:

'I've no idea at all. It was an illiterate letter, misspelt, cheap-looking.'

Poirot waved a hand. 'There is nothing much to that. It might easily have been written by an educated person who chose to disguise the fact.'

These are Agatha Christie stories so we can expect to find even more ingenious methods of subterfuge. In *Murder on the Orient Express*, Poirot examines one of the death threats made to the aforementioned Mr Ratchett:

'It requires the eye of one used to such things. This letter was not written by one person . . . Two or more persons wrote it — each writing a letter or word at a time. Also, the letters are printed. That makes the task of identifying the handwriting much more difficult.'

Firstly, to 'print' letters rather than write in cursive — as would have been standard during Christie's time — is a sure-fire way to try and disguise one's writing, something which Poirot notices immediately. But as for there being more than one scribe, this is a clever extra touch because several people trying to disguise their handwriting on the same note would cause serious confusion. We can assume that in this case Poirot noticed there were slightly different styles to letters which should perhaps have been identical, and different amounts of pressure in various pen strokes, but I would not imagine that different inks were used as this would make the variety of writers too obvious. I think *all of the scribes used the same pen* — which brings me to a very important point about the clue in the above paragraph: the letter is also symbolic of the book's denouement and perhaps is a more important clue when taken as a metaphor rather than a material piece of evidence. If you aren't aware of the ending of this book, then hopefully this will titillate you into starting it!

So, why not abandon the idea of writing with a pen altogether if you want to remain anonymous? Instead, letters can be cut out of publications, ransom-note style, as in *The Moving Finger*, where residents of the village of Lymstock have started to receive similar poison pen letters which appear to be from the same source: ' . . . a local letter with a typewritten address (on the envelope). Inside, printed words and letters had been cut out and gummed to a sheet of paper.'

Poison pen letters appear several times in Agatha's books, of varying materials, and you may think them a bit hackneyed in murder mysteries. I initially felt the same way as Caroline Crampton when she said in her podcast *Shedunnit*, 'I thought that poison pens were mostly a convenient trope used by detective novelists to the point of cliché.' However, they were in fact very common in real life during the golden age of detective fiction, and Caroline goes on to list many cases from the 1920s and 1930s. Indeed, an article was written in 2020 by Curtis Evans on this very topic, titled 'The Poison Pen Letter: The Early 20th Century's Strangest Crime Wave'; there's no doubt Agatha was familiar with this phenomenon which Evans says 'overwhelmed the courts'.

It's not just the physical elements of these malicious missives which are important, it's the psychology behind them, and in *The ABC Murders* we get the common observation, 'Anonymous letters are written by women rather than by men.' But it's in *The Moving Finger* that we encounter a seemingly typical poison pen campaign, targeting the entire population of the usually idyllic village of Lymstock, which appears to begin as brother and sister duo Jerry and Joanna Burton move into a cottage there from London. The sheer volume of vitriolic letters received in the small village causes the local police to call in an expert in these matters — Inspector Graves — who echoes this sentiment exactly. He says of the letters, 'They were written by a woman, and in my opinion a woman of middle age or over, and probably, though not certainly, unmarried.' Obviously we can't tell the age or marital status of a scribe from looking at their handwriting or their method of communication; this concept is more about the psychology of these notes than their appearance. The assumption is that — like poison — these messages would be used by someone of the weaker sex; hence the name 'poison pen' letters. Interestingly, though, the idea that malicious communications (as they're officially called) are usually written by women rather than men is not an opinion shared by psychologists and organisations like the British Institute of Graphologists. I don't think it was actually shared by Christie either, given the culprits behind anonymous missives in many of her books; and indeed the many real-life poison pen campaigns referred to above were perpetrated by men as well as women.

In *The Moving Finger* in particular there is a spectacular amount of forensic document analysis, thanks to Graves's experience, and he pinpoints aspects of the notes that are helpful to the investigation. He observes that the individual characters used to create the text are 'cut out of a printed book. It's an old book, printed, I should say, about the year 1830.' He goes on to explain that although fingerprinting has been carried out 'there are no fingerprints on the letters and envelopes of a distinctive character'. They have, of course, been handled by many people including postal workers and the recipients, but none have a particular set in common. The sender was 'careful to wear gloves'.

He then goes on to say, taking us back to the typewriter examination we discussed earlier,

> 'The envelopes are typewritten by a Windsor 7 machine, well worn, with the 'a' and the 't' out of alignment . . . These envelopes have all been typed by someone using one finger.'

It's usually obvious to experts that a person has typed with one finger because all the letters are stressed equally — there's no variation, which would be expected when several digits of different sizes are used, pressing the keys with varying force, from slightly different angles.

It could be assumed that the typewritten aspect of the envelopes is incredibly helpful because the typewriter and habits of the typist can be identified. But unfortunately it's not the case here because, although these amazing analytical techniques have been used to successfully pinpoint the typewriter, it doesn't matter! It's a communal machine at the Women's Institute which absolutely anyone in the village has access to. Similarly the 'one finger' method of typing doesn't necessarily mean the sender was unfamiliar with this method of communication, it could just as easily be, as Inspector Graves surmises, someone perfectly capable of typing well, but who is trying to disguise that fact. He says, 'They're covering their tracks at every turn: Whoever writes these things has been very cunning.' I would argue that so has Agatha, who has constructed the plot in such a way, using real camouflaging techniques, to keep the investigators — as well as the readers — baffled.

* * *

It's not just envelopes which are frequently typewritten; the message itself can be written with such a machine, meaning no handwriting has to be copied or forged at all. The suicide note of Christian Gulbrandsen in *They Do It with Mirrors* is one such one example. The only real issue here is that document examiners would state that it's just as unusual for someone to type out their suicide note as it would be for them to write it on a 'scrap' of paper. Ultimately it gives the game away.

Experts can easily glean just as much from a typewritten piece as they can from handwriting, as we have seen, and as Christie reiterates frequently. Aside from *The Moving Finger* with its poison pen letters, much of the information regarding typewriters in Christie's books comes from the ingenious *The ABC Murders*, when a murderer makes the mistake of goading Poirot with typewritten letters: 'Don't you know, Mr Cust, that a typewriter can be identified? All those letters were typed by one particular machine . . . and that machine was your own — found in your room.'

But perhaps an unexpected book with some focus on a typewriter is *Evil Under the Sun*, Agatha's twentieth novel featuring Hercule Poirot, who is attempting to have a sun-soaked holiday on Burgh Island, a holiday destination in Devon that was also the inspiration for Soldier Island in *And Then There Were None*. Of course, Poirot is certainly not about to experience the R&R he needs because a rather dramatic love triangle has him suspicious that someone is going to be hurt . . . or worse. Poirot is always right, and the murder victim in this book is the stunningly attractive Arlena Marshall, one third of the love triangle causing Poirot so much concern.

Many of Agatha's plots hinge on people having an ironclad alibi which is sometimes a reason in and of itself to be suspicious. In general people who are innocent don't know they're going to need an alibi so their activities can be a bit wishy-washy! It's the people with unbreakable alibis who have usually planned for it, and it's this which leads to many of Christie's brilliantly convoluted murder stories, the premeditation and planning of which make them different from what she calls 'ordinary, nightclub murders', in reference to drunken violence and lovers' tiffs which might unfortunately lead to murder. I think that, of all the alibis posited in Agatha's books, my favourite is 'alibi by typewriter'. After the unfortunate Arlena is strangled in *Evil Under the Sun*, the police suspect the husband, Captain Kenneth Marshall. But the Captain doesn't really have an alibi. At the time Arlena was murdered, he says, 'I went up again to my room at ten minutes to eleven. There I typed my letters. I typed until ten minutes to twelve', after which he got ready for tennis as he and several friends had a court booked for midday. When asked by the police if anyone can confirm that story, Captain Marshall says the chambermaid probably can as she must have heard him clicking on the keys of the typewriter. In addition to this are the letters the Captain typed and hadn't posted yet. The insinuation is that if a member of the police force was to copy the letters on a typewriter, as a sort of experiment, they wouldn't be able to do it under an hour — therefore confirming Captain Marshall's alibi.

The letters, we're told, were in answer to some business queries which Captain Marshall read in the mail he'd received *only that morning*. (I've always found the most unbelievable aspect of Agatha Christie's novels to be the reliability of the postal service! But it's absolutely true that it used to be much more dependable, and even I'm old enough to remember the days when we'd receive letters in the morning *and* the evening, like clockwork.) So, the police have an interesting alibi to look into; an alibi they think is fairly plausible. They examine the message the Captain was replying to, which was dated from earlier that day. That part checks out, but what about the rest? The police need to establish exactly how long the letters took to type — was it a good hour, as Captain Marshall said, meaning he was in his room when Arlena was killed? Most crucially, they need to know the *content* of the letters in case they were pre-typed, so reading them is important.

We find out later that 'alibi by typewriter' proves true! The police reconstruct it as best they can, and can't find a hole in it. It's rather a surprise given that Christie usually enjoys astounding us in some way with these seemingly unbreakable alibis, and illustrates that typewriters have rather more forensic uses than perhaps we first thought.

*

But what about when there's barely any of the document left for the FDE to work with? Burning documents would be one such way of destroying paper evidence, and in Christie's books there are several examples of this. After all, the cremated remnants of something burned in a fireplace is a typical murder mystery trope, and as such we find fragments of charred documents in Christie's work from the very beginning. *In The Mysterious Affair at Styles*, ' . . . with skill he extracted a small piece of half-charred paper . . . Japp then produced the charred fragment of paper recovered from the grate'; and in 'The Case of the Missing Will', 'All he held was a charred fragment of stiff paper . . . ' Perhaps most exciting is the charred piece of one of Ratchett's threatening notes which Poirot finds in *Murder on the Orient Express*. Not only is this the note Poirot referred to as being pivotal in solving the case, it's also one of the only examples we have of Poirot carrying out a *bona fide* forensic test. We are told that Poirot murmured to himself that he needed a woman's hat-box, of the old-fashioned style, and instructed the conductor to go and find one. When the conductor handed one over, Poirot got to work dismantling the hat-box to reveal the wire netting; a method more commonly used in hat-boxes from over a decade earlier. It's this wire netting he needs for his experiment.

What follows is a wonderful description of Poirot's attempt to, in his words, 'resurrect' what was on the burnt note. He clamps the fragile piece of charred paper between two pieces of wire mesh from the hat-boxes and holds it over a flame with tweezers. The metal begins to glow, as do the areas of the paper where inky words were written. It's only temporary but it's enough for Poirot to see what was written on that paper, and subsequently solve the entire case. It works because of a difference between the written contents and the paper background: ink doesn't burn at the same rate as paper. Nowadays, infra-red filters do the job instead of the eyes.

* * *

Perhaps people who *should* burn documents are those who seem inclined to do the exact opposite: the sentimental lovers who keep their illicit love notes to refer to again and again rather than destroy the evidence. This is alluded to many times in Agatha's works, probably because it was fairly common practice in an era without text messages and emails. In 'The Adventure of the Western Star' Poirot laments, 'She told you that the letters were destroyed? Oh, la, la, never does a woman destroy a letter if she can avoid it. Not even if it would be more prudent to do so!' and in *The Mystery of the Blue Train* he asserts in a similar manner, ' . . . the Comte de la Roche knows one subject à fond: Women. How is it that, knowing women as he does, he did not foresee that Madame would have kept that letter?'

One of the most famous murder cases of the era, which led to the deaths by hanging of Edith Thompson and Frederick Bywaters in 1923, and was also featured in the Notable British Trials series, revolved around love letters between Frederick and Edith, but it was actually *Fred* who kept the letters, in direct contrast to Agatha's quotes above.

Edith was born Edith Jessie Graydon, in London, on Christmas Day 1893. She had a happy childhood, excelled in the performing arts, and was academically bright. After leaving school in 1909 nearing the age of sixteen, she worked first for a clothing manufacturer and then for a large millinery firm. Her natural style and grace, coupled with her intelligence, impressed her employer, and she quickly rose through the ranks to become chief buyer of the company, frequently visiting Paris on their behalf. She had met her husband-to-be, Percy Thompson, the year she left school, and after a six-year engagement they were married. The couple had flourishing careers and lived a comfortable, happy life together.

Frederick Bywaters had been in Edith's life a long time, as he had been a friend of her younger brother; but he reappeared in 1920 after spending time in the Merchant Navy, and became an acquaintance of both the Thompsons. Despite Fred being eight years her junior, Edith is said to have been immediately attracted to him, with his youth, good looks and tales of adventure. Her husband seems to have been oblivious to all of this, happy to invite Fred on holiday and then even allow him to move in with them. Edith and Fred started an affair and finally Percy *did* notice what was going on. The situation led to some arguments and to Percy becoming violent towards Edith, with witnesses reporting her suffering from bruises. Luckily for Percy, Fred was headed back out to sea with the navy, and the only thing Edith could do was write to him from her marital home and look forward to his replies. After Fred's return to London several months later, the affair was back on, but things reached a violent conclusion soon after. While walking home from the theatre together, Edith and her husband Percy were accosted by someone who jumped out of the bushes, threw her to the ground and stabbed her husband. Percy died at the scene. After the crime was reported, the Thompsons' lodger Fanny Lester told police of her suspicions of Fred Bywaters, and he was quickly arrested. When faced with Bywaters at the police station, Edith admitted that — yes — she knew who he was, and she was truthful about their affair, but she always maintained her innocence of the crime. The police investigated Fred's home and discovered more than sixty love letters from Edith; the only physical proof that they were linked to each other in any way because she had destroyed all of his replies. Despite Frederick maintaining that he acted alone when killing Percy Thompson, they were *both* tried for murder in what became one of the most controversial cases in history.

Those letters were a smoking gun. Via missives totalling 55,000 words Edith recalled her daily life and reiterated her love for Fred and how much she missed him, but unfortunately she also wrote about how much she longed to be free of her husband, even going so far as to say she had tried poisoning him and, rather gruesomely, had tried feeding him ground-up glass light bulbs in his food. (None of this was ever proved to be true.)

The jury were scandalised. Despite Frederick insisting that Edith had no idea of his murderous plan, and that her writing of killing her husband was just her vivid imagination, fuelled by the type of books she liked to read, they were both found guilty and sentenced to death. They were hanged at the same time, half a mile apart, in January 1923, and the now-familiar pathologist Sir Bernard Spilsbury carried out her autopsy. The case was a *cause célèbre* at the time and still attracts criticism for several reasons. The contemporary public were shocked at the sentence bestowed on Edith as no woman had been hanged in Britain since 1907. But also, there was no evidence of her being complicit in the murder, and the general feeling is that she was hanged simply because she didn't conform to how a woman 'should act'. She was portrayed in court as a *femme fatale* who had manipulated her young lover and masterminded the plan for the brutal slaying of her husband. In reality, she was probably a naive young woman who lost her head when a new romance swept her off her feet. After experiencing the anger and violence of her husband she retreated into a fantasy world, and kept up the momentum with a series of missives to her young lover — perhaps due to a yearning for freedom rather than a new love affair. The letters were written on paper, but were treated as though written in stone, and when she sealed those envelopes, she sealed her own fate.

Some aspects of Christie's book *Crooked House* read rather like an obituary to Edith and Frederick, even though their story ended long before this book was published. Consistent with that lapse in time, Christie mentions in her autobiography that she had the idea for this book in her mind for a long time before she sat down to write it, and it remained one of her favourites. I think as soon as Christie read about this case, she was inspired by it. Perhaps Edith Thompson stayed with her because at the time she was hanged, aged twenty-nine, Christie herself was only thirty-three. Edith's name is repeated many times in *Crooked House*, with one of the main characters, Magda, continually mentioning her desire to star in a play of Edith's life. In addition, a couple of residents of the eponymous house appear to be having an affair, just as Edith and Frederick did — the woman is older than the man here too — and their relationship seemingly comes to light because of love letters. We're told, in an exact echo of the Thompson–Bywaters case:

> 'A certain amount of evidence has come to light. Letters.'
>
> 'You mean love letters between them?'
>
> 'Yes.'
>
> 'What fools people are to keep these things!'
>
> 'Yes, indeed . . . You couldn't open a daily newspaper without coming across some instance of that folly — the passion to keep the written word, the written assurance of love.'

Just like in the real-life case, and in contrast to her earlier quotes about the sentimentality of women, it's not the woman of the couple in *Crooked House* who ostensibly kept their love letters, it's the man.

The documents in the above examples may have (or unwisely may *not* have) been destroyed by flames, but fire isn't always destructive. There's one substance which may react favourably to heat: ink.

Considering the genre, Christie doesn't overuse tropes such as 'invisible ink', but there is a respectable smattering of appearances. In particular, it's the short story 'The Case of the Missing Will' which illustrates this tool the best. While searching for the titular will, Poirot finds an envelope which seems out of place and acts on a hunch. We're told that 'with great care he cut open the envelope, laying it out flat. Then he lighted the fire and held the plain, inside surface of the envelope to the flame. In a few minutes, faint characters began to appear.'

This is a description of how invisible ink — also called sympathetic ink — works, and Agatha even uses the term 'sympathetic ink' in *The Secret Adversary*, which is only her second book. By definition it's an ink which is invisible on application and is made visible by some means such as applying heat or another substance. (You can make it yourself using lemon juice mixed with a few drops of water and write with it like ordinary ink. Once dry it leaves no visible mark, but the writing will reappear if held next to heat, and a hairdryer or radiator will usually do the trick if you don't want to set fire to the page using an open flame!) More recently this trope has been used by Rian Johnson in his 2019 film *Knives Out*, which is a delicious ode to all golden-age detective fiction, yet it's set in our modern time. The contents of a letter only become visible to Jamie Lee Curtis's character when she happens to hold a lighter near the paper by accident.

Sympathetic ink differs from disappearing ink because it's always invisible, whereas disappearing ink stains paper in the usual way, only to subsequently vanish. It can therefore be used as a joke or to deliberately mislead, something we see in *Crooked House* when it appears that a will may have been signed in disappearing ink. There is a discussion as to whether or not the signature had been erased somehow, but the lawyer present says it's not possible, 'Not without leaving signs of erasion.' And forensically, Agatha is absolutely right about this. In *Modern Criminal Investigation* (1935), author Harry Soderman states:

> Ink may be erased with a knife, rubber or ink eradicator. When the erasure has been made with a knife or rubber, it is generally easy to detect the area involved, as it is translucent . . . and ink eradicators can be easily detected with ultraviolet rays.

Presumably, then, in this situation, we have to assume disappearing ink was used, and we have to marvel at Agatha's thorough knowledge of the topic. I think that's why we see inks featuring in books throughout Christie's canon, written decades apart. In *Three Act Tragedy*, from 1934, there is a chapter called 'Concerning an Ink Stain' which tells us how an unusually located splash of ink in a butler's room leads the amateur sleuths to some possible document evidence: blackmail letters hidden in the fireplace. And twenty years later in *Mrs McGinty's Dead*, the fact that Mrs McGinty recently bought a bottle of ink, which we're told is rather unusual behaviour for a working-class woman at that time, clues Poirot in as to the real motive behind her murder.

In Christie's books, ink provides more information than Rorschach's Inkblot Test to those willing to interpret its meaning!

* * *

From words to splotches to genuine pictures. It was in Agatha's first ever book that she began to practise something she would continue throughout her writing career: drawing attention to document evidence via the use of diagrams in the text. She never includes images of blood spatter, or marks made by a weapon, or the location of fingerprints, for example. She only ever reproduces *documentation*, usually in fragment form: remnants of a charred will, pieces of drug labels, torn scraps of repurposed notes and more.

This is typical of golden-age murder mysteries, which had a genuine puzzle element and set of rules, straddling the gap between crosswords — which were equally popular at the time — and real crime stories. This effectively made detective fiction a longer version of a cryptic crossword, and conversely the crossword a visual representation of the reader seeking clues. Both have their origins in what was known as 'the puzzle craze of the early 20th century', which came after the First World War, and the two were combined by writers such as Dorothy L. Sayers. Although the first crossword printed in a magazine was in 1917, it had its origins in other word grids and puzzles known as acrostics; something which is mentioned in Christie's short story 'Greenshaw's Folly'. Detective fiction and word play in this way go hand in hand, and I can attest to this: as an avid lover of this type of fiction, I also complete a crossword with my husband every single morning, with coffee!

Other illustrations which could also be called 'document evidence' are maps and floor diagrams, which have echoes of Cluedo, and which happily pepper many of Agatha's mystery puzzles and give them an interactive quality (if you're a fan of Cluedo, see Appendix 2 for a list of where you can find them all). These diagrams are even used in whodunnits today, and I happily experienced this on board the Orient Express for a special Murder Mystery day. One of the clues given to us was a diagram of who was located in each carriage, as well as various business cards and actor testimonials. I'm extremely thrilled to be able to tell you that *I solved that mystery* and won a unique copy of *Murder on the Orient Express* for my efforts!

The idea to include a floor diagram isn't Christie's originally; as we've seen, it's something linked to the interactive nature of crossword puzzles and acrostics which naturally evolved to feature in crime mysteries. According to Martin Edwards, it was Lord Gorell — the author of 1917's *In The Night* — who first supplied a floor plan, ' . . . the kind of garnish that became a familiar ingredient of Golden Age novels'. It was this Lord Gorell who was co-president of the Detection Club with Agatha Christie.

Taken in this context we can really see the importance she afforded to documentation evidence in her stories, which is reflected in the trends of the time: the use of puzzles and diagrams which took the threat of violence into a more comfortable, cerebral sphere.

5

Impressions, Weapons and Wounds

'It is like seeing a trail of footprints and they are not all made by the same feet'

— *Hickory Dickory Dock*

When the broken pieces of an ancient clay pot are unearthed, the potsherds are recorded, cleaned and reconstructed by experts. The pot can then be photographed and the images published, or it can even be placed on display in a museum for others to see. Depending on how well the conservation has been carried out, the cracks may no longer be visible; the careful, skilful hands of the archaeologist have done their best to repair the damage.

This was how Agatha's broken heart was repaired by the archaeologist Max Mallowan.

After the most devastating year of her life — in which she discovered her husband was having an affair, her beloved mother died and she suffered a period of genuine psychological and emotional distress (colloquially known as a nervous breakdown) — Agatha Christie found herself on the cusp of forty, alone, and in need of a solitary holiday. Perhaps in modern-day parlance she wanted to 'find herself '. Despite previously booking a ticket to the West Indies for this very purpose, she became entranced by tales of the Middle

East at a dinner party one night, and opted instead to go to Baghdad, via the Orient Express. This journey was to shape the rest of her life and hone her talents, just as a flintknapper shapes pointed tools and arrowheads from arbitrary pieces of flint. It was during her visit to what was then Mesopotamia that she attended the dig site of famous archaeologist Leonard Woolley, then met and eventually married his assistant, Max. Agatha and Max subsequently spent the rest of their years revisiting that most enigmatic part of the world.

While writing her books she also assisted Max's project by cleaning, photographing and drawing the finds, incorporating much of the process into stories such as *Murder in Mesopotamia* and *Appointment with Death*. She assisted in the excavation of well-known artefacts, and interestingly *National Geographic* describes these as 'cases', saying 'Christie's second husband, Max Mallowan, was the lead investigator, and the 'detectives' in this case were not police officers, but archaeologists.' Archaeology is frequently described as 'detective work' so it's perhaps not surprising that Agatha flourished here too. (Indeed, there is a specific discipline, forensic archaeology, which combines the two.)

Toolmarks, footprints and 'cuts' are just as important in archaeology as they are in forensic science and they have slightly different meanings in each discipline. In archaeology, a 'cut' is a physical 'slice' that represents a moment in time and which can be seen as different layers known as 'contexts' via a cross section. When something is dug up — or backfilled — in the past, it corresponds to an action within a specific timeframe in archaeology. For example a grave cut, over many decades or centuries, will end up covered in deposits of earth, but when archaeologists dig down into it they can ascertain when it was initially dug by examining how it looks compared to the layers surrounding it. They will find 'clues' about the subsequent years in those layers of earth in the form of pottery pieces which relate to specific eras, and perhaps dated coins. The contexts and the items within them form a complete picture, such as that which would be revealed at the end of a detective novel or the examination of a modern crime scene.

In the same way that an artefact unearthed in an archaeological excavation has to be assessed from different standpoints — not only what it is, but where it lies in the historical layers, what other objects or organic traces are nearby, and so on — so much forensic evidence is actually a complex mixture of types: a shoe mark in blood combines blood spatter analysis and footprints, and an inky finger mark on paper mixes fingerprint examination with that of questioned documents. Christie frequently combines types of evidence herself, like this quote from Colonel Race in *Cards on the Table*, ' . . . the stained glove, the fingerprint on the glass, the fragment of burnt paper . . . ' This chapter is, likewise, a combination of evidence types which — though seemingly different — relate to each other very closely. Some people who work in forensics in real life may be experts in not just one but two, or even three disciplines. Similarly, many forensic scientists work in tandem: blood spatter analysts with serologists (who work with a mixture of body fluids), or pathologists with toxicologists.

We know that Christie will have seen ancient Mesopotamian finger impressions in her archaeological role, and many sites have been uncovered that feature prehistoric footprints: traces of early humans which have been there for millions of years. The same tools and 'evidence' are used to reconstruct the past whether at a burial site in Ancient Greece or a day-old crime scene.

What are Impressions, Weapons and Wounds?

Within the context of forensics, impression evidence is created when one object comes into contact with another, using enough force to leave a mark or cause an indentation of some kind. Fingerprints, ballistics, even aspects of document analysis have shown us this: the marks our fingers leave in putty, the rifling on a bullet, and written indentations on a notepad page are all impressions. But for the purposes of this chapter we're going to concentrate on a quintessential piece of detective evidence — the footprint — as a form of impression evidence, along with similar indentations such as drag and tool marks and tyre tracks. Then we'll take a look at weapons and the resulting wounds they cause as separate impressions evidence, since the two can be considered to go hand in hand: often at autopsy the pathologist will determine that a certain wound is consistent with being caused by a particular weapon on the basis of the somewhat violent 'impression' it has left in the flesh or bone of the deceased.

Impressions: Footprints, Tyre Tracks (and Drag and Tool Marks)

Impression evidence is classified into two types: damage-based evidence and non-damage-based evidence.

Fingerprints, for instance, are classed as non-damage-based because it is the intrinsic pattern on an individual's finger pads that makes their impressions unique and thus specific, as previously explored.

What I'm concerned with here is damage-based evidence which, as the name suggests, is dependent on an item acquiring or inflicting damage in order to leave a specific impression. This includes footwear and instruments, which are optimised as evidence by the acquisition of marks from wear and tear, including, as previously discussed, the typewriter. We're told in forensic footwear literature, 'Millions of rubber heels will be quite uniform in manufacture when sold in the shop, but after only a few days of wear will develop individual characteristics.' Put simply, the more damage the sole of a shoe acquires, the more unique markings it will eventually create as a footprint.

When it comes to marks and impressions there is a difference between *class* characteristics, which place evidence into a possible broad group of similar examples, like 'knives' or 'hammers', and *individual* characteristics, which connect evidence to a particular individual or item. A pair of trainer prints found at a modern crime scene may be recorded and run through a database which will determine their brand. Say that they are Reeboks; this is the *class* or group they belong to. But further examination may find a particular pattern of wear on the soles of those Reeboks, which will be unique to the way an individual wore them down because of the differences between people's gait, the way they place their weight as they move, the surfaces they walk on, how often they wear a pair of shoes and much more. The police may have a specific suspect in mind, let's call him 'Bill', and if other pairs of shoes from this individual are examined, and the wear pattern matches the prints retrieved at the crime scene, we now have *individual* characteristics and can say that they are very likely to be Bill's Reeboks. Finding the exact pair of Reeboks Bill wore would be the best type of evidence, and now investigators know they're on the right track. If they can't find the Reeboks, maybe they can look in his bank account and see if he ever bought Reeboks, and if that happened before or after the crime was committed.

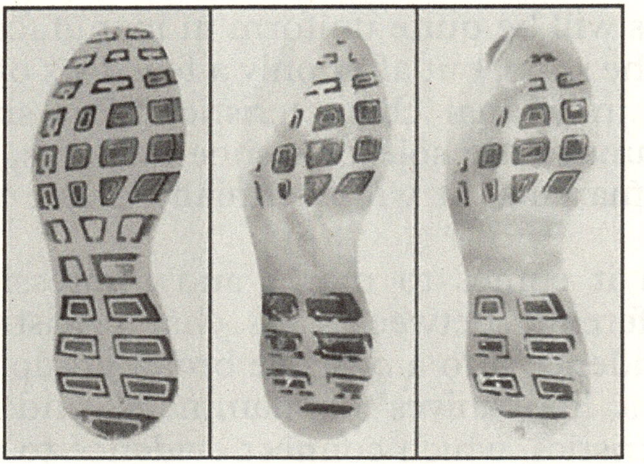

A photograph of the gradual wear of the sole of a shoe

Agatha Christie had a remarkable understanding of this concept which she refers to especially in *The Murder of Roger Ackroyd.* When the shrewd Inspector Raglan gets involved in the investigation into Roger's murder, he seizes some boots belonging to a suspect, saying, 'I've got a pair of his shoes here. He had two pairs almost exactly alike. I'm going up now to compare them with those footmarks.' We're told he lays them over the marks on the window-ledge:

> 'They're the same,' he said confidently. 'That is to say they're not the same pair that actually made these prints. He went away in those. This is a pair just like them, but older — see how the studs are worn down?'

Without even knowing it Agatha is referring to class vs unique evidence! The class evidence is the same brand or type of shoe, 'a pair just like them', and the unique evidence would be the specific way in which the studs are worn down.

Footprints are useful because they can literally situate a perpetrator or a witness at a crime scene, and can illustrate whether more than one person was present — and can thereby corroborate or refute statements and alibis. They can also indicate points of entry and exit. Typical examples may be footmarks in the flowerbed beneath a window and the presence of soil from that flowerbed in the room, indicating an entry point. In *The Secret of Chimneys*, which is really a thriller rather than a murder mystery, Agatha still provides us with a dead body as she does with all of her thrillers. During the investigation into the murder of Count Stanislaus, at the huge country pile known as 'Chimneys', muddy footprints are found clearly visible on the steps outside an open window next to which the body is discovered, as well as 'a second set going away again'.

The conclusion reached is that a perpetrator found an open window and left the footprints when climbing in and back out. The same muddy footprint scenario is repeated in several short stories, indicating Agatha had a clear idea of the concept of footprints as evidence and how they could help to reconstruct crimes.

Crime scene investigators may follow shoe prints at a scene in order to focus their search for other physical evidence too: a footprint trail could lead them to a place where items have been jettisoned by a suspect — items like gloves, a weapon or stolen goods.

More importantly, in the case of multiple crimes, the presence of identical footprints at different scenes can indicate a link between them. Finding the same prints in different places not only connects them all to one individual but the subsequent linkage between the scenes themselves can link other pieces of evidence which, when considered individually, weren't much help, but taken as a whole are crucial to solving the case. One scene may have provided investigators with a footprint and a blonde hair, one a footprint and a blood spatter pattern which suggests a six-foot-tall perpetrator, and one a footprint and fibres from the carpet of a Ford car. Separately these pieces of the puzzle may not be very useful, but, once they are connected, police now know they're looking for a six-foot-tall blonde person who drives a Ford car. Evidence such as this can narrow the list of suspects down considerably, or at the very least suggest a place to focus their investigations.

So, once gathered, how are these pieces of evidence retrieved and analysed?

First, let's take a look at footprints. Their analysis depends on how they're presented and, just like fingerprints, there are three main types:

Patent — These are visible to the naked eye, as patent fingerprints are, and are usually created when a person treads through a substance like paint or mud, and tracks it around as they walk. Therefore, they're in relief. Perhaps, after a particularly horrific murder, bloody footprints — rather than muddy ones — head towards the back of the house and out of the door, suggesting that someone who'd been around blood exited that way. In 'The Erymanthian Boar' this is described by Poirot: 'Footsteps — footsteps that have trodden, I think, in blood, and they lead from the unused wing of the hotel.' For their retrieval they can simply be photographed, which is done at a ninety-degree angle to avoid any distortion or false perspectives. It's important that a scale rule is placed alongside the print to help with sizing it correctly, and therefore sizing the foot of the individual. If the print doesn't quite show up as well as it could for the camera, angled light can be used to make it more visible, in the same way that deep indentations on paper, such as handwriting, can be detected by using a low, oblique angled light to make the impression clearer.

Latent — These are not visible without the use of specialist equipment and are created when a very thin layer of something invisible to the naked eye is transferred from the bottom of an apparently clean shoe. It could be an accumulated mixture of oils and general grime stamped onto glass, linoleum or pieces of paper, or it could be as a result of static electricity, known as static cling. This can be observed on blown-up balloons which have been batted around a room for a few days: hair and dust and small pieces of detritus coat the surface, pulled in by static electricity. Searching for these kinds of prints is difficult but the experts, after years of experience on crime scenes, know how to look for them successfully. They can be retrieved using aluminium fingerprint powder and then photographed or lifted with tape, although a modern-day technique is to use gelatine or an electrostatic lifting device to transfer the print to a lifting film — something which wouldn't have been available during Christie's time. It's clear here the connection between fingerprints and footprints, and why some people are experts in multiple fields.

Plastic — These are perhaps the first type of footprints we think of in detective stories: three-dimensional impressions which are made in substances such as mud or snow. They need to be photographed first, particularly if they're in snow, and angled light can bring out any necessary detail for the camera. Sometimes they are coated with spray shellac or hairspray first, to stabilise the material and bring out contrast. The footprint is then physically collected by creating a wooden frame around it or 'boxing it in' and filling the subsequent rectangle with dental stone, a liquid which flows into all the furrows of the print. It hardens, just like plaster of Paris, and creates a hardwearing 3D representation of the shoe's sole. Plaster of Paris was indeed originally used for this purpose, and Christie references it as early as 1924 in her short story collection *Partners in Crime*. The book showcases the adventures of husband and wife team Tommy and Tuppence Beresford as they're thrown in charge of a private detective agency. During 'The Affair of the Pink Pearl', Tuppence asks Tommy, 'I hope you're going to take plaster casts of footprints?' A crime scene book from the 1930s describes some interesting alternative methods in the absence of plaster. In emergencies we're informed that lard, porridge, or a flour and water mixture can be used to cast footprints. In addition to this, salt added to plaster of Paris will speed up the hardening process, and sugar will slow it down. Who'd have thought the contents of a kitchen cupboard would have quite so many forensic uses?

* * *

Tyre tracks are very similar to footprints in that they can be plastic or three-dimensional when left in the mud or on a grassy verge, patent when perhaps they've driven through blood, tar or paint, and even latent because they leave behind certain oils used in the manufacture of the tyres' rubber. They're also retrieved from scenes in a similar way to the shoe marks above. Surprisingly, though, cars in general aren't a forensic focus of Christie's works despite the fact they became the dominant form of transport in her lifetime, and despite her love for her own Morris Cowley — so I won't dedicate too much time to them. In addition, the science of tyre track impressions is younger than that of shoes, and tracks made by horses and carriages and the like were more the focus of Agatha's predecessor Arthur Conan Doyle. However, it is worth noting that there is one instance in which Agatha uses tyre tracks as a clue, and that is 'Ingots of Gold', a short story about smuggling. One of the main characters, Inspector Badgworth, investigates a possible hiding place for stolen gold and notices some clear tyre tracks at the scene, particularly the individual characteristics which can be so important to an investigation. He points out a defect in the tracks: 'There is a three-cornered piece out of one tyre, leaving a mark which is quite unmistakable.' On a hunch he goes to investigate the lorry of a potential suspect, taking along Miss Marple's nephew Raymond West who narrates the tale (and who makes an appearance or receives a mention in many of the Marple books and stories). On entering the suspect's garage, they see the mysterious triangular piece missing from one of the tyres and Badgworth exclaims, 'We have got him, by Jove! Here is the mark as large as life on the wheel!' This suspect, Kelvin, is duly arrested — on the evidence of the tyre mark.

But that isn't the end of the story. Unfortunately for the inspector, there was a nurse looking out of the window all night willing to testify that she never saw the lorry leave the garage. Nor did her patient hear its engine from her bed. And apart from the evidence of the tyre there isn't much else to connect Mr Kelvin to the crime. It is, of course, Miss Marple who strikes upon the ingenious solution to the mystery — and as ever cracks the case wide open!

* * *

Similarly, Christie's stories aren't particularly full of impression evidence like tool and drag marks, but they do get a mention once or twice so we know she was aware of them.

In *Hercule Poirot's Christmas* from 1938 a rather impressive 'locked room murder' scenario is explained when the key which was found on the inside of the locked door is examined with a magnifying glass. As Poirot peers at it, Colonel Johnson exclaims, 'By Jove! Those faint scratches on the end of the barrel. You see 'em, Poirot?' Of course Poirot, who sees everything, sees *them*. He says,

> 'But yes, I see. That means, does it not, that the key was turned from outside the door — turned by means of a special implement that went through the keyhole and gripped the barrel — possibly an ordinary pair of pliers would do it.'

She also uses the same technique nearly two decades later in her thriller *Destination Unknown*.

Tool marks, in current forensic parlance, are usually referred to as one of three types:

Indentation Marks — These occur when a tool is pressed into something soft like window putty or thick, drying paint.

Sliding Marks — These happen when a tool slides or scratches across a surface, like a chisel on a paint can or a crowbar on a car door.

Cutting Marks — These are left by tools slicing through materials as varied as wood, metals or bone.

Alternatively, tool marks can be split into two categories: friction marks (formed when some part of the tool rubs against a surface) and stamping marks (which show a full impression of the edge or face of a tool).

From the above categories we can see that the key in *Hercule Poirot's Christmas* was exhibiting sliding marks from the pliers, a nice little piece of impression evidence that Agatha included but probably didn't know how to define using the correct terminology. In a modern-day investigation, a comparison microscope might be used to try to match a particular set of pliers with the marks on the barrel of the key, if that was necessary to solve the murder, but for our purposes Agatha gives us just the clue without the need for high magnification.

The impression-based clue Agatha has given here is an example of 'damage-based evidence', and when it comes to human flesh that type of damage can be called an injury or wound.

Weapons and Wounds

Bruising is recorded as a type of impression evidence given that bruises are marks which resemble the 'tool' which left them on the body, whether that be a weapon, a foot or a car bumper. Bruises — technically known as 'contusions' — are created when someone is alive, and this evidence is transient: it changes colour as the body heals, losing its contrast with the skin as it lightens. When a person is dead, their ante-mortem bruises may remain visible for longer because no healing will take place, but the body undergoes the process of decomposition which can destroy this type of evidence in a different way. It's therefore necessary to photograph contusions on the dead, just like tyre tracks and footprints, with a scale rule placed alongside. If the sizing is correct, it may well be possible to compare a bruise with the item suspected of causing it — though there are no instances of this in Christie's books.

Agatha does, however, compare injuries of other kinds with the weapons that may have inflicted them — just as we would at autopsy — and these injuries fit into several distinct categories:

Blunt-Force Trauma includes the aforemetioned contusions as well as:

Abrasions: These are the most superficial injuries as they affect only the epidermis (the surface layer of skin) — the typical 'skinned knee' or similar. Theoretically abrasions shouldn't bleed much as the epidermis doesn't contain any blood vessels, but they do tend to have a red 'spotty' appearance.

Lacerations: When blunt force is applied to some parts of the body, the weaker elements there may stretch and split with the impact. A relatively thin layer of flesh on bone will be lacerated if hit hard enough with a blunt object because the bone beneath reflects some of the force back; the energy can only travel outwards, and it does so violently, causing ruptures. Lacerations will bleed as they tend to be quite deep, and they can be mistaken for sharp-force trauma if the edges are particularly defined. However, it's the different strengths of the elements in the skin which enable pathologists to tell the difference. When a laceration occurs, stronger connective tissues and nerves don't split with the impact, so they can be seen across the base of the wound as 'bridging fibres'. Lacerations are more common in areas of skin overlying bone, such as the scalp, rather than fleshy areas like the buttocks. Blunt-force trauma abounds in Agatha's works and accounts for around thirty separate deaths by my count — it's clearly a quite impulsive and effective way to murder someone.

Sharp-Force Trauma

Incisions or Incised Wounds: These are caused by objects with a sharp cutting edge such as knives and axes, but also shards of glass, razors, anything with a 'blade'. All of the elements in the flesh are neatly cut because a blade is sharp enough to slice through the connective tissue and nerves. They therefore contain no bridging fibres and can be differentiated from lacerations. Incised wounds are longer than they are deep, and this is what separates them from stab wounds.

Stab/Puncture Wounds: These tend to be deeper than they are long which often makes them more lethal than incised wounds (unless incisions are made over areas where major arteries are positioned superficially, such as the wrists.) The most common weapon used in stabbings is a knife, but swords and screwdrivers and the like can cause stabbing injuries as well.

It is stab wounds in particular which can be in some way matched or compared to the weapon that caused them, and we see this in many of Christie's works. Of particular note is her short story 'The King of Clubs', where she overtly differentiates between blunt-force and sharp-force trauma. After the murder of the impresario Henry Reedburn, Poirot asks the attending Dr Ryan, 'Could not the blow on the back of the head have been caused by his striking the floor?' to which the doctor replies, 'Impossible. Whatever the weapon was, it penetrated some distance into the skull.' This illustrates that Agatha was familiar with the differences between these injuries. In fact, according to the Laura Thompson biography, Agatha kept all sorts of notes on injuries from various sources to give her writing more realism. She kept an article from the *British Medical Journal* about a patient living for hours after being stabbed, and jotted down ideas about someone being killed by a steel window shutter acting as a guillotine, and the effect of a stabbing through the eye.

However they're caused in real life, wounds are always photographed with a scale, described clearly, and sketched on a diagram so that their exact location on the body is recorded as part of the post-mortem exam. In Agatha's books the process would be the same, but she stopped short of furnishing us with those particularly gory autopsy details.

According to specialists, footwear impression examination has been carried out with forensic applications for over three hundred years; the first recorded occasion in the UK when footwear evidence formed part of the prosecution case occurred in 1697. The victim, Elizabeth Pullen, was killed in the larder of her own home. Her throat was slit and, as is to be expected in such cases, the scene was incredibly bloody. In the victim's blood was the impression of a foot — a slipper to be exact. From the size of the print, it looked as though the murderer was a woman. Frenchwoman Margaret Martell was suspected of the crime and we can only assume, with such scant information from historical cases, that she was known to the victim. Indeed, the same is still true today: murderers and victims are usually known to each other. Margaret Martell was found to have some of Elizabeth's property on her, as well as a bloody slipper. Martell claimed to be innocent but faced with the overwhelming evidence a jury found her guilty and sentenced her to death. While standing at the gallows, she finally admitted to the murder.

Another recorded case comes from Scotland in 1786. After another Elizabeth, the pregnant Elizabeth Hughan, was fatally stabbed, the investigator at the scene noticed footprints in the mud and followed them. The impressions were described as 'boot prints', and because they were relatively deep into the mud the investigator surmised the person who left them had been running, since running feet do press down more forcefully. In addition to this it was noted that the boots appeared to be 'heavily nailed and patched'. The officer actually made a plaster cast of the impressions: it was crude, but effective. The next day he compared the casts against the boots of individuals who attended the funeral of the victim, and it was through this process that he discovered the identity of the murderer, William Richardson. His deposition states: '1st October, 1786 measure of the print of the foot of the person who murdered Elizabeth Hughan' and '2 October 1786 applied to William Richardson's foot and fits it exactly. That is, it fits the sole of the shoe; the nicks agreeing exactly with the heel.' William Richardson was hanged on this evidence and, like Margaret Martell, finally admitted to the killing just before he went to the gallows.

* * *

The success of footprint retrieval paved the way for the collection of other types of impression evidence at crime scenes, and the murder of Ruby Keen in 1937 is interesting to us for several reasons. First, Christie chose to call the victim in her 1942 book The Body in the Library 'Ruby Keene' and she included some other parallels with the real case. On the broader topic of forensics: the autopsy of the real Ruby was carried out by pathologist Sir Bernard Spilsbury, whom we have already met many times; and, especially pertinent here, the investigation showcased plaster casts of knee marks as well as footprints.

Ruby Keen was a young woman of twenty-three who lived with her brother, sister and widowed mother in Leighton Buzzard (a market town in Bedfordshire). She worked in a local factory and had previously had a regular boyfriend, Leslie Stone, a former labourer who had joined the Royal Artillery. However, when he was posted to Hong Kong her affections waned, and she eventually became engaged to a young policeman. Interestingly, Christie herself had an incredibly similar experience: she was initially engaged, or at least 'had an understanding to be married', to Reginald Lucy, a Major with the Gunners and brother of her friends the Lucy sisters. After he was posted to Hong Kong, however, and despite them continuing their courtship via air mail, Agatha met Archie Christie at a party and the unfortunate Reggie was entirely forgotten.

A photograph of Ruby Keen

Back to Ruby's life: Stone was medically discharged from the army after four years and headed back home to Leighton Buzzard. It was a small town and in April 1937 he inevitably saw Ruby in the company of another man, presumably her fiancé. Waiting until he caught her alone, he asked her out for a drink sometime 'for old time's sake' and she agreed, meeting up with him a week later at a pub called the Golden Bell. Stone was wearing a brand-new blue serge suit and looking dapper, so when he asked Ruby to break off her engagement and marry him instead it probably wasn't a surprise to any of the other drinkers in the pub, or even Ruby herself. Leslie Stone had clearly dressed to impress Ruby, and attempt to win her back.

But we can only assume that didn't work because sadly Ruby's body was found at about 7 a.m. the following morning. She had been strangled with her own silk polka-dot scarf (in Christie's book, Ruby Keene was strangled with the 'satin waistband of her own dress'), and although most of her clothing had been forcibly removed, she didn't appear to have been sexually assaulted. A struggle of some kind had taken place — as could be seen from various marks in the ground — and police took plaster casts of them, particularly in two areas which looked like the depressions left by knees. When Bernard Spilsbury examined these in the lab, he could clearly see the creases from the killer's trousers in these depressions, as well as the twill fabric consistent with a serge suit.

Police arrested Leslie Stone because witnesses had seen him and Ruby together in the Golden Bell, and when his suit was seized the knees had been brushed clean so vigorously that the fabric had practically worn away. Other trace evidence comparisons linking him unequivocally to the crime were made between the soil from the scene and particles found in the suit, and heel marks which had been cast from the soil were likened to Leslie's shoes. It was enough for Leslie Stone to be convicted of her murder and he was hanged in August 1937.

The casts and clothing from this case are now in Scotland Yard Crime Museum and they say of this case, 'it took place only about two years after the establishment of the Metropolitan Police Forensic Science Laboratory under the leadership of its first director Dr James Davidson, and it illustrates the careful crime scene management and analysis that was progressively being developed'.

Evidence from the Ruby Keen case
at Scotland Yard Museum

When revisiting *The Murder of Roger Ackroyd* for the purposes of writing this book, I was struck by the amount of forensic science in it (even if some is at a rudimentary level), which is why I make reference to it so frequently. There are constant discussions of fingerprints, footprints and wounds. When Christie wrote her first book, *The Mysterious Affair at Styles*, she focused mainly on what she already knew — poisons — throwing in a fair amount of forensic investigation, but with *The Murder of Roger Ackroyd*, the one which placed Poirot into retirement then brought him out again, it looks as though she opted to read more about the forensic sciences and incorporate them into the story.

The mentions of footprints which run throughout the novel are of particular interest, because this is a Hercule Poirot book and — just as with the trace evidence we discussed in an earlier chapter — Poirot has a complex relationship with footprints.

When we first meet Poirot, in *The Mysterious Affair at Styles*, his sidekick Captain Hastings is new to the world of detection and presumably is only aware of the clichés he's read about in books. He remains by the door of the bedroom in which a murder was committed, 'fearing to obliterate any clues'. When Poirot refers to him as a stuck pig for staying where he is, Hastings tells him he is afraid he'll destroy any foot marks. Poirot is incredulous at this: 'Foot-marks? But what an idea! There has already been practically an army in the room! What foot-marks are we likely to find?' and in a way this could be considered good forensics. It reminds me of one of the first things I learned on my Forensic Science BSc, which is that fingerprinting a light-switch is practically pointless owing to all the activity it has seen.

However, they are investigating this murder the very next day, so it's not as though months or years have passed and that looking for footprints is futile. We're told that Poirot finds all sorts of evidence underfoot during his search: from a coffee stain on the floor, to a cup smashed into the carpet, to a wax stain — all still present and perfectly intact. So why the disdain for 'foot-marks'?

Poirot says in 'The Incredible Theft': 'Me, I do not concern myself much with footprints and such things but for what it is worth we have that negative evidence.' We know that previously in the story Poirot had deftly stepped out of the window and studied the area with a torch, and that when he was asked if there were any footprints there, he replied in the negative. So, he theorises, '*There were no footprints on the grass*. It had rained heavily this evening. If the man had crossed the terrace to the grass this evening his footprints would have shown.' Although Poirot is very familiar with the kind of terrain required to capture footprints, he's really more concerned with their absence here, rather than their presence.

But in 'Dead Man's Mirror', another short story from the same anthology, Poirot seems to be preoccupied with footprints. We're told he examines the garden at the scene of a shooting and noticed footprints. Later he discusses them with house guest Susan Cardwell:

> 'But observe, mademoiselle, footprints.'
>
> 'So there are.'
>
> 'Four of them,' continued Poirot. 'See, I will point them out to you. Two going towards the window, two coming from it.'

'Whose are they? The gardener's?'

'Mademoiselle, mademoiselle! Those footmarks are made by the small, dainty high-heeled shoes of a woman.'

Over the course of a couple of pages we learn that he eliminates Susan as a possible match to the footprints, instead deciding they belong to another member of the household, Ruth Chevenix-Gore. He even asks her if she has been out in the garden, to which she answers that she did so, twice.

He explains his preoccupation with these shoe marks later on:

'Madame, there were four footprints and four footprints only in the border. But if you had been picking flowers there would have been many more. That meant that between your first visit and your second, someone had smoothed all those footsteps away. That could only have been done by the guilty person, and since your footprints had not been removed, you were not the guilty person.'

To me, he sounds very much like someone who does concern himself with footprints!

Similarly, in *The Murder on the Links* Poirot says of some footprints, 'These footmarks are the most important and interesting things in the case!' although again he may be referring to their absence rather than their presence. He'd previously been preoccupied with two flowerbeds planted with scarlet geraniums, one with a tree which leads to a bedroom where a crime was committed, and one without. The flowerbed containing the tree has no footprints, but the bed without a tree contains the gardener's footprints, which the investigating officer has excluded as a clue. These are the ones which Poirot thinks are 'the most important and interesting things' he has seen and which he vows to look into further, saying, 'I can investigate this matter of the footprints later.'

True to his word, he does, telling Hastings that the criminals in question left by the window and the tree they'd seen earlier. Hastings of course claims this can't be possible, 'But there were no footmarks in the flower-bed underneath,' a comment which Poirot jumps on:

> 'No — and there ought to have been. Listen, Hastings. The gardener, Auguste, as you heard him say, planted *both* those beds the preceding afternoon. In one there are plentiful impressions of his big hobnailed boot — in the other, none! You see? Someone had passed that way, someone who, to obliterate their footprints, smoothed over the surface of the bed with a rake.'

Agatha understood that, like fingerprints, footprints can be wiped away, obscured or even planted. There's always the possibility of *fake* forensic evidence in Agatha's world, and we come back round to the apparently important footprints on the window ledge in *The Murder of Roger Ackroyd.* They are commented on several times, but perhaps they're just a little too convenient? We know that the boots of the suspect, Ralph Paton, were compared to the prints, but we also know that Ralph had two similar pairs of boots — and one issue with shoe prints is that you don't need feet to be in the shoes in order to create them. So when our narrator, Dr Sheppard, sums up some of his thoughts on the case, saying, 'At some time during the evening Ralph Paton must have come in through the window, as evidenced by the prints of his shoes,' he's leaving out that pivotal point that *Ralph's feet* didn't necessarily need to be involved!

Perhaps that's why Poirot is less interested in footprints than we imagine him to be. By now we're familiar with his contrary nature, whatever his genuine feelings — and I don't think his opinions on footprints are set in stone. They really have more to do with Agatha projecting her ingenuity in the way she wants to present evidence, and trying to get us to use our own 'little grey cells' by subverting our expectations of what evidence can actually mean.

As well as footprints, *The Murder of Roger Ackroyd* focuses on a stabbing with an incredibly sharp implement — described as 'something quite unique' and 'a shining piece of twisted metalwork' — which turns out to be Ackroyd's own dagger from Tunisia. We're told that the weapon has a serious edge: ' . . . a child could drive that into a man — as easy as cutting butter'. I do feel this clinical type of stabbing is something Christie favours in her books. Despite the weapon itself being slightly unusual, it's a murder method I'd describe as quite utilitarian: one thrust, from behind, at a point very likely to cause instant death — which usually means the neck or base of the skull.

The position, from behind, is key to the clinical nature of this killing method, as it doesn't require the perpetrator to look into the victim's eyes, whether that's because it makes the process completely unexpected or because the murderer is a coward who doesn't want to see their victim's demise. This gives it an 'execution' quality: it's quick, relatively clean and absolutely lethal.

We learn how a housemaid was killed in this way in *The Moving Finger* from 1942: 'An ordinary kitchen skewer, sharpened to a fine point, was thrust into the base of the skull, causing instantaneous death.'

We also see it in *Lord Edgware Dies*, nine years previously, when Agatha describes the method after we're told that the unfortunate Lord was 'stabbed in the back of the neck just at the roots of the hair'. Inspector Japp informs Poirot that when stabbed in this way 'death results amazing quick. Straight through the cistern into the medulla, that's what the doctor said — or something very like it. If you hit on exactly the right spot it kills a man instantly.'

Poirot therefore concludes, 'That implies a knowledge of where exactly to strike. It almost implies medical knowledge' — and it required Agatha to do some research as it certainly wasn't *general* knowledge.

The 'ordinary kitchen skewer' in *The Moving Finger* would create a very uniform puncture wound for an investigator to examine, but in *Lord Edgware Dies*, the shape of the injury stumps the examining doctor in the first instance. He can tell by the shape of the wound that it wasn't made by an ordinary pen knife; rather something akin to a cut-throat razor but much thinner. Whatever the weapon he surmises it was incredibly sharp.

We later find out that the weapon was a 'corn knife', which is some kind of podiatry tool that I'll admit I wasn't familiar with, and was therefore horrified to discover is used for scraping corns off the feet! A corn knife is indeed like a mixture between a pen knife and a razor, or perhaps could be better described as a miniature cut-throat razor which is very long and thin. It's not to be confused with a knife used to chop down corn, as in the vegetable. That would give you images of a machete or similar, and Agatha didn't write anything about a machete-wielding maniac, particularly in 1933.

Corn knives were — and still are — lethally sharp, and because of that they're not commonly purchased nowadays by anyone who isn't a professional chiropodist. Clearly in the first half of the twentieth century they were carried by people who'd perhaps reached a certain age and weren't quite so light on their feet. In one of Agatha's books a corn knife is used to slice open what we're told is a heavy canvas rucksack, indicating its razor-like quality. One would need to be very wary of little old ladies with foot complaints given the contents of their handbags . . . !

At the very end of *Lord Edgware Dies* we get to read a letter written by the murderer, and all Japp's talk of 'cistern' and 'medulla' starts to make sense. The killer got the idea for this particular cold and swift murder method when a doctor 'had been talking about lumbar and cistern punctures, and he said one had to be very careful, otherwise one went through the cistertia magna [sic] and into the medulla oblongata where all the vital nerve centres are, and that would cause immediate death. I made him show me the exact place.'

This specific quote is why I feel Agatha must have done some research on this particular topic — or at least happened upon a specialist piece of literature. It's very exact and it is correct, except that the 'cistertia magna' is actually the *cisterna* magna. I'm unsure whether Agatha made that mistake herself, whether it's a typo or whether it's in there on purpose to show that the writer/murderer isn't actually medically educated and is repeating this learned titbit to the best of their ability. I'd prefer to adopt that last explanation, in deference to Agatha!

Regardless of possible mistakes in the medical description, this type of stabbing to the base of the brain certainly made an impression on Agatha, no pun intended. As well as using a version of it in the aforementioned books, it was also deployed in *Ordeal by Innocence* published in 1958, illustrating this murder method spanned four decades' worth of her books.

The wound in *Lord Edgware Dies* perplexes the doctor, and in this Agatha has touched upon a generally accepted property of stab wounds, which is their ability to impart some information on the tool that caused them. According to *Simpson's Forensic Medicine*. 'The appearance of a stab wound on the skin will reflect, but not necessarily mimic, the cross-sectional shape of the weapon used.' At the most basic level, Christie knows that a stab wound is easy to discern — in the absence of a weapon — because of its shape. She references this several times, most notably in *Death on the Nile* when Dr Bessner examines a stab wound on a murdered maid and says the weapon which made it is interesting. He goes on to say,

> 'It was something very sharp, very thin, very delicate. I could show you the kind of thing.' Back again in his cabin he opened a case and extracted a long, delicate, surgical knife. 'It was something like that, my friend, not a common table knife.'

We later find out that the victim had indeed been

'stabbed with a surgical knife'.

Dr Bessner is hazarding a guess at what implement could have been used in the stabbing of the maid and, with experience, a pathologist will be able to suggest some weapons which might be consistent with a fatal injury, but caution — as always! — will be exercised. Some points include:

- Knives may be incredibly sharp along the blade, but they also have a blunt edge (unlike daggers). This is reproduced in knife injuries, with the wounds having one pointed 'V' shaped edge and one blunt edge. But interestingly the blunt edge often splits the flesh of one point of the wound, causing what is known as a 'fishtail'.
- If a knife or dagger is fully inserted with extreme force, and there's no clothing in the way, bruising and abrasions can form on the skin around the wound in the shape of the hilt, similar to the way the muzzle of a gun can be identified when pressed against the skin of the victim.
- A blunt object such as a screwdriver will tend to cause more bruising (contusions) than an extremely sharp knife, and particular screwdrivers create different wounds. For example, a cross-shaped or 'Phillips head' screwdriver will create a distinctive cruciate (cross-shaped) wound.
- Sharp but irregular weapons like scissors or chisels leave unique marks which are distinct from those of knives: scissors create a 'Z' shape in the flesh and chisels a rectangle.

The various stab-wound shapes can thus inform the pathologist of the type of weapon used.

Other types of wound too — whether sharp- or blunt-force injuries — can be interpreted in similar fashion. Christie refers to this frequently in her books with confidence: we know she did research on the topic (such as keeping articles from the *British Medical Journal*) and she's bound to have discussed it with members of the Detection Club.

Perhaps the clearest-cut of these are the incised wounds, caused by a tool with a sharp edge. Examples include 'A bigger chopper . . . corresponded only too well with the deep wound in the back of Rogers' head' from *And Then There Were None*; and there's a hatchet deployed in *After the Funeral*. We're told the killer 'attacks Mrs Lansquenet with the hatchet — and attacks her savagely. Six or eight blows were struck.' This is a particularly brutal onslaught and in Christie books one needs to be very wary of such savagery — it's unusually disturbing, so it distracts the reader from a very important point: the body was butchered *beyond recognition*. What are the killer's reasons for doing this?

This wasn't the case for the unfortunate Mrs McGinty in *Mrs McGinty's Dead*, who was struck down violently in a similar manner, but was still recognisable afterwards. The particular instrument with which she was slain isn't found at the scene, but as we go through the book the type of weapon investigators are looking for becomes slightly clearer. The best conclusion they can come to is that it's: 'Something in the nature of a meat chopper, the police surgeon had said — but not, it seemed, actually a meat chopper', which means that during his investigation Poirot is looking for something else, perhaps something slightly unusual — and this is what makes this particular implement a key part of his solving the case.

* * *

Taken at the Flood is a Christie book which illustrates the importance of examining wounds independently of any weapon found at the scene, to ensure there is some sort of correlation. It is set shortly after the Second World War in 1946; Hercule Poirot is called into a village where a stranger, using the literary name Enoch Arden, has been killed. (This stranger had been blackmailing David Hunter, telling him he knows how to find the first husband of Rosaleen Cloade (née Hunter), David's sister, which would illustrate her second marriage is bigamous and cause all sorts of financial problems.) 'Enoch Arden' was killed in his room in the local village pub, and the reader is told he has been struck on the head. Since the body was found near the fireplace in his room, with a pair of fire tongs in the grate, which have some discolouring, the assumption is that he was killed with the pair of tongs.

At the inquest, we are given further information. The Coroner, Mr Pebmarsh, encourages the examining doctor, Dr Cloade, a relative of Rosaleen's husband, to describe the scene and subsequently asks the doctor if he believes the tongs caused the injuries. Dr Cloade believes that some of them undoubtedly were, although he didn't make a thorough examination because — rightly so — he couldn't move the body in any way until the police had been called.

When the police surgeon who carried out the autopsy takes the stand after Dr Cloade, he provides more detail, telling the Coroner that Enoch Arden had been struck at the base of the skull five or six times. He too believes that the tongs could have been the weapon used. But it's not until later that the original examining doctor, Dr Cloade, vocalises some misgivings he had about the wound to Poirot:

> 'Doctors, like everyone else, are the victims of the preconceived idea. Here's a man, obviously murdered, lying with a blood-stained pair of fire-tongs beside him. It would be nonsense to say he was hit with anything else, and yet . . . I'd have suspected something rather different — something not so smooth and round — something — oh, I don't know, something with a more cutting edge — a brick, something like that.'

What follows is a conversation about the apparent discrepancy between the wound and the weapon. It's one long clue for the reader, who is required to use their own detection skills to try to solve the case. But in addition, it's a wonderful testament to the possibilities of forensic pathology and the amount of research Agatha put into the subject matter.

* * *

I've alluded to the fact that injuries recorded at autopsy are carefully examined, described accurately and sketched on a diagram in the relevant position so that their exact location is recorded. It is this information which can help to indicate the height of the assailant, for example, or whether they're left- or right-handed. Although the latter is a particular favourite in murder mysteries, some pathologists would exercise caution in ascertaining the handedness (technically known as *manual laterality*) of a perpetrator except in very exceptional circumstances. Still, it's a trope used frequently by mystery writers and Agatha was no exception. The rationale behind making this distinction between left- and right-handed individuals in these instances is presumably based on common sense. Turning once again to *The Murder of Roger Ackroyd* we are informed, definitively, that 'The blow was delivered by a right-handed man, standing behind him . . . ' Logistically it had to be from behind because Roger is sitting in front of the fire and it's very unlikely his murderer could have stood in front of him without burning his backside (and the other characters could literally follow the smell of singed fabric emanating from a suspect's behind to catch their killer). Since the dagger is sticking out of his neck and we're told at one point only that his head had 'fallen sideways' I'd make the assumption that his head had perhaps fallen to the left and the dagger favoured the right side, hence the murderer was right-handed. It would be very awkward for a left-handed person to stab Roger in this way . . . although that's not to say it's not *possible*. And this is the problem with attempting to allocate manual laterality to a perpetrator, something I think Christie knew. First, as I previously mentioned, *Roger Ackroyd* is no straightforward murder mystery so we don't know if we can trust what we're 'seeing' or what we're told. Secondly, designating left- or right-handedness depends on there being only one attacker involved or a very clear wound/wounds, and later Agatha stories which feature this idea simultaneously debunk it.

In *Murder on the Orient Express*, the stab wounds on

the victim aren't clear and easy to examine because they are erratic. Dr Constantine describes what he says are 'ten — twelve — fifteen' wounds which seem to have been delivered incredibly haphazardly — some are deeper than others, for example, and come from a variety of directions.

And in addition to the blows which have 'glanced off' he says, ' . . . one or two of the blows were delivered with such force as to drive them through hard belts of bone and muscle'.

Because of the variety of wounds, it's difficult to ascertain whether a man or woman created them. Poirot suspiciously points this out:

> 'Did a man, committing the crime, say to himself, 'I will make this look like a woman's crime. I will stab my enemy an unnecessary number of times, making some of the blows feeble and ineffective . . . ' '

This has echoes of the strange, haphazard nature of the handwritten death threats the victim, Mr Ratchett, had previously received, as well as an element of disguise. Later on, Dr Constantine confirms that he counts twelve wounds on Ratchett, a significant number. But there is something else which puzzles both the doctor and Poirot, which is that some of the wounds would be incredibly difficult to execute by someone who is right-handed.

> 'Exactly, M. Poirot. That blow was almost certainly struck with the left hand.'
>
> 'So that our murderer is left-handed? No, it is more difficult than that, is it not?'

'As you say, M. Poirot. Some of these blows are just as obviously right-handed.'

It's a case in which the body is not giving out its clues as easily as one may have hoped, causing Poirot to sarcastically exclaim,

'The matter begins to clear itself up wonderfully! The murderer was a man of great strength, he was feeble, it was a woman, it was a right-handed person, it was a left-handed person.'

Agatha is quite correctly reluctant to offer a definitive opinion on the handedness of the murderer in this book, and is acting in a similarly cautious manner as would a pathologist or medical examiner who may be asked this question. Given that *Murder on the Orient Express* was written four years after the inception of the Detection Club, I'd hazard a guess that this topic may have come up in casual conversation over supper and the general consensus was that it's not quite so easy to allocate a murderer's dominant hand. This would have worked in Agatha's favour, because the 'handedness' of the stab wounds is a huge misdirect anyway!

In *Towards Zero*, written ten years afterwards, we move even further into deliberate misdirection. After Lady Tresillian is murdered by a blow to the head, the examining doctor, Lazenby, explains how the whole thing was 'awkward'. He says, 'She was struck, you see, on the right temple — but whoever did it must have stood on the right-hand side of the bed — there's no room on the left, the angle from the wall is too small.' We're told the Inspector, Leach, 'pricked up his ears' at this, querying if the murderer must be left-handed. The doctor's reply is very understandable and, in fact, commendable in relation to this topic! He says,

> 'You won't get me to commit myself on that point. Far too many snags. I'll say, if you like, that the easiest explanation is that the murderer was left-handed, but there are other ways of accounting for it.'

He proceeds with a variety of explanations, finally concluding, 'I've had some experience in these things and I can tell you, my boy, deducing that a murderous blow was struck left-handed is full of pitfalls.'

It's just as well Dr Lazenby wouldn't commit to making a deduction. The murderer in this case has us scrambling through double and triple bluffs so nothing can be taken for granted here. In fact, all three examples are cautionary tales from Agatha about allocating manual laterality from wounds, clearly aligned with medical expert opinion.

* * *

The same goes for much of the evidence in this chapter: when analysed properly footprints, tyre tracks and tool marks can offer up a plethora of information, but there is always a need for caution. Poirot's slight disdain for footmarks encapsulates this, as does an exhibit I saw on a recent research trip to Scotland Yard Crime Museum. The exhibit was called 'False Feet' and it was a pair of wooden stilts with shoes attached to the bottom. What we know of these is that they were made by a burglar with size 12 feet to act as decoy feet of a much smaller size. His own footprints were so large as to be a liability and make him easily identifiable, so he took these false feet along to his crime scenes to try to confuse the police by creating smaller footprints. It didn't work. While swapping his shoes for these stilt contraptions near the house he was about to burgle, he left his own footprints anyway. The police found them and he was identified.

This is along the lines of something referenced in *Partners in Crime* in the short story 'The Ambassador's Boots'. The boots are stolen for a brief period and it causes Tommy Beresford to remark, 'Boots suggest footprints. Do you think they [the thieves] wanted to lay a trail of the Ambassador's footprints?' — understanding that forensic evidence like this is easier to fake than, say, leaving a person's fingerprints or blood at the scene of a crime. In a nutshell this is perhaps why Agatha Christie has Hercule Poirot display some ambivalence when it comes to 'shoemarks'; they do have a huge amount of forensic value, but only if they contain feet.

The suggestion is that perhaps inanimate, inorganic objects — when not treated carefully at a crime scene — can effectively 'lie', but the *body* will always tell the truth. Agatha clearly knows this, judging by her ambiguous use of all sorts of technical forensic evidence, and Poirot's contrary nature towards it, whereas the clues she affords us from medical examination of the various corpses in her works are always spot on. It is surprising, therefore, that none of her long-term, recurring characters are medically qualified. She has no fictional Dr Bernard Spilsbury equivalent, for example; instead she has different local doctors, police surgeons and even dispensers provide us with the secrets offered up by the various murder victims in her canon — murder victims we'll eventually go on to dissect. But first we'll examine the most dramatic of all the body's organic clues: the blood.

6

Bloodstain Pattern Analysis

> 'Blood — *so much blood* — blood everywhere . . . Blood on the chairs, on the tables, on the carpet . . . An insistence on blood — fresh, wet, gleaming blood . . . So much blood — *too much blood . . .* '
>
> — *Hercule Poirot's Christmas*

In the BBC TV series *A Very British Murder*, Lucy Worsley reads a quote from Agatha Christie's pivotal book *The Murder of Roger Ackroyd*:

> Ackroyd was sitting as I had left him in the armchair before the fire. His head had fallen sideways, and clearly visible, just below the collar of his coat, was a shining piece of twisted metalwork.

She uses this paragraph to illustrate that she believes Christie's works are rather pallid, going on to say, 'Now there are a couple of reasons why this is classic Agatha Christie. Firstly, there's the bloodlessness of it . . . However, after reading *all* of Agatha's mystery novels and numerous short stories I can definitively say I disagree that bloodlessness is 'classic Christie'. In *The Murder of Roger Ackroyd*, the piece of metal sticking out of the victim's neck may well have been shining, but the same can't be said for the blades in many of her other stories. As we progress through the literary years, Agatha uses steadily more vivid terms to describe the amount of blood on a given weapon, initially referring to 'patches of what looked like rust' and moving towards descriptions of actual dried blood. Later still we are told that a blade is covered with 'red, glistening patches' of blood and treated to words like 'spurted' and 'congealed'; eventually culminating in the unexpected blood orgy that is *Hercule Poirot's Christmas*!

Agatha also wrote a short story called 'The Blood-Stained Pavement' which was rather macabrely renamed 'Drip! Drip!' for the US market. The story focuses, as you can imagine, on bloodstains and illustrates that, when it came to blood, Agatha really didn't shy away. Clearly there was a reason Agatha chose to keep some of her novels, *The Murder of Roger Ackroyd* being one of them, quite bloodless. I believe it's because in that book she wanted its spectacular and unexpected twist to be the main feature of the story, and didn't want blood or gore to distract from that. However, in other novels she *did* allow the blood to tell the story — just like it can in real life. She understood that the passage of time would cause exuded blood to congeal and that could indicate time of death; in *One, Two, Buckle My Shoe* a dentist, Henry Morley, is found dead in his workplace, and we're told ' . . . there was dried blood round the wound. That meant Morley had been dead some time.' She also knew that blood which had been shed in different scenarios would cause distinctive stains and tell a tale, like when an original stain is transferred to someone or somewhere else. In one short story, 'The King of Clubs', Poirot theorises that blood on a marble seat shows where the victim was killed, yet 'a stain on the polished floor' shows where he lay for a while before being moved.

Given Christie's idyllic and sheltered youth, she's said to have taken to nursing soldiers in the VAD during the First World War extremely well and wasn't reputed to have been squeamish at all. Laura Thompson states, 'If she was tormented by the wreckage, the beautiful boys with their missing limbs, the dirt and blood and phlegm, she did not say so. Going back to her anecdote about the amputated leg she disposed of to assist a terrified new nurse, she matter-of-factly quotes in her autobiography that she had to ' . . . throw it into the furnace. It was almost too much for the child. Then we cleared up all the mess and the blood together.'

Given these traumatic experiences and her first-hand knowledge of bloody injuries, it's safe to assume that her stories aren't as cosy and 'bloodless' as might be expected.

What is Bloodstain Pattern Analysis (BPA)?

Bloodstain Pattern Analysis is a descriptive term for a discipline which is just that: the interpretation and analysis of bloodstain patterns, usually at a crime scene, in order to reconstruct the actions which contributed to the blood being shed. I say discipline rather than science because BPA requires a level of interpretation and an artistic eye that another blood science, forensic serology, does not. BPA follows scientific rules but with an element of artistic licence. Serology is what we're actually picturing when we envisage forensic scientists in labs, with white coats and test tubes, analysing bloodstains for blood group or DNA. The lucky serologists also get to examine semen, vomit and faecal matter. It's different from BPA but the two disciplines work together so it's useful to understand both.

Bloodstain Pattern Analysis is used to answer important questions, from the basics of whether a crime has been committed to the minutiae of exactly how an accident occurred. At a crime scene, analysts look at the distribution and appearance of the bloodstains and try to provide answers to the following questions:

- How were the bloodstains formed?
- Where did the blood originate?
- What (type of instrument) caused the wounds or bloodstains?
- What was the minimum number of blows?
- How were the victim/s and assailant/s positioned?
- What movements were made during and after the bloodshed?
- Does the bloodstain evidence support or refute witness statements?

BPA as a discipline requires intricate knowledge of several different sciences for the highly skilled analysts to make an interpretation: biology, physics and mathematics to name just a few. Biology dictates the behaviour of blood in terms of clotting and can give information on its viscosity — that is, its thickness. Physics explains how blood reacts under forces like gravity, and why it pools or perhaps spreads depending on the surface or container on which it lands. And mathematics — specifically geometry — is the tool used to measure velocity, the distance blood has travelled, the angle of that travel and so much more.

All of these varied elements come together for BPA analysts to do their job. Blood acts in very specific ways according to these principles, and a blood-soaked scene which may look random to the uninitiated is in fact more like a wall of hieroglyphics ready to be translated by those who are fluent in the language. This language is the variety of stains which can be interpreted by analysts according to the dynamics that caused them.

In *The Hollow*, after the book's only victim — John Christow — is shot to death, the scene is rather artistically portrayed: 'A dark stain welled up slowly on his left side and trickled on to the concrete of the pool edge; and from there dripped red into the blue water.'

What Christie is describing here in the world of Bloodstain Pattern Analysis are **Passive** stains.

These typically result from the action of gravity alone, excluding any other forces. Examples are oozes, drips, flows, spills and pools, and there is no shortage of these in Christie's books. In *Death on the Nile* a crimson stain slowly soaks through a trouser leg and in *The Murder at the Vicarage* blood pools around Colonel Protheroe's head.

In *The Clocks*, however, there's a rather different exchange of blood when poor Sheila the secretary literally stumbles across a corpse in the living room of someone she was asked to act as a typist for. She describes it to the investigator, who's not particularly happy about the process:

'And there's blood on him!' She looked down and loosened one of her clutching hands. 'And on me — there's blood on *me*!'

'So there is,' I said. I looked at the stain on my coat sleeve. 'And on me now as well,' I pointed out.

This is a perfect example of **Transfer** stains, which are caused by objects coming into contact with existing bloodstains and leaving smears or patterns of transferred fluid. These can include a bloody shoe print, bloody drag marks from a body being moved, a bloody print from a weapon being placed on a surface or someone brushing up against someone bleeding. The final type of stain in the world of BPA are **Spatter** stains, which have a very specific and technical meaning, and shouldn't be confused with 'splatter' — spatter is caused by blood droplets being projected through the air and landing on surfaces. There are different types of spatter depending on the mechanics that caused them. Droplets of blood can be flicked or cast off a surface that is wet with blood — such as a bloodied weapon — and leave a distinctive pattern of stains. If a blood vessel is breached or damaged, blood may gush or spurt from an artery due to the circulatory pressure of the heart still pumping. Christie has the rather gruesome sounding 'spurts' covered in 'The Blood-Stained Pavement' and we get splashes in the short story 'Sanctuary'. However, most intriguing and very pleasing to those of us in the forensic community is Agatha's use of the word 'spatter', not 'splatter', a difference which may seem insignificant but is important. It's in the book *Towards Zero*, which has a larger amount of forensic information than any of her other books. The victim of this title, Lady Tressilian, is brutally beaten about the head with a blunt object, ostensibly a niblick, while in bed at her stately home, Gull's Point, and following this savage attack forensic evidence abounds. After the murder, investigator Williams examines the jacket of a suspect, Neville Strange, and says, 'See those dark stains? That's blood sir, or I'm a Dutchman. And see here, it's spattered all up the sleeve.' It may seem like a small distinction because spatter and splatter ostensibly mean the same thing, but in a forensic context they don't. Splatter can be generally defined in many ways, one of the most common referring to a viscous liquid being splashed or trailed over an object or surface. The difference is that spatter, without the 'L', refers *only* to small drops and sprays, and is one very specific type of bloodstain within this forensic science. Or to put it a different way, a 'splatter' can be one huge long trail of mud, or custard, or oil; but a 'spatter' can only be made up of *several small* stains of blood. Spatter includes its own subtypes because of this and Agatha was familiar with some more than others:

Gunshot Spatter — If someone is shot through the head, blood will be ejected from the wounds due to the force of the bullet. It may be forward spatter from the exit wound (and therefore travelling in the same direction as the bullet) or back spatter from the entry wound, travelling in the opposite direction, typically back towards the firearm. Usually forward spatter is a finer mist than back spatter, which is made up of fewer, larger droplets, but there are lots of variables. An important factor is that the back spatter from the entry wound may land on the person shooting the gun, along with the aforementioned gunshot residue (GSR). It's therefore necessary to distinguish between the types because a forensic examination of spatter may contradict the account provided by a person who says they were standing anywhere other than in the shooter's position. Agatha never really describes gunshot spatter specifically, and this could well be because it would be unusual for a non-forensic specialist to know there's a difference. But she did describe the blood from firearm casualties and in 'The Mystery of Hunter's Lodge' we have a description of the victim, Mr Pace, 'all shot and bleeding'. We do also get quotes such as, ' . . . killed — with a great hole in her head and blood everywhere' from *Towards Zero*, and that describes the next type of spatter — cast-off spatter — perfectly.

Cast-off Spatter — When an object covered in blood is swung through the air in an arc, lines of cast-off spatter can be produced. When the object is the weapon, these give information on the direction and number of the blows; also, the droplets may be different sizes depending on what the object is. If you were to play a round of real-life Cluedo (don't actually try this at home!) it might not be easy to tell whether the weapon used in an attack was a wrench, a piece of lead pipe or a candlestick as they are all relatively similar in size. However, there will be a marked difference in the cast-off from a pool cue, say, compared to cast-off from a mallet. Cast-off spatter can tell analysts the minimum number of blows to a person because the distinctive streaks, flicked off each time a weapon is raised to strike another blow, can be counted. Analysts say *minimum* number of blows because they must allow for the fact that the first one or two blows may not make the weapon bloody enough to create the amount of fluid needed for cast-off.

This cast-off spatter can be distinguished from the next type — Arterial Spray — as it tends to be made up of smaller droplets in relatively equal-sized arcs. As a nurse, that's exactly why Christie would be familiar with this very distinctive blood pattern which is expelled from human sources rather than weapons. It's why we're told someone's blood '. . . spurted out on the pavement' in 'The Blood-Stained Pavement' in a rather matter-of-fact way.

Arterial Spray refers specifically to the spray or spurt of blood released after the severing of a major artery, such as the femoral in the leg, or the carotid in the throat, usually from a stab wound or an incision. The pattern created on a wall, for example, is a clear series of arches as the blood is forcefully pumped from the heart, with every heartbeat, through the injury. As the amount of blood in the body and the power of the heart both decrease, the height of the arched bloodstain also decreases, resulting in diminishing arcs.

Agatha falls short of describing this phenomenon but displays in-depth knowledge of the difference between bleeding from veins and bleeding from arteries in her most sanguinary book *Hercule Poirot's Christmas*; knowledge which she will have soaked up like a bloody sponge during her time as a nurse. The book begins with an old, decrepit yet mischievous character who is the patriarch of a typical country household — Simeon Lee — and his spiteful plans to have a rather interesting yet explosive family Christmas. After pitting his offspring and their spouses against each other, and threatening to change his will as soon as his solicitor reopens after the holiday season, it's no wonder he has his 'throat cut like a pig' on Christmas Eve, and we're told 'he bled to death in less than a minute'. The investigating inspector asks the attending doctor,

> 'What about bloodstains? Surely whoever killed him must have got blood on him?'
>
> The doctor said doubtfully:
>
> 'Not necessarily: bleeding was almost entirely from the jugular vein. That wouldn't spout like an artery.'

Although she uses the word 'spout' rather than 'spurt', Agatha clearly knows what she is talking about. According to *Simpson's Forensic Medicine* she's spot on: 'Damage to an uncovered superficial artery is very likely to result in blood spurting some distance from the wound, whereas damage to a similarly sited vein will result in blood merely welling up out of the wound without any projectile force.'

I'm certain, too, that when treating wounded soldiers Agatha would have come up against the final type of spatter, which is *expirated* spatter, but she doesn't really mention it in her books. (The closest we get is when, in 'The Tragedy at Marsden Manor', it's noted that 'There was blood on the lips, but most of the blood must have been internal', meaning it never made its way out of the body.)

Expirated Spatter — When blood from an injury is mixed with the air of the lungs, it may be expelled in a sort of aerosol of tiny droplets through the nose or mouth. This spatter is very specifically breathed out (or sometimes forced out of a wound in the lungs or chest) and is made up of a fine mist which may sometimes contain bubbles, visible to the analyst in the form of 'bubble rings' — outlines within a bloodstain resulting from air in the blood. The spatter may also have a dilute appearance from having been mixed with saliva.

Perhaps now, after seeing the huge variety above, it makes sense why bloodstain pattern analysts may bristle when the word splatter is used rather than spatter, given how nuanced a term it is. I hope they now feel they have Agatha Christie on side!

Interpreting Stains

The first systematic piece written about the interpretation of bloodstain evidence has the catchy title

Concerning the Origin, Shape, Direction and Distribution of the Bloodstains Following Head Wounds Caused by Blows. It was written by Eduard Piotrowski, at the Institute for Forensic Medicine in Krakow, Poland, in 1895.4 It wasn't translated from its original German until much later, with the aid of eminent blood spatter analyst Herb MacDonell (who was involved in the notorious O. J. Simpson case in the US), but that's not to say other investigators weren't refining the discipline in the meantime. MacDonell wanted to translate Piotrowski's work specifically because he was a pioneer of Bloodstain Pattern Analysis from a hundred years before. Herb thought no one 'preceded him in designing meaningful scientific experiments to show blood dynamics, methodology and thoroughness. He had an excellent knowledge of the scientific method and a good understanding of its practical application to bloodstain pattern interpretation.'

It's worth noting, however, that Piotrowski's paper was written using data from the bludgeoning of rabbits, not humans, and the diagrams in the study include depictions of the unfortunate bunnies. The use of rabbits has ethical implications nowadays so these experiments haven't been repeated, but they don't need to be. The principles apply to any blood no matter the origin, so much of Piotrowski's methodology is still in use today.

Take a single droplet of blood: a number of variables govern the way its presence at a scene can be interpreted. First, it's a common misconception that droplets of blood are 'tear shaped'; that's only the case at the moment the drop separates from its source. As it subsequently falls through the air, and is subject to the combined forces of gravity and surface tension, the droplet becomes a perfect sphere. If that sphere drips exactly perpendicular onto a smooth floor, it will leave a perfectly circular spot. If it drips from a greater height or onto a textured surface, satellite spatter may be seen radiating out from that circular spot. (These are smaller droplets distributed around the main blood droplet, usually because the impact has caused a 'splash'.) If it drips or is propelled onto a surface at an angle other than a 90° perpendicular, say 40°, 30° or 10°, the stain will be elongated and will illustrate to bloodstain pattern analysts the direction from which the drop came, because the elongated 'tail' points in the direction the droplet was travelling.

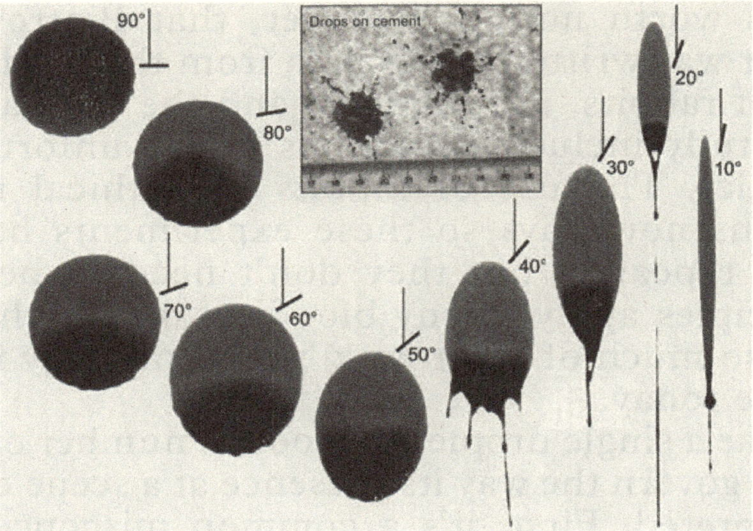

A diagram of blood drops hitting a surface from different angles

Determining the direction in which blood drops travelled can help to reconstruct exactly what happened at a crime scene. If there are a number of bloodstains radiating in different directions and at different angles, the bloodstain pattern analyst can draw lines backwards from them, to give an *area of convergence*, using complex calculations for angles and trajectory — calculations that my brain has never been able to handle! 'Area of convergence' may sound complicated, but it just means the point at which the lines of travel traced back from the bloodstains meet and which they must have all started from; a point of origin. It could be a stab wound, or a head injury, or even someone coughing up blood as a result of natural causes, such as an aneurysm. The results could then be depicted as a 2D drawing, but it's much better if it can be seen in 3D. That's where the visually arresting technique known as 'stringing' is used. You may have seen this represented frequently in the TV show called *Dexter*, about a man who's a blood spatter analyst with Miami PD by day and a particularly unusual — and crafty — serial killer by night . . . Stringing is a time-consuming, manual process in which the analyst uses bright red thread to represent blood, tacks one end of the thread to the blood droplet on the surface of a wall or floor, and fixes the other end at a place they've determined is the area of convergence or origin. This could be a point in what appears to be mid-air, so a tripod or similar will be used as anchorage. A second stain has another thread tacked to it and then across to the area of origin, and a third, and so on for every stain. What results is a striking display which could be part modern art and part 'cat's cradle' as hundreds of strings emanate from walls, floor and furniture to meet in a single place, suspended in mid-air. The reason this method has value is that if that place in mid-air is about six feet from the ground a blood spatter analyst may discern that a person with an injury was hit on the head as they were *standing*. But if it's only about six inches off the ground, that would indicate the person's head was on the floor and they were *lying down* when they were hit. But imagine if the person had been hit several times, or if many people were injured at a scene — it would take an agonising length of time to string all those different blood droplets to their various points of origin. For that reason, the technique has mainly been replaced by computer software with various names like HemoSpat and LeicaMap 360. I just can't believe one of the programmes isn't called 'No Strings Attached'!

Interestingly, BPA also works the other way round.

It can give information on what is *unlikely* to have happened, it can exclude people from being at the scene, and even blood's absence — i.e. a 'void' pattern in the middle of an otherwise bloodstained area — gives analysts information, just as much as its presence. For example, a void pattern will occur when someone is standing in the way of a large amount of blood spatter, meaning they get covered and the space behind them remains clear. They change position, and there is the void pattern as a kind of reverse shadow. The significance of an absence of blood is something Christie understands: in *After the Funeral*, Inspector Morton is unconvinced their suspect is guilty because 'There was no trace of blood on her clothes' and she hadn't had time to change. Once again, the clues which aren't there, as well as those which are, provide us with the full forensic picture.

History of Bloodstain Pattern Analysis

In *The Washing Away of Wrongs*, a coroner's handbook from thirteenth-century China, there is a story that is often cited as the first use of entomology — or study of insects — in a forensic context. But I think it also illustrates the significance of blood distribution in a crime. According to Chinese lawyer and death investigator Sung T'zu, who wrote this astonishingly early text, a fatal stabbing occurred in a village in the year AD 1235 (by the Western calendar). For the investigation, different blades were tested on the carcass of a large animal and it was determined from the wound it made that a sickle was the likely weapon used in the stabbing (as we've just seen in the previous chapter, particular weapons can make recognisable wounds). Subsequently, all the villagers were asked to bring their sickles before investigators to be examined. On inspection, they all appeared to be clean. However, one sickle blade was inexplicably attracting blowflies, though the insects were eschewing all the other sickles. It was clear that, although invisible to the naked eye, remnants of blood from the murder remained on this otherwise clean blade, which only the flies could detect and couldn't resist. The flies — and the blood — helped them catch their murderer.

Despite the significance shown as early as the thirteenth century, it wasn't really until the early twentieth century that bloodstain pattern analysis came into its own. Yes, Eduard Piotrowski had written his paper in 1895, but in order to make use of his findings forensic investigators needed to be able to distinguish human blood from animal (and one human's from another's). It was only when this became possible that bloodstain patterns could be further investigated, and here we have the two strands of serology and bloodstain pattern analysis respectively. We'll focus on serology later, and pattern analysis here.

As with many of the forensic sciences, it took a notorious crime for the usefulness of bloodstain patterns to be projected into the public consciousness. In this instance it was the Dr Sam Sheppard case in 1954.

Marilyn and Sam Sheppard had been high school sweethearts who, ten years later, were living out the suburban dream in Bay Village, a lakeside suburb in Cleveland, Ohio. Sam had been what would be termed in the USA a 'jock': proficient in sports, class president, popular. Despite being offered several athletics scholarships, he'd opted to follow in his father's footsteps and become a doctor of Osteopathic Medicine. He settled down to a career at his father's hospital after marrying Marilyn in 1945, and by 1954 the two had a seven-year-old son, Sam 'Chip' Sheppard, and were living in a two-storey house by the lake.

But their suburban dream was about to become a nightmare.

On the night of 3 July that year, while entertaining friends Don and Nancy Ahern, Sam claims to have fallen asleep on the daybed on the lower floor of the house. Marilyn saw the guests out after the movie they had all been watching ended, and went to bed, upstairs. She was subsequently brutally attacked — suffering around thirty-five blows to the head — and died of the injuries. There also seemed to be an element of sexual assault, as her pyjamas were ripped.

Sam always protested his innocence. He claims to have been abruptly woken up on the daybed by the sound of Marilyn screaming. He says he ran up to her bedroom only to perceive the form of a 'bushy haired man' attacking his wife. He claimed that while trying to stop the assault, he was knocked unconscious, later coming round to the sound of more commotion downstairs. Following the sound again, he chased the intruder through the house and out to the beach, where he struggled with him and was knocked unconscious once more. The next time he came to, he was topless and submerged halfway in the water of Lake Erie. He ran into the house and called his friends and neighbours the Houks and screamed, 'For God's sake . . . get over here quick, I think they've killed Marilyn!'

From the start, the coroner who attended the scene,

Dr Samuel Gerber, was suspicious of Sam. There were many different reasons why Sam was eventually arrested for the murder of his wife: an hour appeared to have passed between the attack on Marilyn and Sam making a call for help; the call for help he *did* make was to his neighbours and not directly to the police; the Sheppards' dog hadn't barked during the attack (which it would likely do if there was an intruder); the ransacking of the house looked 'staged' and some stolen items — a fraternity ring, a key and a blood-stained wristwatch — were found in a bag dumped in the garden.

Then the press discovered that Sam had been having an affair with a beautiful hospital technician called Susan Hayes . . . and that his wife had been pregnant at the time of the attack. Public, professional and press opinion of Dr Sam Sheppard was extremely negative, and Dr Gerber's very apparent bias didn't help. He noted the many bloodstains at the scene but felt it unnecessary to have them analysed — as far as he was concerned, they had their man. Sam Sheppard was sentenced to life in prison for the brutal murder of his pregnant wife.

But Sam's brothers never stopped believing in his innocence, particularly after some unusual events unfolded regarding a man called Richard Eberling — a handyman and window cleaner who had been to the Sheppards' home. Throughout his life, Richard Eberling was what we'd call 'known to the police': a suspicious character associated with women who had questionable deaths. During what passed as an investigation into Marilyn Sheppard's murder, Eberling was at least questioned, and the reports state he had apparently felt an attraction towards her.

Because of the work he'd done for the Sheppards, Eberling knew the layout of the house well and wasn't a stranger to their dog. Rather more crucially he was being interviewed by police who suspected him of carrying out a series of burglaries in the Sheppards' neighbourhood and they found in his possession several of Marilyn's rings. He volunteered information that his blood would likely be found at the scene of Marilyn's murder if police were to look for it, saying he'd cut himself while washing their windows. Of course, the blinkered coroner Dr Gerber hadn't had any of the blood analysed at the time even though it certainly wasn't beyond the realms of investigation in the 1950s to do so. Swabbing stains to determine blood types wouldn't have taken more than an hour. This information was important but it was ignored by Dr Gerber.

Because of this, Sheppard's defence lawyer, Bill Corrigan, eventually called in the now familiar Dr Paul Leland Kirk, an esteemed criminalist and head of the criminology programme at the University of California Berkeley. By now Sam was behind bars and the murder had taken place a year before, so Kirk was dealing with an old crime scene. Still, Kirk was able to conclude that the void pattern, or blank area, on the blood-soaked wall near Marilyn's bed meant that something — or someone else — should have been covered in a matching amount of spatter . . . but Sheppard hadn't been, like our suspect in Christie's *After the Funeral*. He also affirmed that the void meant the assailant had been swinging the weapon in a left-handed manner, but Sheppard was right-handed. We've seen that there can be difficulties in determining a suspect's dominant hand, and Agatha Christie very infrequently committed to it in her fiction by this time, so we can't say this is solid evidence — but it's another piece of the puzzle that could have been looked into. Furthermore, a bloodstain on a pillow which coroner Dr Gerber insisted was the outline of a surgical weapon, and therefore tied medical professional Sam Sheppard to the crime, was shown to actually be a pattern simply caused by part of the pillow case being folded over.

Most important was the wristwatch, which had been described as 'bloodstained', and the assumption that Sam had worn it as he attacked his wife. Yes, it was stained with blood spatter on the face, but it also had spatter on the metal *underside*. This is Blood Spatter Analysis 101 — it meant there was no way Sam had been wearing it when Marilyn was attacked, and in fact it must have been sitting on the bedside table in order for blood to splash onto it in that way. Crucially, a bloodstain which didn't seem to be consistent with the distribution of the rest of the spatter was analysed thanks to Kirk, and the conclusion was that it wasn't from Sam or Marilyn Sheppard — a third person had been at the crime scene. Could this have been Eberling's blood? Could this have been the reason he'd insisted his blood was 'probably at the scene' and invented an innocent reason for its presence?

After many appeals, a retrial was finally conducted in 1966, twelve years after the first trial. This time, Dr Sheppard walked free, making headlines all over the world. He talked on some chat shows and even wrote a book, which leads me to believe Christie would have been familiar with this case, as does the fact that it brought blood spatter analysis to the fore all over the world as a forensic tool.

What makes this case particularly gripping is that all the information — including all Paul L. Kirk's investigation photography — is now available via Digital Commons from Cleveland State University, meaning you can examine all the evidence and act as an armchair detective. If you are tempted to look them up, though, be warned: some of the pictures are quite graphic.

This case put me in mind of Agatha's *Ordeal by Innocence*, which features Jacko Argyle insisting he was innocent of bludgeoning his mother, but being thrown in jail and dying after a couple of years — before his innocence is proved in spectacular fashion. The original investigation and trial of the Sheppard case took place four years before *Ordeal by Innocence* was written, and could even have been an inspiration for the book. Sam Sheppard's real-life story is similarly tragic: two weeks after Sam was originally sentenced for the murder of Marilyn his mother committed suicide. A week after that his father died of a haemorrhaging ulcer. Marilyn's father also committed suicide in 1966 and Sam himself died of alcohol-induced liver failure in 1970, aged only forty-six. As Christie reiterates several times in *Ordeal by Innocence*, 'It's not the guilty who matter, but the innocent.'

* * *

In *Mrs McGinty's Dead* the police describe the clothing of a man under suspicion of murder: 'Finally there was blood on his cuff . . . said he remembered brushing up against a butcher's shop the previous day. Baloney! It wasn't animal blood.'

We can infer that the accused in this story doesn't

know enough about medicolegal advances to think the investigating team will be able to tell the difference between human blood and animal blood. And it's true there was once a time when a murderer whose clothes and hands were covered in blood could simply say, 'Oh *this*? This is actually blood from when I slaughtered a cow earlier,' and there wasn't any way for investigators to disprove the statement.

In our modern era of DNA testing, blood transfusions and more, it may seem ridiculous that perpetrators of gruesome human slaughter could ever have got away with it by simply claiming the blood was from an animal, and not human in origin. In fact it happened all the time. How could early investigators tell the difference? It wasn't until 1863 that German-Swiss chemist Christian Friedrich Schönbein started to experiment with blood and various chemicals, and noticed that blood effervesced or 'bubbled' with the addition of hydrogen peroxide — but so did other biological substances like semen and saliva. This hydrogen peroxide discovery by Schönbein helped in the subsequent creation of what are called *presumptive tests* for blood, in the early 1900s (which were used during Christie's time of writing, and which are still in use today). Presumptive tests determine whether blood or biological matter is present at all and this does include animal blood. Examples Christie-era investigators used include:

The Kastle-Meyer Test — The chemical phenolphthalein is added to a presumed blood sample on a clean swab and, after a few seconds, hydrogen peroxide is added. If the swab turns bright pink rapidly, blood is likely present.

The Leucomalachite Green or LMG Test — LMG is a colourless liquid but when added to a presumptive blood sample on a clean swab, along with our friend hydrogen peroxide, it turns green.

The reason they're called *presumptive* tests is because investigators may get a positive response from substances which are not blood — not only the bodily fluids like semen and saliva mentioned earlier, but also from material which contains natural peroxidases, of which, bizarrely, horseradish is one. Investigators can *presume* there's a chance blood is present when they carry out these presumptive tests and experience a positive reaction, but they can't confirm it. However, they're one step closer. *Using Taken at the Flood* as an example, we're told that a pair of steel fire tongs were at a murder scene '. . . the heavy head of which was stained a rusty brown'. Now, a 'rusty brown' stain could be anything, couldn't it? So early crime scene investigators — those working during the time this book was written in the 1940s — would have carried out a presumptive test, like the ones listed above, using simple chemicals and swabs to give an answer within minutes. If there was a negative response, the poker would be dismissed as dirty in some other way — perhaps it just had paint on it or genuine rust and was therefore irrelevant to the murder. But if there was a positive response, then there's a chance the rusty brown stain *is* blood, although we know it could still be something else. The next step, then, would be to carry out complicated confirmatory tests to *prove* the presence of blood. These tests were usually carried out in a lab, and they were more time-consuming and more expensive than presumptive tests, all good reasons why they're not just done straight away. A dark stain at a crime scene could turn out to be paint, and the quickest way to eliminate it from the exhibits list was to undertake a presumptive test first. A negative reaction would mean that further confirmatory tests would not be needed, therefore no time or money would be wasted. A positive reaction would mean that the stain *could* contain blood (or semen, or saliva — or horseradish!) and at least now investigators would know where to focus confirmatory tests to determine if some type of blood was present. This is why in *Towards Zero* we're told that the spattered jacket is going to be tested: 'The blood on the sleeve has gone for analysis, Sir. They'll ring us up as soon as they get the result.' They will have decided the jacket is worth sending off for analysis not by guessing there may be some type of blood on it, but by presumptively testing first.

A key phrase here is 'some type of blood'. To return to the explanation of the suspect in *Mrs McGinty's Dead* that he 'remembered brushing up against a butcher's shop the previous day': how *did* investigators eventually differentiate between human and animal blood in order to lay to rest the excuse 'It's animal blood, guvnor'?

Around the same time as these presumptive tests were being introduced, in 1901, a German doctor called Paul Uhlenhuth created what is known as 'The Precipitin Test', building on previous biological research by other scientists. He discovered that if he injected the protein from a chicken egg into a live rabbit, then mixed this rabbit's blood serum (the liquid part of blood) with chicken egg white, the egg proteins separated or precipitated out from the liquid together to form 'clumps' of a type of substance known as precipitins. But these clumps only formed in chicken egg whites, not those of a duck or a goose or any other bird. The significance of Uhlenhuth's work, for our basic forensic purposes, was to establish that the blood of different animals contained proteins unique to them, and this eventually allowed analysts to differentiate between human and animal blood. (It also meant that rabbits were still on scientists' hit lists, it seems!) This is the 'analysis' referred to by Christie in *Towards Zero* when discussing the bloodstained jacket; this is the complicated confirmatory test which would determine what animal the blood present came from, and which is why we're told later in the book, 'Blood on the coat sleeves is human.' After creating this 'Precipitin Test', Uhlenhuth established a specific protocol on how to use it, which included conducting a control every time (just as we always used to have a control in school science experiments). He also created standardised serums from a specific recipe, which he made available via official sources, to significantly reduce wild variety in testing results no matter which investigator carried them out. These controls meant that the test was infallible every time and was first used in a forensic context just a year later, when several children were brutally murdered in Germany.

In September 1898, two young girls had gone missing from a village called Lechtingen one afternoon. By evening, the body of seven-year-old Hannelore Heidemann was discovered in the woods, gruesomely dismembered. Just an hour later, her eight-year-old friend, Else Langmeier, was also discovered mutilated and dismembered in a similar fashion. Ludwig Tessnow, a local carpenter, was quickly suspected after he'd been seen returning to the village from the woods with bloodstains on his clothes. But during the police interview he said the dark brownish stains were 'wood dye' and investigators had no way to prove otherwise. Tessnow was released and headed further afield, to the island of Rügen. In July 1901 two young brothers, Peter and Hermann Stubbe, were found dead there. They'd been mutilated, beheaded and disembowelled. Once again Tessnow was suspected as he'd been seen talking to the two boys earlier in the day, and he'd once again been seen wearing clothing covered in dark stains. (How brazen people could be before testing!) But Tessnow's luck was running out. This time, one of the interviewing magistrates remembered his name being linked with the murders of the girls in Lechtingen, and a local farmer claimed he'd seen Tessnow running from his field in Rügen after several of his sheep had been slaughtered.

The police needed real evidence to tie this monster to the gruesome slayings, or he'd go free and almost certainly murder again. Paul Uhlenhuth was contacted and asked to examine Tessnow's clothing, along with the rock he'd likely used to crush the poor boys' skulls. Uhlenhuth was able to detect the wood dye, but amongst it he found stains he identified as sheep and human blood. It was enough to have Tessnow tried, found guilty and executed — and it made Uhlenhuth a household name. His work in bacteriology and immunology was prolific, and he was nominated for the Nobel Prize in Medicine more than forty times in his career. Unfortunately, I have to note that he was also a member of the Nazi Party, and his application to carry out medical experiments on non-white POWs in 1944 casts a serious shadow over what was otherwise a litany of monumental achievements. It's possible for scientists to make incredible discoveries, but unfortunately good science can be applied in appalling ways depending on the motivation of the scientist.

* * *

Although human blood could now be identified as human, there was still an issue. Anyone caught red-handed (or red-shirted, or red-floored) could lie and say they had just injured *themselves*. 'Of course it's human blood, sir — I cut myself shaving' could still be the excuse of a wily killer. What was now needed was a way to identify whose human blood it really was.

Enter Karl Landsteiner and the ABO blood grouping system.

Around the same time that Paul Uhlenhuth was differentiating human from animal blood, Austrian-born Karl was working at the Institute of Pathological Anatomy in Vienna.

It had previously been demonstrated that when a human was given injections of blood from other animals, the red blood cells clumped together and this led to very low levels of successful transfusion. However, Landsteiner determined that a similar reaction occurred when one human was transfused with the blood of another human too, not just with that of a different species. He'd used samples of his own blood and that of his colleagues to show this 'clumping', or agglutination as it's scientifically called, and began to look into why it happened. He concluded that at least two antigens (substances which are capable of stimulating an immune response: the body's way of fighting infection) must exist, and he called them anti-A and anti-B. He then went on to classify four different blood types, or blood groups, which he named A, B, AB and O. The names come from those antigens or 'markers' he first discovered. Put simply, Type A blood has A antigens on the red blood cells, and Type B blood has B antigens on the red blood cells. Type O blood has neither of these antigens on the red blood cells, and Type AB has both. Another antigen which Landsteiner went on to discover was the Rh or Rhesus factor; a person may test positive for the Rh antigen, or they may be negative, and this is why we classify an individual's blood as 'O-negative', 'A-positive' and so on. What Landsteiner was able to illustrate is that the clumping or agglutination he'd previously seen in his blood transfusion experiments didn't occur when two bloods of the exact same type were mixed. These landmark discoveries made blood transfusions possible, because knowledge of these markers enabled medics to provide the right blood to the right patient.

These varying proteins also enabled medicolegal investigators to categorise people into groups via their antigen types. There may have only been relatively few groups compared to the possibilities we now have with DNA analysis, but it was enough to make a difference to how certain cases were investigated. Suspects could be eliminated if their specific type wasn't present in blood at the scene, on victims or on weapons, or could become prime suspects if they were covered in blood of the same type as a known victim's.

Blood groups are mentioned frequently in *Towards*

Zero, which really showcases Agatha's increasing forensic knowledge by the 1940s. After finding a blood-stained item which could be the murder weapon, a niblick, Superintendent Battle is keen to speed up the investigation, but the police surgeon Dr Lazenby — in very typical fashion of forensic examiners! — is more cautious: 'I can only swear that it *might* have been the weapon. I'll analyse the blood on it, make sure that it's the same blood group . . . ' It's a good job Dr Lazenby is being thorough because in Battle's opinion a golf club in the room with blood and hair on it is enough for him to identify it as the murder weapon, and we subsequently find out that wasn't the case. This book is full of faked evidence, bluffs and double-bluffs.

This exchange is interesting because in early Christie it was indeed enough for the characters to be made aware of clues in this way: it's bloody and it's at the scene of the crime so it stands to reason it must have been the weapon. 'He had fallen forward, struck down by a terrific blow on the head from behind. The weapon was not far to seek. A marble statue stood where it had been hurriedly put down, the head of it stained with blood,' for example, from 'The Adventure of the Italian Nobleman' published in 1923. However, with the known advancement of forensic science had come two new avenues for fictional crime writing. First, the story had to echo the reality of the situation and a piece of evidence like this would no longer be taken for granted without the relevant tests being carried out. Second, it opened up the idea that evidence like this could be falsified — by someone on the wrong side of the law who also knew of these forensic advances.

Agatha addresses the first issue by having several

items from the scene — or 'exhibits' as we call them in forensics — sent for analysis, including items of clothing and the suspected murder weapon.

Superintendent Battle later confirms that the blood on the spattered sleeve is of the same blood type as the victim's, thus referencing the pivotal forensic discovery of Landsteiner, and showing the importance of establishing these facts about the blood early. (It's only insinuated that the outcome of tests on the golf club similarly indicated human blood, but it's not as important once investigators realise it's a faked murder weapon.) No one staying at Gull's Point can pretend they were stained with blood while tenderising a raw steak with a mallet, so we can move forward through the story safe in the knowledge that we have our facts absolutely straight, at least scientifically speaking.

We also find a mention of blood group in *Mrs McGinty's Dead*, but does the blood belong to the unfortunate Mrs McGinty? According to our investigators, it does: 'Bentley's coat sleeve had blood on it and hair — same blood group and the right hair.' Excluding the fact that Bentley's own blood may be of the same type as his supposed victim, things don't look good for Mr Bentley. And we *can* exclude that possibility because Bentley never suggested the blood was his own; you may recall he tried to explain the blood away by saying he'd brushed up against meat in a butcher's shop. The Inspector says of the sleeve, 'It was washed, of course — but they don't realise now that a microscopic amount of blood will give a reaction with the latest reagents. Yes, it's human blood alright.'

And this is what I love about Christie, dropping new forensic discoveries into the story as casually as village gossip. This book was written in 1952, and just a year before, a pivotal and iconic substance in the world of blood detection was perfected: **luminol**.

Haemoglobin is key to the use of the substance luminol in the detection of blood. It's the oxygen-carrying molecule present in the red blood cells of all vertebrates, and it contains iron; which is why some people take iron supplements if they're anaemic. Enter luminol, a synthesised, complex compound which, when mixed with blood and good old hydrogen peroxide, which we know about from early presumptive tests, temporarily glows pale blue via a process called chemiluminescence. It's actually the iron in the blood reacting with luminol that causes the ethereal glowing effect. Although it was developed in stages from the early 1900s, it wasn't called 'luminol' until 1934, and it was in 1937 that German forensic scientist Walter Specht extensively studied luminol as applied specifically to blood at crime scenes. Testing with luminol works best in a darkened room, as it's easier to see the chemiluminescence without light intrusion. The reagent mixture needs to be sprayed finely and evenly onto suspected bloodstains and (if the stains are blood) it will glow blue for only around thirty seconds. This gives time for photographs to be taken to be analysed by experts and further used as evidence in court. If necessary, the stains can be sprayed again and again and again giving an identical reaction. That's to say, luminol doesn't degrade the blood in any way and the luminous reaction can be repeated over and over, meaning as many photographs as are needed for evidence can be taken.

Christie's book *A Sittaford Mystery* is set in one of her favourite places: Dartmoor. It's also one of my favourite books. Sittaford House is a large manse which becomes snowbound in winter, and there are some rather spooky goings-on in this mystery with a very closed circle of suspects. After the murder of Captain Trevelyan, which drives the plot, a young boyish character called Ronnie says, 'I thought you could never wash out blood stains. I thought however much you washed them they always came back.'

In a way Ronnie is absolutely right: using luminol on aged and decomposed blood actually gives a stronger and longer-lasting reaction than fresh blood, and it's particularly effective at detecting blood which someone has tried to wash away — making it ideal for crime scenes which the perpetrator had tried to clean of all evidence. Of course, I can't be certain that this is what Agatha was referring to when Superintendent Spence describes 'new scientific methods of determining bloodstains' or 'the latest reagents' in *Mrs McGinty's Dead*. But his quote in that book — and really the comment Christie makes — is more advanced than words put in Inspector Japp's mouth to describe a blood-soaked floor in *One, Two, Buckle My Shoe* from twelve years earlier: 'There was a trace of blood on the linoleum — in the corners where it had been missed when the floor was washed over. After that, it was just a question of finding the body.' This earlier reference to bloodstains implies that they were discovered due to sloppy cleaning — that is, leaving small amounts of blood visible to the naked eye — and not due to reagents able to increase the visibility of latent bloodstains, showing the advancement of analysis and Christie's knowledge of it, over that time.

Grodsky's 1951 paper on luminol was published

in the *Journal of Criminal Law, Criminology, and Police Science*, and with an enticing name like that there's a chance that avid crime researcher Christie may have read a copy of the journal or discussed it with the Detection Club. She iterated several times in her autobiography that she became a student of criminology, effectively, because of her detective fiction.

* * *

In the short story 'The Man in the Mist', Tommy and Tuppence stumble unexpectedly across the body of a woman killed by a blow to the head. According to Christie 'a heavy blow with some blunt instrument had crushed in the skull. Blood was dripping slowly onto the floor but the wound itself had long ceased to bleed.' This perfectly illustrates the importance of blood and its ability to clot or congeal, and what this means in a forensic context. Our blood clots or 'coagulates' in order to stop us from simply bleeding and bleeding until we die from the tiniest wound. In people who are alive, there are many coagulation mechanisms, involving proteins, calcium and platelet cells, which means that in individuals who don't have a blood disorder the clotting rate is fairly predictable. In blood that has left the body after someone has bled, the clotting process is also fairly predictable depending on environmental circumstances. (But remember, whenever it comes to biology there are many variables!) Very generally, once blood has left the body, the first signs of clotting appear between, say, three and fifteen minutes later: the blood gets darker and forms a jelly-like mass. Over time the clot itself — made up mainly of red blood cells — begins to contract and separate from the watery element of the blood: the serum. This can give investigators — whether BPA analysts, police officers or pathologists — a rough idea of time since death or bloodshed when observing the blood on a wound:

> Blood still liquid = bleeding likely occurred a few minutes previously
> Blood gelatinous and shiny = bleeding probably occurred less than an hour ago
> Blood separated into clot and serum = bleeding likely occurred several hours ago

As with all forensic sciences, caution needs to be exercised and this mnemonic aid isn't definitive, but over time and with lots of experience crime scene investigators become proficient at estimating when the bleeding started. We do see this in Christie's works, for example with the shooting of Colonel Protheroe in *The Murder at the Vicarage*:

> 'When do you think Redding shot him?'
> 'A few minutes before I got to the house.'
> The doctor shook his head. 'Impossible. Plumb impossible. He'd been dead much longer than that . . . Redding lies. Hang it all, I tell you I'm a doctor, and I know. The blood had begun to congeal.'

What the doctor is saying is that by looking at the condition of the blood which had exuded from Colonel Protheroe's head wound, he could tell there was no way — in his opinion — Protheroe had been shot only 'a few minutes before'. This tells us that rather than being still liquid, the blood must have been 'gelatinous and shiny' as in our list above. The fact that the doctor won't budge on this distinction is absolutely pivotal to how the murder is eventually solved.

What I find fascinating is that Agatha Christie not only knew about this coagulation process and its usefulness for estimating time of death, but she actively researched and included a chemical way to counteract it — and therefore give her killer a very unique alibi — in her bloodiest book: *Hercule Poirot's Christmas*. On finding the deceased Simeon Lee with his throat cut 'right up under his ear', after hearing his inhuman scream from his locked room, some of the members of his family seem to reflect upon the situation quite lyrically, with one, Lydia, quoting Shakespeare: 'Yet who would have thought the old man to have had so much blood in him?' Others, however, exclaim more pragmatically: 'Oh so much blood everywhere!' and '. . . Grandfather lying in a lot of blood.'

These quotes are important: Poirot insists there is *too much* blood. Would an old man really bleed quite this much? Would he put up this much of a struggle given how physically decrepit he is? And, more pressingly, how was he murdered in a room with a locked door and no window egress?

The murder seemed to have been committed mere minutes before the body was found: the entire family had heard the scream; had heard the furniture crashing to the floor in the struggle and, more importantly, had seen the blood once they'd forced the door open. There were pools of it, red and glistening, which — according to our rough estimates above — suggested that bleeding occurred 'a few minutes previously'. But we later find out that this time of death was impossible, so what was the real scenario? Why was the blood telling lies?

When Poirot figures it out, he subjects everyone involved to a drawing-room denouement of the sort which Christie has become famous for, but which actually features in a smaller number of her books than you'd imagine. He says to the culprit:

> '. . . you cut his throat . . . you had with you a bottle of some freshly killed animal's blood to which you had added a quantity of sodium citrate. You sprinkled this about freely and added more sodium citrate to the pool of blood which flowed from Simeon Lee's wound.'

Sodium citrate! Did you guess that? No, neither did I! I can't imagine even the most astute reader would.

Sodium citrate is an anticoagulant which works by binding the calcium in the blood, calcium — which we've seen — is needed for clotting. The actual substance is made up of the sodium salts of citric acid that come from citrus fruits. In its pure form, sodium citrate is used in the food industry as an alternative to vinegar or lemon juice when a tang is needed, usually labelled as an E Number (E330) on any ingredients lists. But really most of us will probably be more familiar with it from having our blood taken. After the initial process, our blood is usually distributed between several different plastic tubes with various coloured tops, and the blue tops contain the sodium citrate which stops the blood coagulating before it can be tested.

It's an unusual plan for our murderer to carry out

in order to make it look as though the blood of the victim was freshly spilled, therefore giving them an alibi by 'altering' the apparent time of death. But as unusual as it may seem, Agatha did have that nursing experience during the First World War — a particularly pivotal time for this discovery to be made. It was in November 1914 that an article appeared in the *New York Herald Tribune* explaining the uses of sodium citrate to stop blood coagulating, and by 1916 there was an article in the *British Medical Journal* on the topic entitled 'The transfusion of whole blood. A suggestion for its more frequent employment in war surgery'. As a military nurse, it's highly likely Agatha would have learned about this substance and its ability to stop blood coagulating from the doctors she was working with, or perhaps even read the paper herself (we know she kept notes from the *British Medical Journal* in later life). However she learned about this interesting process, she immortalised that knowledge in this 'festive' book.

* * *

Finally, the blood distribution *inside* the body after death is an important post-mortem artefact for death investigators of any kind. Most people have heard of the stiffening of the body which happens after death — rigor mortis — but may not have come across the term livor mortis. Also called hypostasis or lividity, this is the process of blood settling in the lower areas of the body due to the effect of gravity, once the heart stops and is no longer propelling blood around the corpse. The word 'livid' actually means 'bluish', so when we sometimes say colloquially that a person is livid (angry) we're implying that they're so furious they're going purple in the face. Agatha uses the term correctly when describing the murder victim in *The Murder on the Links*, 'His lips were drawn back from his teeth and an expression of absolute amazement and terror was stamped on the livid features.' She's explaining that the face was bluish and corpse-like, not irate — although I'm sure feeling angry at being murdered is pretty justified.

Livor mortis is important because it begins as soon as the heart stops and blood starts to settle in the vessels lowest to the ground, whether a person is lying down or hanging, or in any other position. It's simply due to gravity. In the first scenario, blood will pool at what we'd call the posterior, or back, of the body, except for the parts which touch the floor (these vessels are squeezed closed by pressure against the floor); in the second it would pool in the legs, the lower arms and fingers (if the hands are hanging straight down) and even in the earlobes. The purplish pattern of livor mortis is different from bruising and it can actually become fixed in place as decomposition progresses. If an investigator is called to a death scene and the deceased is lying face up on a bed, a relative says they died in their sleep and the livor mortis pattern is on the back, back of legs and buttocks this would make sense. But if the pattern showed extreme blue or purple in the face, neck and shoulders and pale legs it could be ascertained that the deceased fell out of bed head first and was stuck like that for several hours, before being found and possibly put back in bed by the relative.

* * *

Agatha featured blood in her books and stories from very early in her career, as early as 1923 in fact. Initially, in short stories, she tried out different tactics to portray bloody crimes in a way that was suitable for the era. In the earliest example, 'The Tragedy at Marsden Manor', we simply get a droplet of blood on the victim's lip and the possibility of internal bleeding. But thirty years later in *After the Funeral* our victim 'had been savagely attacked . . . and the henna dyed fringe was clotted and stiffened with blood'. Between these two was the extraordinary *Towards Zero*, peppered with all sorts of forensic references with particular attention to the location of blood, whether or not it was human and even what blood type it was — the first time Christie ever actually mentioned blood *type*. This is unusual, though, since blood groups had been well known for forty years by this point: Agatha was therefore slower to add this particular piece of scientific knowledge to her murder mysteries than she was luminol, for example. Perhaps it's because Christie — as previously mentioned — liked to vary her murder methods and didn't want to overshadow some plots with too much gore.

It's true that perhaps Agatha sometimes needed some encouragement to write particularly sanguineous murders. In the prologue to Hercule Poirot's Christmas, she wrote a note to her brother-in-law:

> You complained that my murders were getting too refined — anaemic, in fact. You yearned for a 'good, violent murder with lots of blood'. A murder where there was no doubt about its being murder! So this is your special story — written for you. I hope it may please.

But in *Cards on the Table* (1936) her character Ariadne Oliver — based on Agatha Christie herself — describes one of the methods of her writing process, 'If the thing's getting a little dull, some more blood cheers it up!' Agatha is the one who chose to set this bloody Poirot case rather incongruously during the festive period, for maximum impact — which shows a cheeky sense of the macabre! She is the one who researched an unusual way of stopping blood from clotting and incorporated it into this rather ingenious slaying, and she is the one who wrote fantastic lines about 'fresh, wet, gleaming' blood and referenced blood-soaked Shakespeare quotes. So, I believe that as well as pleasing her brother-in-law, it pleased *her*, too.

7

Autopsy

'What are they? They are not men and women — they are just bodies. That reminds me very much of the morgue in Paris. Bodies — arranged on slabs — like butcher's meat!'

— *Evil Under the Sun*

The human body is like a painting: the canvas of our skin stretched over the frame of our bones. For pathologists — and the anatomical pathology technologists (APTs) like myself — this canvas appears daubed with features which not only tell us how a person died, but also how they lived. Pathology, after all, is the study of *disease*, as opposed to the commonly held view that it's the study of death alone. The visual puzzle aspect of the human cadaver is what drew me not only to the field of pathology as my chosen career, but also to the books of Agatha Christie.

She gives the reader a fighting chance of solving her mysteries, as they are usually filled with clues. Some of them are so obvious that on looking back after finishing the book you wonder how they didn't slap you in the face at first reading. Others are buried so deeply in the text they need to be excavated — something only her archaeologist husband Max would have the skills to reveal. But when

I first began reading her books as a child it was the many clues she provided about dead bodies — the blood, wounds and complex decomposition artefacts — which I found the most ingenious, and this cemented the love of forensic pathology which would go on to shape my whole life.

In *Partners in Crime* (in which Tommy and Tuppence Beresford take over a private detection agency), each short story is given a humorous twist by Agatha who has her married protagonists portray different fictional detectives to solve each case. Not only does it make for amusing reading when Tommy tries — and fails — to be as astute as Sherlock Holmes, for example, it also creates a satisfying meta loop when they reference Hercule Poirot's 'little grey cells' and Tommy uses the phrase 'Mon ami' in an attempt to emulate him! There's a fictional world of Hercule Poirot *within* the fictional world of Tommy and Tuppence! The reason I mention this is that one of the literary sleuths that Tuppence considers emulating is Reginald Fortune, a surgeon and detective created by the writer H. C. Bailey, who was a member of the Detection Club, and who was mentioned by young Peter Carmody in *The Body in the Library*. In 'The Ambassador's Boots' Tommy warns against this impersonation, saying, 'You will have to examine horribly smashed faces and very extra dead bodies a good deal.' Martin Edwards, the current president of the Detection Club, states that 'even during the 1920s a strong sense of evil had pervaded H. C. Bailey's writing' far more than it perhaps would in Christie's works.

Christie admired Bailey's Reggie Fortune stories, despite this slightly darker content, but in her own murder mysteries you won't find gratuitous violence and gore. She said in her posthumously published autobiography, when looking back on the golden era of crime, 'No one could have dreamt then that there would come a time when crime books would be read for their love of violence, the taking of sadistic pleasure in brutality for its own sake', referencing, perhaps, contemporaneous police procedural fiction, which had a grittier element than its 'cosy crime' forebears. This, however, doesn't mean that during the era she's reflecting on *she* wasn't considered rather wanton in her description of some murders, and a *Times* review of *One, Two, Buckle My Shoe* in the 1940s supports this. It describes the book as 'joyless, dry and colourless' and goes on to say,

> it quickens into life only when a revolting corpse is discovered. This is characteristic of Christie's school. The 'full horrible details' that bring people to death are accounted of more importance than details which bring people to life.

This is not the sort of review most people would associate with a 'cosy' Agatha Christie book, but she was writing at a time very different from ours.

For this reason, anything violent or gruesome which was or is perceived to be in an Agatha Christie story is there *for a reason*. Dorothy L. Sayers, Christie's fellow Detection Club member, also used this technique, saying that in detective novels 'where the writer has exerted himself to be extra gruesome, look out for the clue', and it's within the discipline of forensic pathology that clues abound.

What is Autopsy and Forensic Pathology?

Anything which occurs after death is given the Latin epithet 'post-mortem' — a straight equivalent, since 'post' = 'after' and 'mortem' = 'death'. So much of our vocabulary consists of 'post-*something*' that it's easy to confuse it with other phrases. When I was in my third trimester, a taxi driver told me a hilarious story about his wife's pregnancy. He said she'd arrived at her hospital's reception desk and announced that she was there for her 'post-mortem', to which the stunned receptionist replied, 'I don't think you are!'

The taxi driver's wife, of course, meant her 'post-*natal*'.

Because the phrase post-mortem is so well known to us, we refer to autopsies as 'post-mortems' even though the full description of the process is 'post-mortem examination'. No one who works in the field says all three words, and in fact it's usually shortened still further to 'post' or even 'PM' depending on how terribly busy we are and how little time we have to waste on syllables! Christie herself uses all the different iterations, but she also frequently uses the word 'autopsy' too, which means the same thing. The word 'autopsy' comes from the Greek *autos* which means 'oneself' and *opsis* which means 'sight' or 'viewing', so literally means 'to see for oneself' or 'self-examination'. The main purpose of an autopsy is to find the cause of death.

Or perhaps that's a little simplistic? One of the questions I get asked most frequently is 'Why is an autopsy performed if the cause of death is obvious, such as a hanging or a person being hit by a train?' and the answer is that, in truth, an autopsy is about *more* than just finding the cause of a person's death. There are a few different types of autopsies and the ones we need to know about here are forensic (or medicolegal) and routine (or coronial). We know that forensic means 'in relation to the law', so forensic autopsies are carried out when a crime has been committed and a person has been killed. This means finding out exactly how the person died, if they suffered any trauma before or after death, if they were sexually assaulted and if so by how many people, and, in the same vein, if the assailant or assailants left any evidence of themselves on the body. People who *die unexpectedly* will also need an autopsy (at the order of a coroner, hence 'coronial') to establish what exactly happened, even those who appear to have died a natural death, which is why they're also called 'routine' (although that's a bit of a misnomer as it's not 'routine' for absolutely everyone to have a PM. There are differences in criteria). These types of post-mortem examination don't take into account how the family feels about the process from an emotional perspective, or any religious leanings the deceased may have had.

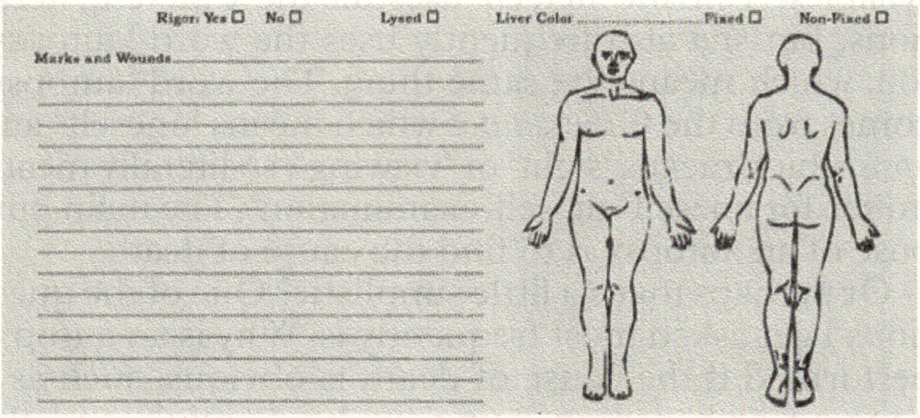

Image of a typical autopsy record or examination form

When you think about it, there are many ways to murder a person and have it look as though they may have died naturally — and Christie was well aware of this. In *Appointment with Death* one of the characters describes a possible case of poisoning by digitalis, which comes from foxgloves. He says 'the active principles of the digitalis may destroy life and leave no appreciative sign' as can be the case with several types of poison. In *Five Little Pigs*, Agatha explains via one of her five main characters: 'I read up coniine, and it hasn't got any distinctive post-mortem appearances. It might have been thought to be sunstroke.' If professionals just took one look at a dead body and said, 'There's no bullet wound, therefore it's a natural death' or some such thing, there'd be a lot of very successful murderers wandering about the world! Similarly, if a family member was allowed to put their foot down and say 'No' to a coronial autopsy, they could quite easily cover up their own murders of relatives, which, sadly, far outweigh the number of stranger-on-stranger murders in the world; you're far more likely to be killed by someone you know than by someone you don't.

Nowadays, the criteria for you or me or anyone else to escape having an autopsy in the UK are incredibly tight and both have to be met:

1. The deceased must have seen a doctor at some point during the two weeks before death.
2. That doctor must believe that death is a result of natural causes.

However, as careful as the whole system appears to be, it came under review after the notorious homicidal doctor Harold Shipman caused the death statistics in the UK to spike (although this was only noticed retrospectively); murders which he got away with because his victims were old and, after being drugged, looked as though they'd died a natural death. Before he was stopped, Shipman managed to kill at least 250 patients. Interestingly a similar series of crimes occurred during Christie's time when a GP called John Bodkin Adams 'lost' 163 patients to coma then death between 1946 and 1956. He was investigated and actually got away with it, which is perhaps what inspired Shipman? Since the Shipman case, and in order to make autopsies far more common than they once were, various studies were carried out on the accuracy of diagnosis without examination, and the modern textbook *Simpson's Forensic Medicine* asserts, 'It should be remembered that at least 50% of the causes of death given by doctors have been shown to be incorrect by a subsequent autopsy.' At *least* 50%! The criteria determining who did and didn't receive a post-mortem were far laxer in Agatha's day, and she shows this in her short story from the 1920s 'The Tragedy at Marsden Manor':

> 'By the way, you saw no need for an autopsy?'
>
> 'Certainly not!' The doctor became quite apoplectic. 'The cause of death was clear, and in my profession we see no need to distress unduly the relatives of a dead patient.'

In this quote, the doctor — without carrying out a post-mortem examination — believes that the cause of death was clear because the victim had 'had one haemorrhage already, and another one would prove fatal'. This is in line with the more relaxed standards of the era. Later in the story, however, the deceased has to be exhumed when a very clever method of murder is suspected, and we are told that the post-mortem confirms what they thought. This is a fictional account, but over the years similar exhumations did occur in real life which led to the need for more stringent autopsy guidelines. In a later short story, 'The Lernean Hydra', Poirot is asked to help a physician whose life is being destroyed by malicious rumours that he poisoned his wife. About the deceased wife, we have this exchange:

> 'What was the cause of death?'
>
> 'Gastric ulcer.'
>
> 'Was there an autopsy?'
>
> 'No. She had been suffering from gastric trouble for a considerable period.' Poirot nodded.
>
> 'And the symptoms of gastric inflammation and of arsenical poisoning are closely alike . . . Get the body exhumed and an autopsy performed.'

Throughout Christie's body of work, she illustrates an intricate knowledge of the coronial process and of inquests, so I suspect she attended a few of them, possibly in her capacity as a pharmacist — although they are open to the public, and many of the characters in her books refer to attending inquests as simply 'something to do' in a usually quiet town when a scandalous murder has been committed. We see this in works as far apart as *Why Didn't They Ask Evans* from 1934 and *Postern of Fate*, the last book Agatha ever wrote, in 1973. Attending inquests would be useful as active research for Agatha's literary work, as well as dinner conversation for the Detection Club. It may explain why her inquest and autopsy information is so technical and well executed in later books such as *Taken at the Flood* and *Endless Night*, and yet the courtroom scene from her very first book, *The Mysterious Affair at Styles*, was removed because the publishers thought it wasn't realistic. Instead, the ending was played out with all the characters in one room of the house, forever cementing the idea of the 'drawing room denouement' in her books.

In routine coronial cases an autopsy seeks to determine the true cause of death, exclude any foul play, establish the identity of the deceased in some cases and — quite importantly — record any other pathologies they may be displaying. To take the example of a hanging, it may appear that the cause of death is consistent with hanging (although a PM will corroborate or refute that depending on what is discovered at detailed examination) but the person may have been suffering with an underlying disease, cancer for example, and, in fact, perhaps the reason they hanged themselves was *because* of this disease. Alternatively perhaps they, or their next of kin, didn't know they had it. This information all goes to the coroner, and becomes a matter of record. It's perhaps not as glamorous as scenes you may see on *Silent Witness* or similar TV shows, but collating this data, and sharing it with relevant health organisations, is how we build up a statistical knowledge of death and disease.

* * *

When a body is about to be autopsied by a forensic pathologist, the assistant, an anatomical pathology technologist, will be present, as well as, among others, various police officers, exhibits officers and a photographer. There'll usually be a set order in which the team carries out the process to glean as much information from the victim's remains as they can, but that varies depending on who's in charge, or the circumstances of the case. Ultimately the body will offer up a myriad of clues and intriguing details to those who know what they're looking for, and slowly the picture before them will become clearer. There are many times that Poirot shows skill at putting the pathology picture together in his deduction, for example in *The Murder on the Links* when he observes foam on the lips of a victim. He goes on to explain, 'He died, if I am not mistaken, of an epileptic fit' — and foam around the mouth can suggest a seizure of some type. Christie describes victims of strangulation very accurately in multiple instances, for example the 'blue congested face and protruding tongue' in *A Murder Is Announced*. Indeed congestion (excess venous blood), oedema (swelling) and cyanosis (blueness) are all characteristic of murder by strangling.

The pathologist is able to differentiate genuine injuries sustained by the victim from processes which naturally occur after death, and it's important to do so. To the unqualified, some of the natural post-mortem artefacts which present on the body could be mistaken for injuries. In the blood chapter we looked at livor mortis — also known as hypostasis and lividity — which happens when the heart stops and blood settles in the vessels of the body, due to gravity. This could be misconstrued as bruising, as they can look the same in some instances, since both processes occur due to the movement of blood — but there is a difference. Bruises, medically known as contusions, are caused by blood leaking into the tissues from small vessels which have been ruptured due to an injury. Once the blood is in the tissues, we see it beneath the skin in the form of a bruise because it's highly pigmented. But this blood is considered foreign by our living bodies' protection mechanisms and the haemoglobin in it is gradually broken down in the live patient, causing it to shift through a kaleidoscope of purple, red, brown, green and yellow, and eventually fade completely. In contrast the colour of hypostasis in dead patients is caused by blood which remains in the vessels which in this case are still intact, as they haven't suffered an injury. The colour may resemble early bruising in the living, but once you know what you're searching for, contusions and hypostasis appear different from each other to the naked eye, due to the pattern and spread. They also appear different under a microscope. In this way, a pathologist can distinguish something which might look like a suspicious injury as being in fact just natural decomposition. That said, livor mortis can take on quite unique hues in certain circumstances. If it entirely appears to be cherry red that can indicate carbon monoxide poisoning, or if it's on the brown side, phosphorus poisoning.

Other early decompositional changes include the more familiar rigor mortis, a stiffening of the muscles of the body in a specific sequence between approximately 12 and 36 hours after death. The word 'approximately' is very important when discussing post-mortem changes because there are so many factors which affect their manifestation. The main thing to hold in your mind is that rigor is a physicochemical change which occurs when the body's muscle cells no longer have an oxygen supply and begin to stiffen.

Agatha alludes to rigor mortis in an early short story, 'The Affair at the Victory Ball', when Inspector Japp asks Poirot to help investigate the murder of Lord Cronshaw at a costume ball. Japp tells Poirot of a comment the attending doctor made: 'He did mention that there was a tension and stiffness about the limbs . . . ' indicating that rigor mortis had begun to set in. This information means that Lord Cronshaw had been dead for some time, which is pivotal in helping Poirot solve the case.

Christie more explicitly references the phenomenon in *Towards Zero* when the doctor estimates time of death:

> 'I'd put it between ten o'clock and midnight.'
>
> 'You can't go nearer than that?'
>
> 'I'd rather not. All sorts of factors to take into account. We don't hang people on *rigor mortis* nowadays.'

Of course, no one was ever 'hanged on rigor mortis', in the same way that no one was ever hanged just on a fingerprint as Poirot disdainfully commented in a much earlier story. The doctor is making the point that the physical evidence of the body, although important, isn't always absolutely conclusive, and investigation into a murder is based on multiple strands of information being woven together. These comments are accurate, but Christie does make an uncharacteristic slip regarding rigor in one of my favourite books. *The Body in the Library* starts with a maid dashing into Mrs Dolly Bantry's bedroom, screaming that she's found the dead body of a young woman inexplicably lying on the hearth rug in the library. Police Constable Billy Palk is called in shortly after — along with Dolly's friend Miss Marple. We learn the victim has been strangled, and at this point we don't know her to be Ruby Keene. Dr Haydock is asked to estimate time of death. He says, 'Depends. There was a fire in the grate — the room was warm — all that would delay rigor and cadaveric stiffening.'

This isn't the case at all, though I do think it's a forgivable mistake. Many people associate stiffening with freezing, so an understandable assumption might be that rigidity in the form of rigor mortis — which happens alongside the body cooling — would be delayed by a warm room. It may seem paradoxical but it's actually the *cold* which delays rigor: rigor mortis has nothing to do with the type of stiffening caused by low temperatures. As mentioned earlier, rigor is physicochemical, meaning that heat speeds up that process whereas cold delays it, alongside other decompositional changes which are also physicochemical — that's why bodies are kept in mortuary refrigerators and freezers to keep them 'fresh'.

While on the subject of the cold, another Latin term to complete the post-mortem trio within pathology is 'algor mortis' which is used to refer to post-mortem cooling: the body decreases in temperature after death because the heart has stopped beating and our physiological processes begin to shut down. This is the most well-known indication that death has occurred, and as a result is referenced frequently by Agatha, most notably in *The Clocks* when the unfortunate typist Sheila Webb, who literally stumbles upon a dead man, experiences the algor mortis of his flesh, first hand. We're told she is unsure if the man is dead or alive so, 'almost mechanically, Sheila bent down. She touched his cheek — cold — his hand, the same.' It's notable here because the resident of the house in which the dead man was discovered is blind, and has absolutely no idea who the man was or why he was there. In order to glean some idea of his identity, at the police's request she has to touch the dead man's face to feel his features in case they're familiar, which wouldn't have been a pleasant experience for her if the man was cold. However, perhaps less well known is that in order to record the temperature of a cadaver with medical accuracy, touching won't suffice because the surface of the body — which is subject to influence from the outside environment — will be cooler than the body's core. In order to carry out calculations which relate to body temperature and the relationship with time of death, the pathologist has to insert a thermometer somewhere they can retrieve a deep temperature reading from the body . . . usually the rectum.

Unsurprisingly, Christie doesn't mention this, although as a nurse I'm certain she would have known it.

These two bedfellows of the mortis world — algor and rigor — can be used together to loosely estimate time of death (TOD); a basic aide-memoire used by some pathologists is:

Body feels warm and flaccid = dead less than 3 hours
Body feels warm and stiff = dead 3–8 hours
Body cold and stiff = dead 8–36 hours
Body cold and flaccid = dead 36 hours or more

This is a very simplistic way to estimate TOD. The mnemonic aid ends at 36 hours because after this time the body begins to warm up again, mainly due to microbial activity. This is why we have to keep the dead in fridges and freezers — they don't stay cold. In reality estimating TOD is fraught with difficulty, but it's one of the questions an investigating pathologist is most often asked to answer during a forensic autopsy. It's also the most requested piece of information in Christie's stories, because the time the person died will directly correspond with stories and alibis relayed by suspects — whether in real life or in books. It's one of the most important pieces of the whole puzzle. For this reason, in Agatha's books, there is a fourth way to estimate TOD which can be added to the mortis trio: digestion.

In *The Mysterious Affair at Styles* one of the first things Poirot asks of his companion Hastings is an account of the food which had been eaten by the victim, and when it was consumed. The issue is brought up several more times in the book, making it seemingly important. 'You have not told me if Mrs Inglethorp ate well last night,' Poirot reprimands Hastings. Later, Hastings wonders why he was even asked for that information at all, but it takes some time before Poirot finally satisfies Hastings's curiosity, reminding him that he does not usually reveal his thinking until the end.

Agatha uses this device several times in her mystery puzzles. In *Lord Edgware Dies*, the wonderful Inspector Japp waxes lyrical on this particular topic to Poirot and Hastings after the death of the unfortunate Carlotta Adams. Hastings informs us that 'we'll have to wait until the autopsy' to 'see where the dinner had got to'. Later:

> As a result of the analysis of the stomach [contents], the time of death was fixed as having occurred not less than an hour after the completion of dinner, with possible extension to an hour after that. This put it as between ten and eleven o'clock, with the probability in favour of the earlier time.

Agatha was clearly quite convinced that as well as progressing physical changes, progressing digestion could also be used to estimate TOD. This is relevant because, at the time of her writing, the analysis of gastric contents was commonly thought to be a reliable indicator of when a person had died, assuming that most meals would take a predictable length of time to digest. But we can't assume that, and the process of gastric emptying has since been completely discredited as a means of estimating time of death. There's far too much individual variation between 'bodies', under what we might consider to be 'normal conditions'. Added to this is the fact that stress in any form causes digestion to slow or stop. A correlation between time since death and level of food digestion has never been proved. But, even though it's incorrect, Agatha's use of this concept — particularly the specific nature of the example from *Lord Edgware Dies* — indicates that she was thorough in her contemporary post-mortem research.

When doctors in Christie's books estimate TOD they are probably taking all of these post-mortem factors into account: level of decomposition, post-mortem changes and digestion of food. And boy do they like to estimate time of death! Of all the questions which an autopsy can attempt to answer, the one Agatha focuses on the most frequently is this one. As we have seen, in real life and in Christie's stories, the TOD is important for establishing suspects' alibis — or lack thereof — and is therefore usually the peg upon which the rest of the story hangs. This is an important point to remember. In *The Sittaford Mystery*, street-smart character Emily Trefusis tells us that she's aware of the importance of an accurate time of death, as it 'might make a considerable difference to the question of alibis'. This doesn't necessarily tell us that every single person who reads detective mysteries is aware of that fact, but it shows us *Christie* is, and she's making a point of letting the reader know this will be pertinent to the story. Indeed, in *The Sittaford Mystery*, the TOD of Captain Trevelyan was absolutely pivotal to the case — so much so that it was apparently predicted by spirits during a 'table-turning' session (equivalent to using a Ouija board).

On average, medical examiners in Christie's novels are able to place death to within a couple of hours. The most notable example is from *The Body in the Library*, the same book in which Dr Haydock incorrectly states that the fire in the grate would 'delay rigor and cadaveric stiffening' of Ruby Keene's body. He postulates that the death occurred 'between ten o'clock and midnight'. When asked by Inspector Slack if he could 'get nearer than that' Haydock tells us, with a slight grin, 'I won't risk my professional reputation. Not earlier than ten and not later than midnight.' But this is already an exceedingly precise estimation of time of death! Current accepted practice in forensic pathology is the utilisation of temperature as the most reliable way of estimating when a death occurred. Using this algor mortis, or post-mortem cooling, it's possible to determine time of death with a window of 2.8 hours either side, which leaves a margin of error of approximately 5.5 hours. This calculation is currently done using Henssge's Nomogram, a chart that shows the correlation between three variables: ambient temperature, rectal temperature of the body and weight of the body. When these data points are added the nomogram can be used to estimate time of death to a 'confidence factor' of 95 per cent, which sounds very impressive, yet actually means there is a window of those 5.5 hours.

This nomogram has been in use only since the early 2000s, so Christie would never have been aware of it, but she does understand the importance of algor mortis in time of death estimation, as evidenced in many stories. *Death on the Nile* is a shining example of this: after Linnet Doyle is found dead, the examining doctor says, 'I would not care to be too precise. It is now eight o'clock. I will say, with due regard to the temperature last night, that she has been dead certainly six hours and probably not longer than eight.' This TOD estimation isn't as tight as the previous one, and is more in line with something a modern pathologist would say.

Clearly the specificity of her estimations has nothing to do with ignorance on Christie's part. She was well aware of the pitfalls of calculating the time of someone's demise in the real world, but in order to write a compelling story and provide what appear to be unshakeable alibis to her suspects, she chose to use artistic licence.

In only her third book, *The Murder on the Links*,

the examining doctor says, 'Death must have taken place at least seven and possibly ten hours previously,' which is a much more realistic estimation than we get in some of her later stories. The assertion that there are — as one character puts it — 'too many individual idiosyncrasies' continues into later books like *Appointment with Death*:

> 'It is difficult to be exact . . . There must necessarily be a margin of several hours. Were I giving evidence on oath I could only say that she had been dead certainly twelve hours and not longer than eighteen.'

But my particular favourite is the following exchange from 'Murder in the Mews', in which Poirot is trying to work out if a murder was made to look like a suicide, or the other way round. Inspector Japp is enquiring into the time of death of Mrs Barbara Allen, and receives a rather more exact answer from Dr Brett than he was expecting:

> 'She was killed at eleven thirty-three yesterday evening,' said Brett promptly. Then he grinned as he saw Japp's surprised face. 'Sorry, old boy,' he said. 'Had to do the super doctor of fiction! As a matter of fact eleven is about as near as I can put it — with a margin of about an hour either way.'

With this conversation, Christie pokes fun at herself and her contemporaries, as she knows perfectly well how much artistic licence they take, when they need to.

Even using the most reliable method of post-mortem cooling and Henssge's Nomogram, the 'idiosyncrasies' involved make exact time of death estimation difficult. Variables include posture of the body, the type of clothing worn at the time of death, if the body is obese or emaciated, whether they had a fever just before death and much more. But a master storyteller like Agatha Christie isn't going to let that stop her in absolutely every book, because we're reading to be entertained as well as informed. The times she sticks to realistic forensic death estimation far outweigh the times she doesn't, and we can forgive her for bending the rules of science just a little bit to create the perfect mystery.

A final relative of the triad of algor, livor and rigor mortis is the concept of cadaveric spasm, which is a sudden stiffening of the muscles of the deceased that occurs before rigor mortis proper sets in, yet occurs in a similar chemical way. In medical circles there is much discussion about this process and whether it exists independently from true rigor, because it's only observed very rarely. Examples include a victim of drowning still clutching some leaves and twigs in their hands which they've torn off, perhaps while trying to save themselves via a hanging branch. Most scientists theorise that it can happen as a result of extreme emotion or stress at the time of death, and it tends to occur in the hands and arms. Christie seems to be aware of the rare phenomenon, and alludes to it in *Hercule Poirot's Christmas* when Poirot observes of the dead man, 'The lips were drawn back from the bloodless gums in something that looked like a snarl. The fingers were curved like claws.' Christie may well have seen this curving of the fingers during her time as a nurse in the First World War, but she is likely exaggerating for artistic effect when she writes that a corpse's face can tell you something about how they died, or how they felt when they died. It's something she includes on a few too many occasions to reflect reality, but as mentioned previously we have to allow for poetic licence in Agatha's books, and it certainly doesn't negate the fact that her stories were full of accurate science.

* * *

There are features other than livor mortis visible on a dead body which could be mistaken for injuries: extreme friction on the skin can cause it to become 'parchmented', meaning it looks like flat yellow-brown blisters where this has occurred. Bodies left exposed in the open air or in water may be subject to the attention of scavengers, such as badgers, foxes and crabs, and the resulting damage can have the appearance of wounds or even look as though parts have been severed — although this is a camouflage technique used by Dorothy L. Sayers rather than Agatha Christie. It's important to be able to tell the difference between flesh which may have been gouged when the victim was *alive*, and gouges which are due to hungry opportunists.

Christie seemed to know the difference. When Poirot says in *The Murder on the Links*, 'It is a strange wound, this! It has not bled . . . It is most simple. The man was stabbed *after he was dead*!' he's noticed something key when it comes to damage inflicted on the human body. Genuine injuries can usually be distinguished from something more sinister, because of the time they were inflicted. Those carried out when a person was alive tend to exhibit bleeding and reddening of the edges, which is the body's immune response to the trauma: inflammation — which isn't the case when dead flesh is damaged. This allows doctors to be confident which wounds occurred before death. Christie directly addresses this several times, something she will have picked up as a nurse and during research, and it is basically correct. A doctor can usually tell the difference, which is perhaps why Dr Sheppard is indignant in *The Murder of Roger Ackroyd* when his sister questions him about the murdered Roger's wound: 'My good woman, I examined the body and I know what I am talking about. That wound wasn't inflicted after death — it was the cause of death, and you need make no mistake about it.' In *The Mystery of the Blue Train*, Poirot boards a train bound for the French Riviera, and befriends a young woman travelling alone, Katherine Grey. On the train, Grey meets Ruth Kettering, an American heiress, and finds Ruth dead in her compartment the next morning. In the story, we learn of her awful fate:

> A heavy blow had disfigured the features almost beyond recognition . . .
>
> 'When was that done, I wonder?' [Poirot] demanded. 'Before death or after?'
>
> 'The doctor says after,' said M. Caux.
>
> 'Strange,' said Poirot.

Finally, in *One, Two, Buckle My Shoe* we learn that the 'injuries were definitely inflicted after death, I should say. But I shall know better when I've got her at the mortuary,' which is certainly a sensible proclamation by the doctor examining the body at the scene, and also cements the idea that Christie genuinely knew there was a difference between ante-mortem and post-mortem injury. This is the sort of 'clue' we should be paying attention to in terms of violence — as mentioned by members of the Detection Club — because one of its primary purposes is to obscure the identity of the victim, which is usually pivotal to the most ingenious plots.

Visible decomposition is not a pretty subject but it's not one from which Agatha Christie shied away. We can assume that her work as a nurse during the First World War — and the fact that she grew up during a time when death wasn't quite as hidden from view or sanitised as it is now — taught her of the many different physical effects the cadaver undergoes once the heart stops. (Indeed, in modern parlance she may have even been considered 'Death Positive', which is a death acceptance movement lauded mainly by young, Western females. She writes in her autobiography, 'it must run in one's blood to enjoy funerals and funeral observances'.) She wrote about decomposition effects enough to give her deaths a certain authenticity. She also peppered her prose with mentions of it just to add colour, quite literally! In *Murder Is Easy* our protagonist Luke Fitzwilliam is concerned about leaving his love interest in the company of local occult fanatic Mr Ellsworthy. His narrative informs us he 'had an unreasoning sense of fear. Bridget — alone with the man whose hands had that unhealthy hue of greenish decomposing flesh.' I think this concern is justifiable, and if you find yourself alone in the company of someone whose flesh is reminiscent of decomposition it would be prudent to run. In *One, Two, Buckle My Shoe* we're told that Poirot and Japp 'looked a shade pea green' on viewing the 'natural process of decomposition' of the murder victim who'd been dead a month (and who also, after this length of time, would have been a distinct shade of green). The young female character 'Egg', in *Three Act Tragedy*, is much cheerier when discussing the conspicuous scent of decomposing flesh:

> It was not Egg's way to avoid unpleasantness. She dealt immediately with the point in Sir Charles's mind. 'Smell goes up, not down. You'd notice a decaying body in the cellar much sooner than in the attic. And, anyway, for a long time, people would think it was a dead rat.'

It's certainly true what one character, Ronnie, considers in *The Sittaford Mystery*: 'Inconvenient thing, a human body.' Perhaps that's why, rather than choose between an attic or a cellar, or anywhere else for the disposal of human remains, serial killer John Haigh settled upon the method of sulphuric acid. In *Ordeal by Innocence* we're told that he 'does one woman in, pickles her in acid, gets pleased with himself and starts making a habit of it'. This is a rather irreverent way of describing John George Haigh who came to be known as the 'Acid Bath Murderer' after he was convicted of killing six people between 1948 and 1949 (although he admitted he killed nine). After stripping them of their valuables to sell, he then disposed of their 'inconvenient' bodies by dissolving them in acid, something he was inspired to do after hearing of a French killer using this method in 1925. According to his account it took around two days for an entire human body to become a ‘sludge’ which he would then tip down various manholes. It’s all rather gruesome considering the way he was described in *The Mirror Crack’ d From Side to Side*: ‘ . . . and that man, Haigh, who pickled them all in acid — they said he couldn’t have been more charming!’

History of Autopsy and Forensic Pathology

Anatomical dissection of the dead — perhaps understandably, given its contentiousness — has a storied past, to say the least. Autopsies as an investigative tool have consistently fallen in and out of favour, unlike other forensic sciences which mostly experienced a more exponential improvement upon discovery. This means that there were centuries-long periods when our knowledge of the human body, in life *and* in death, perhaps didn’t advance as much as it could have done.

The first dissections of humans — at least, the first done to discover cause of death — are recorded as far back as the third century BC by noted Ancient Greek physicians Herophilus and Erasistratus. Together they founded a school of anatomy in the bustling metropolis of Alexandria, thought to be the only place carrying out dissections (and, controversially, vivisections — the dissection of the *living*) until the Renaissance.

Notably, Julius Caesar was autopsied in 44 BC after he was stabbed to death. But the journey of discovery is just that — a journey. All sciences involve researchers covering perhaps a small distance of that journey then passing that baton on to someone else who will go a little further. But for the discipline of human anatomy, a great chasm opened up in the scientific world between about AD 500 and the 1500s; a chasm called 'Christianity'.

It's perhaps rather too simplistic to say that all pathological investigation staggered to a halt just because of a prevailing belief that bodies not physically intact after death would likely be denied access to Heaven or rise from the grave in pieces. But what is recorded is that generally accepted beliefs about our anatomy which had been held since the time of Ancient Rome persisted, and accurate knowledge didn't really improve until the 1500s, because any studies were based on the dissection of animals — human dissection wasn't allowed. It was pioneering Renaissance anatomists like Andreas Vesalius who retrieved dead bodies from gibbets in the dead of night to dissect and draw, eventually publishing epic tomes which illustrated that the previous thousand years of assumptions about the human body were wrong.

In the UK, this clandestine nature of dissection continued into the nineteenth century. Anatomy schools were flourishing and in response the Murder Act of 1752 granted the bodies of those who suffered capital punishment to these schools for dissection — it wasn't just as an educational tool for the students, it was a punishment for those who'd been killed by the hands of justice. But this didn't provide enough bodies for the number of medical schools and students. Just like their anatomical forebears, students often had to resort to body snatching — stealing fresh corpses from their graves — as a way to advance their studies, and in some cases actually fund them by paying for their classes in corpses. The need was so well known, and supplying it so very lucrative, that professional body snatchers — 'Resurrection Men' — came on the scene, making a tidy profit from the medical schools. This continued until 1828 when the infamous Scottish duo Burke and Hare decided to cut out the back-breaking faff of digging up fresh bodies to sell and just kill people instead. After they were caught and it was discovered they were responsible for at least sixteen deaths, Hare turned 'King's evidence' by admitting guilt and giving information about how they committed the crimes, effectively 'making a deal' so that he'd be spared the death penalty. Hare therefore escaped the hands of justice — although he died destitute not long after. Burke, on the other hand, suffered poetic justice: he was dissected (as his victims had been) and flayed, so that his skin could be used to create items like a small pocketbook and a business card holder which are still on display — along with his skeleton — at various Edinburgh museums today. But this didn't satisfy the understandable public outrage. It was recognised that surgery and medicine needed to advance, and that cadavers were necessary for this, but pilfering bodies from graves in the dead of night — and worse, murdering people — was abhorrent and unacceptable. The subsequent Anatomy Act of 1832 provided medical schools with additional bodies beyond the previous allocation: the workhouse poor and those which were unclaimed.

This effectively put an end to the need for body snatchers, and finally the study of medicine and pathology could advance unhindered.

* * *

Lucy Worsley calls the forensic pathologist a Victorian invention, and this is a fairly accurate statement. Arthur Conan Doyle had created his character Sherlock Holmes after studying under the Edinburgh surgeon and lecturer Joseph Bell in 1877, nearly fifty years after the Anatomy Act was passed. Bell was an incredibly perceptive man whose 'eyes twinkled with shrewdness'. He taught his students the importance of observation and deduction by determining the occupations and recent activities of patients — without asking questions — and using this information to build up a more complete picture of their cases. Conan Doyle said that Dr Bell 'prided himself that when he looked at a patient, he could tell not only their disease but very often their occupation and place of residence'.

He's considered to be a pioneer in forensic pathology, even assisting in the Jack the Ripper investigation in London, and it was widely known amongst his contemporaries that he'd inspired Conan Doyle. As a Sherlock fan, Agatha would certainly have been aware of him and his accomplishments and most evidently was inspired by his work when it came to her knowledge of trace evidence.

The 'golden era' of forensic pathology really reached a zenith in the public eye as Agatha was becoming a world-renowned author, so the two occurred concurrently. Of all the pathologists advancing the science and investigating the murders which would go down in the history books, none was more like a character from the pages of a whodunnit than the now familiar Sir Bernard Spilsbury, and of all the well-known murder cases occurring at that time perhaps none is more famous than that of Dr Crippen.

In 1910, Dr Bernard Spilsbury was thirty-three years old, and already a successful pathologist at St Mary's Hospital in London's Paddington. He was handsome, talented, commanding and well dressed — so when he was thrust into the limelight as an expert witness in the Dr Crippen case, the press and the public loved him. Dr Hawley Harvey Crippen, in contrast to someone like Spilsbury, was a mousy-looking bespectacled American, with a drooping walrus moustache which made his face look rather mournful. He was known as 'Dr' Crippen despite being unable to practise as a doctor in the UK (he'd qualified in homeopathic medicine overseas, and homeopathy isn't medicine). Instead, he'd initially made a living as a purveyor of patent (read 'quack') remedies. He was married to a fellow American, a budding music-hall performer called Cora, but spent so much time attempting to help her thus far unsuccessful career that he was fired from his job and started work at a centre for the deaf. Cora repaid this dedication by openly having affairs. Perhaps unsurprisingly given their divergent lifestyles, their sixteen-year marriage was in trouble, and Crippen began an affair with his typist at his new office, Ethel le Neve.

Then Cora suddenly disappeared.

When friends of the Crippens started to ask after Cora's whereabouts, Hawley told them she'd gone back to America. A few weeks later he told them she'd died there, hoping to put an end to the questions once and for all. Rather unwisely, Crippen then moved his mistress, Ethel, into the house he'd previously shared with his wife, and Ethel began wearing Cora's furs and jewellery. The previously curious friends became highly suspicious that Crippen had harmed Cora. Far from being appeased by tales of Cora's 'convenient' death in the USA, they contacted Scotland Yard. The Yard sent Chief Inspector Walter Dew to do a bit of digging — at this point just metaphorical digging.

When questioned by Dew, the mild-mannered doctor explained that he was simply embarrassed about being cuckolded and had told friends only part of the truth. He said Cora had left to go to America with one of her lovers, and — wanting to save face — he had simply obscured that fact from their mutual friends and gone about his business.

Inspector Dew seemed to understand the situation, perhaps viewing Crippen as a rather emasculated and weary man. As one of Christie's characters in *Three Act Tragedy* observes, 'An inferiority complex is a very peculiar thing. Crippen, for instance, undoubtedly suffered from it.' Maybe Inspector Dew felt the same while interviewing the man.

Having found nothing untoward at Hilldrop Crescent, Dew left. But for reasons known only to himself, Crippen panicked, and he and Ethel fled to Belgium. He shaved off his moustache and she dressed as a boy, then they boarded the SS *Montrose* in their 'clever' disguises to start a new life in Canada . . . or so they thought.

It was this moonlight flit which made the police far more suspicious of the pair, rather than any of the other circumstantial evidence. Inspectors returned to search Crippen's house again and this time, after a little physical digging, they made a gruesome discovery in the cellar: several kilos of a 'greasy, grey pulp' which had once been a human body. The remains were missing the head, arms, legs and genitalia, and were impossible to identify by sight, except to tell they were wrapped in a man's pyjama top and there was some dyed hair in rollers mixed in with the mess.

At this point the St Mary's Hospital pathology contingent were called in by Scotland Yard and Dr Bernard Spilsbury became the lead pathologist. The crime was already being called 'The North London Cellar Murder' by the press, and a crowd was gathering outside the house to catch any snippets of information they could.

Meanwhile, on the SS *Montrose*, Captain Henry Kendall had become increasingly suspicious of two of his passengers who claimed to be father and son, yet acted inappropriately towards each other. He needed to inform the police, and yet he only had access to wireless telegraphy as a form of communication. Racing against time as the ship was nearly out of range, he sent a message stating he had 'strong suspicions' that the 'Cellar Murder' fugitives were on board — the first time telegraphy was used in this way. They were caught spectacularly. After receiving this information from the *Montrose*, Inspector Walter Dew, the original investigator, took a faster White Star Liner to the *Montrose*'s destination, where he waited. All the world's press and public were aware of this, except the passengers on the *Montrose*. He met Crippen and Le Neve, surrounded by a mass of press and onlookers, as they disembarked their ship a short time later. Crippen is reported to have simply said wearily, 'Thank God it's over.' They were both returned to England on the SS *Megantic*, for trial.

Had Twitter existed in 1910, it's fair to say that Dr Crippen would have been trending, a phenomenon Christie noted herself in *Five Little Pigs*: 'People read with interest that Dr Crippen murdered his wife . . . '

and he's mentioned in around fifteen of her works. He's also in the Notable British Trials series along with Edith Thompson, Buck Ruxton, John George Haigh and many more of the true cases Agatha featured in her books, which leads me to believe she certainly consulted them. So many factors came together in the Crippen case that it had the public captivated: the cuckolded man, the missing wife, the affairs, the mistress and more. Sex sells, then just as much as it does now. Add to the mix the cutting-edge technology used in attempting to apprehend the absconding couple, and the slightly bizarre way in which they tried to disguise themselves, it's no surprise that the public were following the investigation at every stage via the newspapers. Particularly interesting is the forensic science which was applied to the human remains, and the fact that even now — one hundred years later — it's still enthralling.

At a time when DNA testing wasn't possible, and there were no hands to be fingerprinted, the butchered remains from the cellar could only be given a presumptive identification, helped along by the bleached hair in rollers — hair which looked just like Cora's. It was a small piece of human tissue which Spilsbury noted to be abdominal that helped clinch the ID: there seemed to be a scar on this portion of the abdomen and Cora was known to have had an operation there. Spilsbury had actually spent two years studying the formation of scar tissue and was an expert on the topic, so he was utterly convincing in court when describing his careful analysis of this skin — and the jury was rapt. Crippen was found guilty of the murder and dismemberment of his wife and hanged a month later, and Bernard Spilsbury became a household name.

But here's the twist!

The microscope slides containing this scar tissue still reside in the Royal London Hospital Museum, part of Barts and the London NHS Trust, and they were DNA-tested in 2008 after investigators traced members of Cora Crippen's biological family.

Not only were the remains in Dr Crippen's cellar not Cora's, according to analysts they *weren't even female*. The hair found with the remains, which some theorists think was planted by the police, is held in Scotland Yard's Crime Museum, but they won't allow it to be submitted for testing. I've seen it myself and asked them why, but I wasn't graced with an answer . . .

Who on earth was buried in that cellar? And what happened to Cora if it wasn't her? That's a mystery for another time, though. Agatha also references the case in 'The Lernean Hydra', when a character muses, ' . . . and then Crippen, of course. I've always wondered if Ethel le Neve was in it with him or not.' We'll never really know. Ethel was charged not with murder, but with being an accessory after the fact, and acquitted — unlike the unfortunate Edith Thompson a decade later. She sailed back to the United States after giving several lucrative interviews that didn't reveal any new details to the public, and appears to be the inspiration for one of the four 'Where Are These Women Now?' characters in *Mrs McGinty's Dead*, called Eva Kane.

It is with an enormous dollop of irony that we consider the Crippen case as the one which catapulted Bernard Spilsbury into the public eye and made him into someone who was described by *The Lancet* in his 1947 obituary as a man who had 'stood alone and unchallenged as our greatest medico-legal expert'. At the time, however, his work and his cases were known the world over and Agatha Christie mentions many of them directly and indirectly in her books. This would simply have been because he was the most famous pathologist in the country, known for his ability to communicate to the laymen of the jury and given the nickname 'The People's Pathologist' by the press. He therefore worked on all the high-profile cases we've come to associate with the golden age of crime.

A photograph of Sir Bernard Spilsbury

One particularly well-known one is the 'Brides in the Bath Murders', which took place between 1912 and 1914. George Joseph Smith, described by Poirot in *The Murder on the Links* as '[t]he English murderer who disposed of his wives in succession by drowning them in their baths', was always a problem child. Born in London in 1872, he was already in reform school by the age of nine and spent most of his life a con man and swindler under different aliases. His modus operandi was originally to marry women for their money, which resulted, therefore, in several bigamous nuptials, as he stole from them and left, seemingly without trace, only to do the same to another woman somewhere else. However, it was with his wife Bessie Mundy that his MO changed. After becoming her husband 'Henry Williams', and ensuring he was the beneficiary of her will, he was able to convince a doctor she suffered from epilepsy. In an elaborate plot, only seven weeks after their marriage Bessie died in the bath, and without any physical signs of violence on her the examining doctor put her cause of death down to drowning during an epileptic seizure while bathing — purely an unfortunate accident. However, it wasn't so unfortunate for 'Henry Williams', who received nearly £2,580 in Bessie's will, a whopping amount at the time: it's the equivalent of over a *hundred times* that in today's money.

Smith went on to marry Alice Burnham, this time under his own name — George Smith — and she too met an untimely end similar to Bessie's, leaving Smith with her life savings and a £500 life insurance policy (equivalent to nearly £60,000 nowadays). By now, his successes were becoming an addiction, but his next victim, Margaret Elizabeth Lloyd, would be his last. It was his perfect yet unchanging murder method which was to be his undoing, as Poirot observes in *The Murder on the Links*.

In January 1915 Joseph Crossley, the owner of a boarding house in the northern town of Blackpool, sent a package to a detective in London called Arthur Neil. Included in the package was a letter outlining his suspicions about an incident which had happened at his establishment in 1913: the death of Alice Smith (née Burnham), discovered by her husband George.

Crossley included two newspaper clippings in his

package to the detective: one about Alice, and one about the incredibly similar death of a Margaret Elizabeth Lloyd who'd been found in the bathtub by her husband 'John Lloyd' a year later, in 1914. Without any signs of violence on her body, her death had been declared an accidental drowning. However, the similar circumstances were just too coincidental and police began to investigate. They finally tracked down Smith/Lloyd/Williams — who admitted bigamy — but the battle was still only half won. How could they prove that these women were murdered, and moreover that George Joseph Smith did it? It's 1915 and there's a pathological conundrum, so who are you gonna call: Bernard Spilsbury! Once he was on the case, he requested that the various baths from the different establishments be delivered to him so he could examine them. He also examined the victims' exhumed bodies. After toying with several different modes of murder he concluded that if Smith simply held the women under water until they were dead, using varying methods of brute force, there would be signs of struggle in the victims — which there hadn't been. Clearly a more sophisticated approach was being used: one which was causing instant death. Spilsbury eventually settled on a method which involved inhibition of the vagus nerve in the neck: a medical effect which is very surprising for someone like George Joseph Smith to have known about — he probably stumbled on the MO quite by accident.

During Smith's trial, Spilsbury was determined to illustrate what this complicated-sounding, lethal procedure was, so he had one of the bathtubs brought before the entire court, and installed inside the full tub was a female PC who was a very strong swimmer.

As she lay in the bath as the 'victim', Spilsbury acted out the role of Smith and simply positioned himself at the foot end of the bathtub, grabbed the 'victim's' ankles and pulled. Her head immediately slid underwater and it was the devastating force of the fluid flooding her mouth and nostrils simultaneously which put pressure on the vagus nerve — known as vagal inhibition — and she immediately blacked out. (The real victims would have done the same, and died practically instantaneously, explaining the minimal signs of drowning and asphyxia.) In fact this experiment was so successful it took nearly an hour for the unfortunate volunteer PC to be revived and the trial was front page news; as was the cruel murder method of George Joseph Smith.

Nowadays, such a courtroom demonstration would be highly unlikely due to the risk of danger to the stand-in. We now tend to treat people, whether alive or dead, with far more care when it comes to forensics.

* * *

In 'Dead Man's Mirror', the chief constable, Major Riddle, asks the unnamed police surgeon if the body can be moved, and the surgeon replies, 'Oh, yes — I've done with it until the P.M.' (that is, until he has a chance to do the post-mortem). This is absolutely perfect standard protocol. Before an autopsy can even occur, there will be some examination of the body at the scene, usually by a doctor known as the police surgeon (in some Christie books the divisional surgeon, a term which was also used at the time). Sometimes this dedicated police surgeon — or as we'd more likely say nowadays, the forensic pathologist — makes his living via suspicious cases like this, examining the corpse both at the scene and then in the mortuary, and then giving evidence at the inquest and/or court. In *Taken at the Flood* we're told: 'Then came the police surgeon — giving a full and technical description.' But other times the examining doctor is a local GP or similar; someone who can declare the person dead and perhaps make some cursory observations and notes before the body is further examined and then moved, after which another doctor — equivalent to a forensic pathologist — carries out the autopsy. Examination at the scene is important for several reasons: the decomposition of the body is a process which occurs over time, and there may be post-mortem artefacts visible at the time of the body's discovery which may not be evident later at the mortuary. It could be that the position of the cadaver is important and needs to be noted by a professional before it is altered in any way, or it might be that the identification of a corpse would be expedited if certain observations are made and tests carried out before it's moved, meaning some investigators can get on with their work while the body is in transit. For example, in various Christie books we're told that photographs have been taken of the body in situ, or that the 'fingerprint men' have already taken the prints of the corpse to speed up the process of identification. Agatha makes many references to protocol in this way, always correct and clearly well researched.

* * *

Agatha knew that the first thing that can often guide police straight to the perpetrator of a murder is the body itself. Criminals will often go to great lengths to hide, destroy or damage the victim and therefore destroy their identity. In *After the Funeral*, the weapon used to brutally batter someone's skull in is, we're told, 'a hatchet or something of that kind', in what is described as 'a very violent sort of crime'. It's also described as a 'brutal and rather senseless murder', but one thing we can be certain of in a Christie mystery is that it wasn't senseless. Neither was the murder in *One, Two, Buckle My Shoe*, in which the victim 'had been battered out of all recognisable shape'. As early as *The Murder on the Links* and *The Mystery of the Blue Train*, Poirot gets to the crux of this type of savagery, theorising that it is to disfigure the victim and make them difficult to recognise; and in *One, Two, Buckle My Shoe* in particular, Inspector Japp echoes this very important point:

> ' . . . After all, you don't go smashing a dead person's face and head about for nothing. It's messy, unpleasant work, and it was pretty plain there must be *some* reason for it. And there's only one reason there could be — to confuse the identity.'

Even though Agatha tries to confuse the sleuths — and the readers — with these attempts at hiding identity, the clues are there if we look for them. In *The Body in the Library* it's difficult to tell what the strangling victim lying on Colonel Bantry's hearth rug looks like because of her 'blue, swollen face', and yet she is identified by her *teeth*. In this story it's a small observation by Miss Marple which helps to solve the mystery. She explains that a witness 'said her teeth ran down her throat. But the dead girl in Colonel Bantry's library had teeth that stuck *out.*' This process is actually echoed in real life. Even now, in the world of forensic investigation, the examination of teeth — forensic odontology — is the first method used to identify unknown victims, for several different reasons: it's accurate, it's relatively inexpensive (compared to DNA comparison) and it's non-invasive. I spent many an afternoon in the mortuary with the odontologist rolling one person after another out of the body fridge for a quick, ten-minute inspection and can attest to its speed. In *The Body in the Library*, then, Agatha is referring to an incredibly important primary identifier still used today, but in a more primitive form: it's Miss Marple's visual comparison and quick brain which utilises the teeth as clues, rather than complicated dental charts and X-rays. The use of dental charts in *One, Two, Buckle My Shoe* from a couple of years earlier is of paramount importance to the plot, and indeed this is connected to the reportedly rather decomposed and unidentifiable body. I can't go into too much detail here as it may ruin the story, but suffice to say this is one occasion in which Agatha subverts the use of forensic evidence which she is familiar enough with to manipulate.

The relationship between teeth and crime is something that was used in Christie's day, and not just for the identification of unknown victims. Bite marks are prevalent in cases of particular types of offence, such as sexually motivated murder, sexual assaults, and child or elder abuse. Although the comparison of bite marks to a perpetrator's teeth goes back as far as the Salem witch trials of 1692, the first published case of a conviction being secured in this way was in 1948, when George Gorringe was found guilty of murdering his wife, Phyllis, because of a bite mark on her breast. The pathologist in this case was another eminent British gentleman called Keith Simpson who, after the death of Bernard Spilsbury, effectively took his place, and who wrote the book *Simpson's Forensic Medicine* I frequently refer to. It was he who carried out the autopsies on what little was left of the victims of the Acid Bath Murderer, John George Haigh.

* * *

When it came to the victims of murder, Agatha had a wealth of resources to consult in order to amass the amount of amazing detail she relates in her work. The first half of the twentieth century was when the nascent forensic sciences boomed into popular culture along with famous practitioners like Bernard Spilsbury and Francis Camps in the UK, and E. O. Heinrich in the US. Brutal crimes like the Brides in the Bath Murders, the Crumbles Murder, the Acid Bath Murders and more were front page news when they occurred, and the pathologists who investigated them became the faces of the cases; the real-life equivalents to Sherlock Holmes. Details of circumstance, injury and even floor plans of crime scenes were printed in newspapers and periodicals, and trials like those of Edith Thompson and Fred Bywaters and of Dr Crippen were the subject of radio programmes such as *The Black Museum*, a set of fictionalised Scotland Yard case files narrated by Orson Welles in 1951. There was even a corresponding TV show about the Yard in 1960. So as well as discussing the topic with fellow Detection Club members and being in correspondence with professionals in order to get her fiction as factual as possible, Agatha would have listened to these shows and read about the cases in the papers voraciously. When I visited The Black Museum at Scotland Yard, I did look through the visitor log book to see if she'd ever been to see the exhibits there. It surprised me that she hadn't, given the amount of their cases she discusses in her books! But even without visiting that famous repository of objects associated with the country's most heinous crimes, in typical Agatha fashion, when it came to forensic investigation, she had her finger on the pulse — even with the dead.

8

Forensic Toxicology

'But I'm not a nurse, thank heaven, I work in the dispensary.'

'How many people do you poison?' I asked, smiling.

Cynthia smiled too.

'Oh hundreds!' she said.

— *The Mysterious Affair at Styles*

In the grounds of Torre Abbey Museum in Torquay, the birthplace of Agatha Christie, there is a homage to the Dame herself in the form of a garden. Agatha adored gardens in general, and particularly loved camellia flowers, but there are no camellias in the Torre Abbey garden. Instead, this plot of land is planted with borders more likely to blot out lives than bloom. It's called the Potent Plants Garden, and its flower beds are more akin to 'death beds', filled with poisonous plants which can stupefy, convulse and kill. The garden is home to toxic shrubs such as monkshood, which contains aconite; deadly nightshade, which is dripping with atropine; and foxgloves, from which digitalis is made. But why this particular tribute to the woman who was often called the Duchess of Death?

It could be because the murder method she chose for her inaugural work, *The Mysterious Affair at Styles*, was poisoning. After it was published Christie received several positive reviews, but the one which she says pleased her the most was from the *Pharmaceutical Journal*, praising 'this detective story for dealing with poisons in a knowledgeable way, and not with the non-sense about untraceable substances that so often happens. Miss Agatha Christie knows her job.'

Often fledgling writers will begin their careers by writing what they know, and Christie was no exception. Her encyclopaedic knowledge of poisons was garnered through the hours she spent working in a dispensary during the First World War (and again in the Second). The idea for her to write this first novel came from her older sister Madge (nicknamed 'Punkie' by the family). The sisters both enjoyed writing as a pastime and Madge thought it would be very difficult to write a detective story in which it was practically impossible to guess the culprit. Agatha thought she could do it, so her sister both encouraged and dared her to try, even lending Agatha her typewriter for the purpose. Agatha therefore dreamed up various aspects of her plot during down time in the pharmacy, and in her auto-biography she says, 'since I was surrounded by poisons, perhaps it was natural that death by poisoning should be the method I selected'.

* * *

Christie's war service began when she started practising as a volunteer nurse with the Voluntary Aid Detachment during the First World War, but when a dispensary opened up at the Torquay hospital in which she was based, she underwent further training and passed an exam in order to work there instead.

Prescriptions were made up by hand at the dispensary and Agatha found herself surrounded by a plethora of dangerous and fascinating substances such as morphine, strychnine and cyanide — most of which were removed from the British Pharmacopoeia by the mid-twentieth century. In *Five Little Pigs*, Meredith Blake — one of the five main characters who make up the metaphorical 'pigs' — has more than a passing interest in the power of botanicals. He references the British Pharmacopoeia in relation to a particularly dangerous substance: coniine, which is derived from hemlock. He says:

> 'Coniine, you know, is a drug that's dropped out — I don't believe there's any official preparation of it in the last Pharmacopoeia — but I've proved the usefulness of it in whooping cough, and in asthma for that matter too.'

Christie was evidently very familiar with the Pharmacopoeia from the beginning of her careers as both writer and dispenser, and injected this knowledge into some of her stories.

Unlike our modern era of pharmacies which distribute clinical-looking boxes of rigorously trialled prescription drugs, the inter-war years were still reliant on unpredictable remedies, with concoctions mixed together by each individual dispenser rather than arriving pre-packaged: strychnine was taken in small doses as a liquid tonic to 'pep' users up, and morphine powder was handed out (willy-nilly it seems) to tackle any aches and pains. Up until that point in her life, Agatha's writing career consisted only of some short stories and poems, along with one unpublished novel. Inevitably, working among all these unusual substances, she was inspired to write about them, and began with a poem entitled 'In a Dispensary'. It contains the evocative lines:

Here is sleep and solace and soothing, of pain Courage and vigour new!
Here is menace and murder and sudden death In these vials of green and blue . . .

It's clear she recognised the paradoxical nature of these myriad preparations, which could heal or hurt the individual depending on the amount administered. Anything can be a poison, depending on the dosage — even water — and it was Renaissance physician Paracelsus who said 'the dose makes the poison', something Agatha would certainly have been taught during her training.

When she started writing her first detective novel, poison was the natural route for her murderer to take. In fact, out of her sixty-six murder mystery and thriller books, forty-one contain poisonings, and she has dispatched a multitude of characters with familiar substances like cyanide, arsenic and morphine, as well as some less common compounds such as eserine, taxine and oxalic acid.

But there's another reason why poison was such a convenient murder weapon. In the earlier part of Agatha's career, it was a 'go-to' not just for writers of fiction but for murderers themselves. Before the mid-twentieth century, substances which gradually became restricted were available to everyone — as Miss Marple says in the short story 'Greenshaw's Folly', 'Arsenic is of course quite a possibility; so easy to obtain. Probably present in the tool shed already in the form of weed killer.' Eventually, safer and (in some cases) less addictive options were discovered. For the most part poisons were meant to be used as pesticides: cyanide was used to kill wasps, for instance, and flypapers were arsenic-soaked. In *Three Act Tragedy* nicotine is described as a pure, odourless alkaloid, a few drops of which are 'enough to kill a man almost instantaneously . . . And yet it's in common use, as you might say: solutions are used to spray roses with,' indicating its effectiveness on pests like aphids. Although strychnine was a controlled substance from the early twentieth century it was still available to customers who had what was considered to be a valid reason for using it, again for pest control, but in this case bigger pests than aphids: perhaps rats or foxes. I think this is one of the reasons Agatha chose it for her first offering *The Mysterious Affair at Styles*. In the book, we are told it's essential that any procurer of strychnine signs a register at the pharmacy in order to receive it. They had to write their name and address, and the reason the strychnine was needed: in this case 'to kill a wild dog'. This was intended to create a record of the transaction, so that if any homicidal high jinks occurred with the same substance at a later date there was a place for the police to start their search. However, in the plot, Christie's choice of strychnine and this record of its purchase is important for an additional reason and we end up back in 'handwriting analysis territory' — you'll have to read the book to find out why!

Our modern scientific capabilities have changed the face of the poisoning landscape. To go back to the Potent Plants Garden at Torre Abbey, there is a fantastic disclaimer on one of the information posts:

> Where possible we have substituted safer varieties of toxic plants, or acceptable alternatives, to ensure the safety of staff and visitors alike. A number of plants have also been omitted entirely. These include:
>
> Hemlock — which is really very toxic.
>
> Cannabis and the Coca plant — as we have no desire to go to prison.
>
> For those of you who may be tempted, modern forensic science can detect all the above types of poison. In any case, considerable specialised knowledge is required for the successful extraction of viable poison.

Then in red, bold letters: ***Don't even think about it!***

I love this because it's absolutely true. Although these poisons sound pleasantly vintage and one may be forgiven for thinking, 'Surely they don't test for hemlock any more — for goodness' sake, it's so old it killed Socrates!' the fact remains that many of our modern therapeutic and toxic compounds have their basis in these more primitive shrubs. Morphine, for example, is famously present in opium poppies and can be chemically altered to form heroin. Atropine, from the plant belladonna or deadly nightshade, still has some pharmacological applications in ocular medicine: it's used to dilate the pupils of the eyes for optical examination. Digitalis, from foxgloves, is present in cardiac medication.

One of Agatha's most veneniferous books is *Appointment with Death*, not just because of the amount of toxic substances mentioned in it, but because of the poisonous nature of the book's sadistic antagonist, Mrs Boynton. When she is inevitably murdered, it's poison that comes to the fore, and Agatha really illustrates her knowledge when discussing the likelihood that digitoxin was used: 'Digitoxin,' said Poirot, 'is a heart poison, is it not?' Dr Gerard replies:

> 'Yes. It is obtained from digitalis purpurea — the common foxglove. There are four active principles — *digitalin — digitonin — digitalein — and digitoxin*. Of these digitoxin is considered the most active poisonous constituent . . . '

The book was written in 1938, between the wars, and it's clear that we're dealing with a master of poisons in Agatha Christie! According to Kathryn Harkup in *A Is For Arsenic*, Christie's science is 'top notch'. She elaborates, 'Of the compounds listed by Christie . . . digitoxin and digitalin are still prescribed today. Digitalin is now known as digoxin.' Harkup also warns that although digitalis is a very effective way of committing murder, it's also detectable in minute quantities. In the UK, many coronial autopsies will include what we call a toxicology or 'tox' screen to look for poisons, such as digitalis, in the deceased, particularly if there are no obvious indicators as to how the person died . . . something to keep in mind if you're looking for any ideas here!

What is Forensic Toxicology?

Toxicology is a combination of chemistry and physiology, and is defined as the study of the adverse effects of chemicals or physical agents on living organisms. The term 'toxic substances' is so broad we could include water, caffeine and even oxygen if they were found in significant quantities. It's therefore an incredibly extensive subject, and one which mortuary workers like myself need to be well versed in. In modern mortuary science we group poisons under the umbrella term of CBRN, which stands for Chemical, Biological, Radiological and Nuclear, when undergoing special training for what we call High-Risk autopsies (as they have a risk to us if we're not wearing full protective suits, sometimes with respirators). But we might also categorise poisons as man-made and biological. For our purposes we'll stick to the poisons we'd be likely to see in an Agatha Christie book and how they'd be investigated, and she's not known for her overuse of nuclear energy! Here we'll separate them out into Corrosive and Systemic substances, although there's every chance Agatha would have used different groupings when she was studying to be a dispenser back in the First World War.

Corrosive Poisons

These include acids and alkalis, and other substances which cause corrosion or necrosis (cell death) of the body's tissues when in direct contact (which is why the 'Acid Bath Murderer' Haigh used corrosive substances to dispose of his victims). Lysol, a disinfectant which was invented in the late nineteenth century, is corrosive, as are sulphuric and hydrochloric acids. Corrosive poisons cause severe, visible damage to the soft tissues and excruciating pain to the victim. They're not as commonly encountered in medicolegal cases as they once were, and you'd sadly usually see symptoms of this type of poisoning when investigating a suicide or, more disturbingly, malicious attacks and torture. In addition to the damage corrosives cause to the internal organs after ingestion, there will usually be injury to the tissues around the mouth, nose and chin. Deaths by corrosive poison are incredibly violent and painful, and although Agatha didn't use them often in her books, she *did* include them — for instance the hat paint containing oxalic acid ingested by Amy in the prolifically homicidal *Murder Is Easy*. The most notable example is the accurately described death of Mrs Johnson, in *Murder in Mesopotamia*, who drank hydrochloric acid in the middle of the night, by mistake, from a glass on her bedside table (she thought it was water, but it had rather cruelly been switched by the murderer). We're told by the story's narrator, Nurse Leatheran, who found her dying:

> ' . . . her whole body contorted in agony . . . her lips moved and she tried to speak — but only an awful hoarse whisper came. I saw that the corners of her mouth and the skin of her chin were burnt a kind of greyish white.'

These are all absolutely spot-on symptoms of corrosive substance ingestion. The severe, visible damage I mentioned above is necrosis or 'death' of the tissues, caused by extreme irritation to our delicate living flesh. Inside the body — the mouth and oesophagus — this would be akin to being sandpapered from the inside or swallowing razorblades. It would be extremely painful, which explains why Mrs Johnson 'contorted in agony'. In addition, the corrosive fluid would severely injure the larynx, explaining her 'hoarse whisper'. In these cases, the corrosive fluid is inevitably purged from the mouth as the body tries to push it back out again, causing further injury to the external tissues of the face and neck. This presents as greyish white — just as Christie described — as the skin's cells are obliterated and cauterised.

Systemic Poisons

The effects of these substances are not localised in one spot but spread to all body organs and systems in varying degrees, the major damage being manifested in one or two organs (they're not site-specific, like corrosive poisons). They're also responsible for most of the poison deaths in Agatha Christie's books, as they include substances like arsenic and thallium, which are metallic poisons; and cyanide, ricin and digitalis.

In 'The Lernean Hydra', Poirot is investigating the murder of Dr Charles Oldfield's wife, who the village suspect was poisoned by her husband. During a discussion about exhuming her body, intelligent young dispenser Jean Moncrieffe — whom Agatha undoubtedly modelled on herself — says to Poirot:

> 'I know what I'm talking about. You're thinking of arsenic poisoning — you could prove that she was not poisoned by arsenic. But there are other poisons — the vegetable alkaloids. After a year I doubt you'd find any traces of them even if they had been used.'

Jean Moncrieffe is referring to a type of systemic poison Christie utilises in her works frequently, and which gives them a real sense of authenticity: the alkaloid. Alkaloids are naturally occurring compounds which contain nitrogen, produced by a huge variety of organisms such as plants, fungi and bacteria. Many poisons — and indeed many medicines — are alkaloids, which have a pronounced effect on human physiology and work on the nervous system, leaving very few discernible traces in the body. They may cause a variety of different symptoms, but one thing that seems to be true across the board is that alkaloids have an exceedingly bitter taste — which can be an issue when trying to administer them secretly. In addition, many of their names end with the suffix '-ine', including atropine, strychnine, caffeine, morphine and cocaine to name just a few. This is notable as it's a way for the reader to understand that the presence of an alkaloid is being indicated if a substance ends with this suffix, or a bitter taste is referred to, and can often be a clue when trying to solve a murder in a detective story.

In *A Pocket Full of Rye* — one of Christie's more successfully navigated 'nursery rhyme' titles — we have the whole saga of 'four and twenty blackbirds baked in a pie' as well as a 'King in his counting house' (Rex Fortescue), and the 'Queen in the parlour' (his wife Adele). When Rex dies suddenly, we learn what alkaloid he was poisoned with and the examining doctor, Professor Bernsdorff, seems absolutely — and perhaps rather morbidly! — thrilled about it. When investigating officer Inspector Neele asks him, 'Is that what it is? Yew berries?' Professor Bernsdorff replies:

> 'Berries or leaves. Taxine, of course, is the alkaloid. Don't think I've heard of a case where it was used deliberately. Really most interesting and

unusual. You've no idea how tired one gets of the inevitable weed-killer. Taxine is a real treat.'

It's significant in the case because someone was accused of putting it in Rex's tea at the office, but we now know that alkaloids are exceedingly bitter: Rex would have tasted it and immediately left his tea alone. So what bitter food could this taxine have been introduced to in order to kill Mr Fortescue? The reader has to use their own little grey cells to work that out!

In addition to this very realistic conundrum, at the time of Christie's writing she was correct when she put those final sentences in the doctor's mouth: taxine *hadn't* been used in any murder cases. And this wouldn't be the only time she would innovatively write about a little-known poison and use it for murder . . .

'Tox' at Autopsy

Nowadays, once an autopsy is broadly deemed completed — and often before it even begins — there will be an opportunity to take specimens from the body for toxicological analysis. All suspicious deaths will have a 'tox' screen associated with them, as will a high proportion of routine cases. Poison doesn't always leave its mark on the victim, so screening will be done as a backup to the pathologist's findings. In order to check for a variety of substances, a similar array of specimens needs to be taken from the body, and this is frequently the role of the assisting technician or APT. Common specimens include:

Blood — At autopsy this is usually taken from

the femoral or iliac veins in the legs, but from *inside* the lower part of the body once the organs have all been removed. This is because there is usually a larger quantity available there than elsewhere in the body and at the same time it's least likely to be contaminated.

Urine — Often the bladder is still full during autopsy; it's not necessarily true that when a person dies they void its contents, nor those of the bowel. It's prudent to collect urine as soon as it is exposed by the Y-incision: by removing a quantity with a large needle and syringe before there is too much free-flowing blood or fluid from the lungs and abdomen, cross-contamination (and general messiness) is avoided. Drugs and their metabolites are often detectable in urine far longer than in blood, so it's important to keep it unadulte-ated.

Vitreous Humor — This jelly-like substance in the eye is aspirated (sucked out) using a large syringe and needle. (By introducing the needle to the side of the eyeball at a horizontal angle and pushing through any resistance the needle can be seen through the pupil,behind the iris, when in optimum position.) It is always collected if there is no urine in the body, as it is a reliable substitute. Removing this vitreous humor will deflate the eyeball slightly, so water or saline is injected back into the eye for cosmetic restoration, even though the eyelids will then be closed over.

Bile — The gall bladder, which produces bile,

is situated at the back of the liver, so this is a specimen the pathologist will routinely take themselves. Bile is usually used specifically to detect morphine and opiates.

Stomach Contents — These are taken only in the absence of other samples as they are rarely of use, although undigested capsules or tablets can be found provided the person died soon after ingestion.

Lung (tissue) — This is usually removed by the pathologist if solvent abuse is suspected, because we breathe solvents and gases into our lungs. To ensure the solvent vapours don't escape, the tissue is placed into impervious nylon bags similar to those used by fire investigators who collect clothing from a scene: it's important to keep gases in the bag for analysis, and for safety.

Liver (tissue) — This is usually removed by the pathologist and can be useful because there will be higher concentrations of many poisons directly in the liver tissue, as this is where substances are metabolised. For example, when we drink alcohol, which is chemically termed ethanol, the liver metabolises or breaks it down into a different chemical structure, acetaldehyde. This then becomes acetic acid (which is actually vinegar) and then eventually water and carbon dioxide. All substances have different metabolites and their presence in liver tissue can indicate the original poison or drug.

Hair and nails — These two samples are particularly useful in determining if a person has a chronic opiate problem or has been exposed to particular metallic poisons such as arsenic or thallium for a long time. This is because these substances will often be deposited in parts of the body where they can do relatively less harm. The keratin in hair and nails is therefore ideal.

Hair has an approximate growth rate of 1 cm per month. It's best to use pulled hair as a sample. If it's cut from the head, the proximal end — i.e. the part closest to the scalp — needs to be clearly labelled and then the hair can be analysed with the assumption that the most recent dosage of a substance will be nearer the roots. It may also be possible to determine *when* the poison was administered, because of the growth rate. If there is nothing to be found in the hair, but there is a positive tox result from the other organs, this would indicate one large, acute poisoning rather than one occurring over a chronic period.

Nails will first be examined macroscopically, i.e. with the eye, because there may be indicators of the presence of drugs, such as Mees Lines (white, horizontal marks) in chronic use or exposure. Nail clippings will then be taken to be analysed in the same way as the hair.

There is an indication of Christie's knowledge on this topic in *They Do It with Mirrors* when Carrie-Louise tells Miss Marple her stepson, Alex, was so enthusiastic about his new pair of scissors he made her try them on the spot. Miss Marple is immediately suspicious: 'And I suppose he gathered up the nail clippings and took them tidily away?' she asks, later clarifying that she had realised Alex was looking to see if arsenic had been administered to his stepmother over a period of time.

For the forensic examiner, a combination of all of the above sample specimens is the ideal because samples vary in the length of time they retain useful information on drugs, and different drugs are found in different parts of the body. These samples will then be sent to a toxicology lab and the pathologist will await a call when the results are available, usually at least a week later (unless it's a very high-profile case). Unlike the impression we're given from TV shows like *CSI*, the results of tests like this aren't immediately available. This was the case even in Agatha Christie's time. In *One, Two, Buckle My Shoe*, Inspector Japp bemoans the lack of results from a case of poisoning by adrenaline and novocaine: 'They haven't got the exact amount yet — these quantitative analyses seem to take a month of Sundays.' Clearly our pathology teams have never managed to keep up with our murderous appetites.

History of Forensic Toxicology

In all likelihood, people have been poisoning each other as long as we have inhabited the earth, and written tales of victims being dispatched in this way go right back to antiquity.

It was Jacobean playwright John Fletcher who famously called poison 'the coward's weapon', referring to the fact it was such an underhand way of murdering someone, and could be carried out without risk of immediate retaliation. Of course, this doesn't only mean the poisoner is cowardly, not all poisoners are simply cowardly, it could just be that they lack the brute strength necessary to murder someone in a physical manner. For this reason poison is often considered a 'woman's weapon' too. As Christie herself writes in *Three Act Tragedy*: 'Poison is as much a woman's weapon as a man's — more so.' In seventeenth-century Italy, it's said that one woman made a living for nearly fifty years selling a deadly liquid to would-be widows so they could kill their husbands without arousing suspicion. Her name was Giulia Tofana and her mythical potion was named *Acqua Tofana*; it was supposedly marketed as a ladies' cosmetic tonic. In reality this colourless and scentless liquid contained a mixture of toxic and, importantly, undetectable ingredients — though since no one is absolutely sure it truly existed, I can't tell you for certain what was in it. However, arsenic purportedly made up a good bulk of the potion and it was well known enough for Mozart to lament, on his deathbed, that someone had poisoned him with it. According to one account of the popularity of *Acqua Tofana*, 'There was not a lady in Naples who had not some of it lying openly on her toilette among her perfumes. She alone knows the phial, and can distinguish it.'

Over the decades, Tofana and her female helpers are said to have killed more than six hundred men in this manner, but there are so many different stories about her demise that it's impossible to say whether or not she really existed. She wasn't the only one, however. Just a decade after Tofana's death, the French sorceress known as La Voisin had all of Louis XIV's court at Versailles in her thrall with her ability to tell fortunes, provide aphrodisiacs and — of course — help her clients dispose of their enemies with the poisonous concoctions she sold. But even if these stories are slightly embellished, it tells us about the mindset of those perpetuating the tales and the danger people felt from the threat of poisoning. It was such a common murder method that poisons such as arsenic were often referred to as 'poudre de succession' by the French, or 'inheritance powder' by the English, and anyone with any status at all employed food tasters to check if their meals contained poison before they themselves ate it. Of course, they could really only presumably check for fast-acting poisons! If the taster dropped dead within seconds then the person employing them would likely avoid that meal. But the taster could also note the presence of unexpected bitterness and send the dish away, thereby protecting their employer from possible lethal alkaloids.

* * *

The first forensic book written on the topic of toxicology was called *On Poisons*, attributed to the Indian scholar Chanakya who lived as early as 350–283 BC. However, it wasn't really until the eighteenth century that tests to detect a toxic substance were created and subsequently improved upon, becoming the framework for the series of screenings for poisons at autopsy today. This era — the late eighteenth and early nineteenth centuries — was known as the Golden Age of Poisoning, and is where most of Agatha's knowledge would have come from when studying for her dispenser role at the Worshipful Society of Apothecaries. She passed the Assistant's exam in 1917.

Toxicology tests are so common now — whether at

autopsy, or a drug test at work, or even a breathalyser in a car — that it's difficult to believe there were once no reliable scientific techniques for detecting poisons. But, in 1775, a German-Swedish chemist changed all that with a test for the poison we're perhaps most familiar with: arsenic.

Carl Wilhelm Scheele was already well known for his discoveries of elements and his research into acids. During his routine work he found that it was possible to make an acid by heating white arsenic powder (*arsenic trioxide*, which was the white powder used to poison people) with nitric acid and zinc. The acid formed a gas which we call *arsine* and, now that it had been discovered, this process of isolating it meant that the same method could also be used to detect arsenic trioxide in the bodies of possible poison victims. The stomach contents just needed to be heated with nitric acid and zinc, and if the garlic-smelling arsine gas was formed, it meant the stomach had contained arsenic trioxide. This was the first time a test could be used to detect a poison, *any* poison. But the fact it was arsenic was particularly relevant given its notoriety at the time. (It also seems particularly relevant in *this* book because arsenic is the poison most associated with Agatha Christie, but this is rather misleading and I think has more to do with our familiarity with it as a poison in many other books and films, rather than in Christie's works specifically. Throughout her entire canon, Christie dispatched only thirteen characters with arsenic — although it is very frequently mentioned in rather flippant and humorous comments. When referring to the evil Mrs Boynton in *Appointment with Death*, the young doctor Sarah King complains, 'That old woman ought to be murdered! Arsenic in her early morning tea would be my prescription.')

Many of us feel we are more than just nine-to-fivers when it comes to our jobs, but Scheele quite literally died for his work: as one of the great scientists operating in a time long before enforced wearing of personal protective equipment (PPE), the cumulative exposure to toxic substances like arsenic, mercury and lead took their toll and he died aged just forty-three. But his initial discovery is what motivated British chemist James Marsh to create his famous 'Marsh Test' in 1836, and subsequently led to the specialised field of forensic toxicology. Agatha was well acquainted with the Marsh Test and even mentions in her autobiography that, during her Apothecary's Examination studies, she blew up a Cona coffee machine while trying to practise the test with a friend. So what exactly was she trying to recreate and how did it come about?

James Marsh was a promising scientist based at the Royal Arsenal in Woolwich in 1832 when he was asked to examine the contents of the stomach and morning coffee of a recently deceased man. The man, George Bodle, was a farmer from Plumstead — at the time a village near London — who had been in perfectly good health before he abruptly keeled over and died. The suddenness of his death, the fact that nobody in his family seemed particularly sad about it, and the knowledge that there had been some hostility between George and his grandson John, caused the local justice of the peace to become suspicious. He wanted Marsh to analyse George's stomach contents and the remains of the coffee he'd been drinking at the time of his death to see if arsenic was present. Marsh agreed and used Scheele's method to establish there was indeed arsenic in both the coffee and

George Bodle's stomach contents. This scientific evidence, along with witness statements revealing that the grandson, John, had purchased arsenic trioxide from the local chemist, seemed ironclad. However, when the case came to trial, the specimens Marsh had created to demonstrate the presence of arsenic in both the stomach contents of the victim, and his morning coffee, had degraded. With nothing to go on except hearsay, the jury acquitted John Bodle, who emigrated to Australia — and who later admitted he had indeed murdered his grandfather George.

This initial failure infuriated Marsh and inspired him to create a test for arsenic which could be used in court. He was looking for some incontrovertible process which could be understood by laymen and examined again and again. He did this by modifying Scheele's method to include hydrochloric acid, and burning the resulting gas, which caused a silvery-black permanent stain to form on a surface such as porcelain: this was metallic arsenic, and material proof of the presence of the substance.

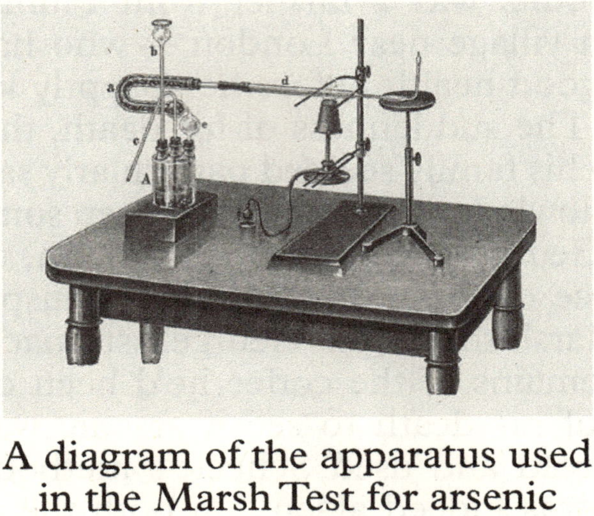

A diagram of the apparatus used
in the Marsh Test for arsenic

James Marsh died ten years after publishing his test, aged only fifty-two, leaving a destitute family behind. Although not appreciated in his own time, he is now described as 'one of the great unsung heroes of crime detection' for creating the first practical test for arsenic. He deserves a place in the Forensic Science Hall of Fame alongside others who didn't quite get the recognition they deserved for services.

Instead, it's the Spanish physician and chemist Mathieu Orfila who is credited with being the founder of toxicology. Like James Marsh, Orfila was called in to act as a medical expert in a case of suspected arsenic poisoning, this time in Paris, in 1840. The accused was Marie Lafarge, who had married Charles Pouch-Lafarge under the assumption he was very rich, when in fact he lived in a dilapidated estate and had assumed *she* was the one who was wealthy. The resulting marriage was understandably fraught given the deception on both sides, and things appeared to come to a head when he went in search of financial backers in Paris. Marie sent him a cake which made him seriously ill, and when he was finally able to return home, he became ill again and subsequently died. Arsenic poisoning was suspected, as Marie was known to have purchased arsenic as rat poison for their dilapidated mansion. (This story may well have inspired Agatha to have one of her characters in *After the Funeral* poisoned by a slice of arsenic-laced cake.)

Orfila used the Marsh Test during the trial and demonstrated to the jury that there was indeed arsenic in Charles Lafarge's body, enough for the jury to convict Marie and sentence her to life imprisonment. From there, the testing for arsenic became commonplace and the era of getting away with these kinds of poisonings was over. But this wasn't only good news for the potential victims, it was an improvement for investigators too. In *The Mysterious Affair at Styles*, we're told that Poirot samples the dregs from various coffee cups, but Christie elaborates, 'With infinite care, he took a drop or two from the grounds in each cup, sealing them up in separate test tubes, tasting each in turn as he did so.' Tasting each in turn? This seems like a rather risky move given that some poisons can act incredibly quickly! But it was common practice at the time. Often the police or investigating doctors would taste substances found near the victim or suspect, or, most revoltingly, would taste the stomach contents! We see it again in 'The Lernean Hydra' when we're told Detective Sergeant Grey finds a mystery substance:

> 'This stuff isn't face powder.' He dipped a finger and tasted it gingerly on the tip of his tongue. 'No particular taste.'
>
> Poirot said: 'White arsenic does not taste.'

This is absolutely true: arsenic doesn't really taste of anything — something Agatha references frequently — which is perhaps why it was so commonly used. Thankfully in such a small amount it wasn't harmful to Sergeant Grey in this instance. In fact, it's rather like modern Drug Enforcement Agents who, on finding a package of suspicious white powder, gingerly dip their little finger into it and dab it on their tongue to see if it's cocaine or heroin. (It's not ideal professional practice, but it is done!) Nonetheless, why *did* investigators risk tasting unidentified substances and even body fluids to try to detect a poison which could possibly turn out to be one which has no taste? It was simply because they had no other way to do it.

* * *

In the nineteenth century, new poisonous compounds were being discovered at a startling rate; notably strychnine and chloroform both appeared in the course of the 1820s and 1830s. It's exceedingly lucky, then, that the burgeoning field of toxicology was keeping up with this influx. By 1850 it had been discovered that curare (an obscure poison usually associated with the tips of arrows, and mentioned in *Death in the Clouds* among other Christie books) could counteract the effects of strychnine poisoning, and around 1900 it was noted that hydrocyanic acid, which contains cyanide, could be used as an antidote to chloroform.

But there isn't usually time to get hold of an antidote when you've been poisoned, unless you work in a well-stocked chemical laboratory. In fact the average murder victim isn't likely to know what they've been poisoned with, never mind what the antidote is — if it's happening over a length of time they might not even know they're being poisoned; they might just think they're ill from a mystery disease. But *Agatha* knows, because poisons are her metier, and there's one story in particular where she shows off that knowledge to the full. In 'The Thumb Mark of St Peter', Miss Marple is stumped — only temporarily, mind — when trying to clear the name of her niece, Mabel, who feels she's suspected of murder. The victim in the story is Mabel's husband, Geoffrey, who had been taken ill — it's suggested as a result of eating 'bad mushrooms'. (This must have been a common complaint at the time because we're told in *The 4:50 from Paddington*: 'People are always obsessed with the idea of mushroom poisoning.') According to this story, Geoffrey had died in the night yelling something obscure about a 'heap of fish'. It takes Miss Marple a while to realise that the 'heap of fish', 'heap of haddock' or 'pile of carp' that the nurses think they overheard Geoffrey shouting about was actually the word *pilocarpine*, the antidote to atropine (better known as belladonna or deadly nightshade). Evidently, while in the agonising throes of death, Geoffrey realised what he'd been poisoned with and remembered the name of the antidote. I'm not sure why he chose to yell out such an obscure word, rather than 'I've been poisoned, get help!'

Unfortunately, there was someone in real life who read this story, 'The Thumb Mark of St Peter', and considered it a source of inspiration . . . In Créances, situated in Normandy, France, 58-year-old Roland Roussel believed the death of his mother was murder, and decided to avenge her by killing the woman he thought to be responsible. Mysteriously, we don't know the victim's name; reports at the time state, 'Police would not disclose the name of the woman Roussel had chosen as his target or elaborate on what he told them about her.' He seems to have taken deadly inspiration after reading Christie's short story and opted to add atropine, which was available in eye drops, to a bottle of wine. He left this wine at his uncle Maxime Masseron's house because — and this part baffies me — his intended victim was known to visit from time to time and drink wine at their house.

(I'm no murderer, but I'd imagine 'step one' when poisoning someone specific is to ensure they definitely receive the poison.) Roland's logic came from his knowledge that his aunt and uncle didn't tend to drink wine unless in company, so the likelihood was they would open the bottle and serve it to his victim. Presumably this plot would also rely on the fact that aunt and uncle Masseron had absolutely no other friends?

As could be predicted, things went drastically wrong: Uncle Maxime and his wife saved the wine for themselves to drink at Christmas. They did so, and Maxime died instantly while his wife fell into a coma. She was rushed to hospital and medics assumed they'd both succumbed to food poisoning. It wasn't until a few days later that the police's suspicions were aroused. A local carpenter and Maxime's son-in-law went to the Masseron house to place Maxime in his coffin for the funeral, and saw the wine open on the table. They, too, drank a small amount to toast the deceased, and both became violently ill. The police's focus eventually fell on Roussel, and when his house was searched, officers found various articles on poisons and — crucially — a copy of Christie's 'The Thumb Mark of St Peter' with relevant paragraphs on atropine underlined.

* * *

When Christie first began training as a pharmacist she learned on the job and received tuition from several people, one a private pharmacist Agatha refers to only as 'Mr P'. He was a rather eccentric character, and a particularly disturbing interaction is referred to in Agatha's autobiography. She says that one day, perhaps seeking to impress her, he took a dark-coloured lump out of his pocket asking, 'Know what this is?' When she answered in the negative he proceeded to tell her it was curare, the substance used in South America to poison the tips of arrows or blowpipe darts. When ingested it's harmless, but if introduced directly into the bloodstream it causes paralysis and death. 'Do you know why I carry it in my pocket?' he asked a bewildered young Agatha, before explaining, 'Because it makes me feel powerful.'

He must have made a very distinct impression on her because curare comes up several times in her books, and in *They Do It with Mirrors* we're informed: 'Curare has to be introduced into the bloodstream . . . not the stomach.'

Many decades after working with 'Mr P', Agatha would resurrect him in the form of a character in *The Pale Horse*. Just as he was an influential character in her life, *The Pale Horse* was an influential book in the world of toxicology — in fact I'd say it's possibly one of the most important detective mysteries ever written.

It's incredibly difficult not to reveal some of the key twists of *The Pale Horse*'s chilling plot, based around the malevolent misdeeds of a trio of supposed witches, and yet the topic of this chapter already provides a clue. Given that Agatha was a founder and member of the Detection Club, and their second commandment for writing stories was 'all supernatural or preternatural agencies are ruled out as a matter of course', I think it's safe to say that we know in this case it wasn't actually the witches 'whodunnit'. We need to look to more earthly methods of killing people from afar — and that really only leaves poisoning.

When Agatha wrote *The Pale Horse* in 1961 she chose to use a substance called thallium as the toxic agent, partly due to a suggestion by a colleague, Harold Davis, the Chief Pharmacist at University College Hospital. It was little known before the publication of Christie's book, but afterwards the poison — and the book — would become notorious.

It's often believed that Christie was the first writer of detective fiction to employ thallium as the method of murder, but that isn't actually the case. New Zealand writer Ngaio Marsh had done so nearly fifteen years before Christie in 1947, in her book *Final Curtain*. It's also often assumed that there'd been no real-life murders with thallium, but that's not true either. The first recorded case of homicidal thallium poisoning was in 1930s Austria: Martha Marek killed her husband, two children, an aunt and a lodger with a thallium-containing pesticide called Zelio, and was hanged for the crimes in 1938. Then in Australia there was a bizarre spate of thallium poisonings — again all by women — in the 1950s. Between them the three women, in unrelated crimes, dispatched eight victims. The reason Christie's *The Pale Horse* stood out was because of her unique experience in the dispensary and her attention to detail. Her descriptions of thallium's specific symptoms were so accurate — particularly the fact it caused the hair to fall out — that her *fictional story* is practically a textbook on its effects.

The depilatory property of thallium featured prominently in the book and is perhaps the poison's best-known effect, and it's also one of the phenomena which the protagonist, Mark Easterbrook, notes early on without knowing what it means. Mark — whose narrative makes up most of the book — eventually realises the witches' victims are being poisoned and works out what is being used after he remembers something he once read. He refers to this lucky recollection, explaining it was an article he encountered when he was in America which was all about the effects of thallium poisoning at a factory:

> 'Their deaths were put down to astonishingly varied causes . . . The symptoms vary a good deal, I understand. They may start with diarrhoea and vomiting, or there may be a stage of intoxication. It may begin with pain in the limbs . . . sometimes there's pigmentation of the skin. But one thing always happens sooner or later. *The hair falls out.*'

Recognising the huge variety of symptoms as those being suffered by *The Pale Horse's* victims, as well as the crucial one all cases have in common, he puts two and two together and solves the case.

Remarkably, in a true representation of 'life imitates art', the same thing happened in real life — in reverse — when two cases of thallium poisoning were identified solely because readers of *The Pale Horse* recognised the symptoms. In 1975, Christie received a letter from a young woman in South America who thanked her for helping to save a life. This woman had been witnessing the deterioration of a friend for some time and it was only after reading the book she realised what she was seeing was the effects of thallium poisoning. After the authorities were alerted to this new information, the man was saved and it was discovered his young wife had indeed been poisoning him with thallium.

Just two years later, a nurse in a London hospital had a similar revelation about one of her patients, this time just a small child. The 19-month-old was from Qatar and had been taken suddenly ill, with a condition that seemed to mystify local medics. After she took a turn for the worse, the anxious parents flew to London with her in the hopes that UK doctors could do better — but the toddler's illness baffied them too. Then, when one of the toddler's nurses, Nurse Maitland, had finished reading her copy of *The Pale Horse* she could see the similarities between her patient and the victims in the book. The toddler's urine sample was sent to Scotland Yard to be analysed, and she was indeed suffering from thallium poisoning, thought to be due to accidental ingestion of pesticide at home. Thankfully, she made a full recovery.

But perhaps the person who gives thallium — and therefore *The Pale Horse* — the largest portion of its notoriety is the 'Teacup Poisoner' Graham Frederick Young: the first person in Britain convicted of committing murder with thallium.

Photograph of Graham Young

It could be said that, as a child, Young's intelligence, curiosity and dedication would have led to him being a very successful scientist. He was interested in chemistry and his father bought him a chemistry set as a reward for passing his 'eleven-plus' exams. But as with many similar cases Young's natural interest in the macabre and apparent lack of conscience meant that his hobby manifested itself in the desire to manipulate and eventually murder; in his case to poison people. He spent several years privately studying the topic and is described as having a university-level understanding of toxicology before he was in his teens. It's unfortunate that he started actively carrying out experiments on his family in 1961 aged only fourteen, the same year Agatha's *Pale Horse* was published, as this led some to accuse Agatha's book of being a direct inspiration for him. I would vehemently disagree with this. Young was already studying poisons extensively before *The Pale Horse* was published, he denied ever reading the book, and when he started using his family as guinea pigs for his toxic tomfoolery that year he used antimony and atropine to cause them to be quite seriously ill, *not* thallium. It was only in 1962, to bring about the death of his stepmother Molly, that Young became impatient and gave her a dose of thallium, which as we have seen had been employed in several murder cases previously. Oddly, her death was put down to natural causes and she was cremated — rather ingeniously at Young's own suggestion! Soon after, his father also became seriously ill and when he was examined antimony was found in his body. He was told at the hospital that just one more dose would have killed him. At this, family members and a science teacher at Graham Young's school finally became suspicious, and on the advice of a psychiatrist the disturbed young man was arrested. Deemed to be suffering from a personality disorder, he was detained at the psychiatric hospital Broadmoor for a recommended period of fifteen years — with the accolade of being the youngest inmate in the high-security facility since 1885. Here the story could have ended, if it wasn't for his release just eight years later.

His prison psychiatrist deemed Graham to be 'no longer obsessed with poisons, violence and mischief' and secured his release after what he considered to be years of good behaviour. The fact that there were four poisoning cases at Broadmoor during the time Graham was incarcerated there, and which he was suspected of committing, seemed to have escaped the psychiatrist's attention, as did the chilling farewell promise Young gave to a nurse on his way out: 'I'm going to kill one person for every year I've spent in this place.'

By then aged twenty-four, Graham Young secured employment at John Hadland Laboratories, based in Bovingdon, Hertfordshire. They manufactured infrared lenses, and an important component in the process was thallium. He was able to pass on to his employers some stellar references from Broadmoor as part of their offender rehabilitation programme — references that made no mention of his poisonous past. His slate was effectively 'wiped clean' in order to give him a chance at a normal future.

But Graham Young didn't want a normal future. As soon as he started work, Young made good on his eerie promise and poisoned eight people, killing two of them. The victims reported their symptoms and between them were examined by a total of forty-three doctors. Not a single one considered that the cases could be due to poisoning — without knowledge of Graham Young's background, why would they? — and the mystery illness was reported as 'The Bovingdon Bug' in the local press. Graham was caught for two reasons. One, as is the case with many psychopathic narcissists he was far too cocky and subconsciously wanted those around him to know what he was capable of, so he asked suspicious and inappropriate questions of his employers, and drew far too much attention to himself. Concurrently, a doctor conferring with Scotland Yard about the case had read *The Pale Horse* and recognised 'The Bovingdon Bug' as thallium poisoning because of Christie's accurate description of the symptoms.

Thankfully, then, by 1972 Graham Young was back in prison for his crimes, this time at the notorious Parkhurst, on the Isle of Wight. Poisoning aside, he was *not* a nice man, and is best known for befriending notorious child killer the 'Moors Murderer' Ian Brady. Agatha Christie was said to have been 'very upset' by the unfounded associations between Young and *The Pale Horse*. *Time* magazine, which reported this, also quoted her husband Max as wondering 'if this fellow read her book and learned anything from it'. I would posit this is absolutely not the case: Graham Young had an encyclopaedic knowledge of similar metallic poisons before *The Pale Horse* was published, and plenty of real-life cases to draw from: such as the Marek case in the 1930s and the antipodean housewife thallium craze in the 1950s. What Agatha *did* do is save lives and draw so much attention to thallium as a poison that it's rarely — if ever — used in deliberate poisonings any more.

* * *

Christie may have been inspired to use thallium as a weapon at the suggestion of a colleague, but she also drew upon real-life poisoning cases, and referred to a plethora of them in her books. Numerous mentions go to Herbert Rowse Armstrong, the 'Hay Poisoner', whose victim was examined by pathologist Bernard Spilsbury and whose story is also a case on the Scotland Yard radio show *The Black Museum*. Armstrong, a solicitor practising in the small town of Hay-on-Wye near the Welsh border, was accused of trying to murder a professional rival with arsenic, and this drew attention to the earlier death of his wife. After she was exhumed, Spilsbury discovered copious amounts of arsenic in her tissues despite her being ten months in the grave, and Armstrong was tried and hanged. He remains the only solicitor in the UK ever to be hanged for murder. (Incidentally his hangman was Britain's chief executioner at the time, John Ellis, who also hanged Dr Crippen and Edith Thompson. Ellis, apparently unable to live with the guilt of his vocation, committed suicide in 1932 by slitting his throat with a razor.)

Interestingly Christie seems to mention a half-fictional version of this case in *Murder Is Easy* when she refers to ' . . . the Abercrombie case — of course *he'd* poisoned quite a lot of people before any suspicion was aroused'. There is no real 'Abercrombie case' but nevertheless Christie cites him again later in the book: 'She mentioned the Abercrombie case — you know, the Welsh poisoner.' The name beginning with an 'A' and the location of the poisoner — Wales — lead me to think she created a fictional version of Armstrong. As we've seen previously, this is quite common in Christie books; sometimes she refers to a well-known case explicitly and other times she changes a name slightly. She knew so many poisoning cases and was clearly interested in them — having been a dispenser — that she even had Hercule Poirot try to solve historical ones from his armchair during his retirement. In one of her later books, *The Clocks*, Poirot tells Colin Lamb that he has a newfound interest in reading and trying to solve old murders. (*The Clocks* was published in the 1960s so these really were old murders by then.) Colin asks him, 'You mean like the Bravo case, Adelaide Bartlett, and all the rest of them?' and this Bartlett case still baffles people to this day. The Bartlett poisoning is also known as 'The Pimlico Mystery', because it took place in Pimlico, London, on New Year's Eve 1885. But it seems that the way was paved for the poisoning to happen long before the actual event.

T. Edwin Bartlett and his young French-born wife had been married in 1875, but it was in 1885 that they met the Reverend George Dyson — and things took a turn for the weird. Dyson was a Wesleyan minister who began frequently visiting the couple, became Adelaide's 'tutor and spiritual guide' and even the executor of Edwin Bartlett's will. He was encouraged to romance Adelaide by Bartlett himself, who also said they should marry each other if he was to die. This may have been because Edwin, who was eleven years older than Adelaide, wasn't a well man. He was convinced he had syphilis and was taking mercury for it, which was likely doing far more harm than good. He also had a long-standing dental issue because his decayed teeth had broken off at the gumline, and — to top it off — he had tapeworms. Perhaps in this context it makes sense that he would encourage Adelaide to satisfy any sexual desires she had with an upstanding minister, under Edwin's own watchful eye . . . This is why it's so surprising that when Bartlett was found dead in bed on that fateful New Year's evening, Adelaide was accused of poisoning him. It doesn't seem as though it was necessary!

At his autopsy, Bartlett was found to have the extremely corrosive substance liquid chloroform in his stomach, but the main question was: how did it get there? Chloroform is damaging to soft tissues, particularly in large quantities, so if it had been forcefully administered to Bartlett there should have been injuries to the soft tissues of Bartlett's oesophagus and even around his mouth — as we saw earlier in *Murder in Mesopotamia* — due to the struggle. But there were none. It seemed more likely, then, that Bartlett had ingested it *himself* — whether intentionally or not — in one deliberate gulp.

After a sensational trial, it was this unsolvable aspect of Edwin Bartlett's death which led the jury to find Adelaide not guilty, although they still had some misgivings about her. At the verdict, the foreman is recorded as saying, 'Although we think grave suspicion is attached to the prisoner, we do not think there is sufficient evidence to show how or by whom the chloroform was administered.' The case puzzled medical men of the era, and Sir James Paget — whose carved bust overlooks me while I work in the pathology museum at Barts — famously said, 'Now that she has been acquitted for murder and cannot be tried again, she should tell us in the interest of science how she did it!'

Another notable real-life poisoning case which

Christie not only had Poirot mention explicitly in the story, but also clearly based the plot of the book *Sad Cypress* on, was the Hearn case, which could alternatively be called 'The Case of the Poisoned Sandwiches'.

Sad Cypress is one of Agatha's more substantial detective mysteries, described as 'more emotionally involving than is usual in Christie' by crime writer and critic Robert Barnard. In the same review we are told 'her knowledge of poison is well to the fore'. When we meet our protagonist, Elinor Carlisle, she is already in the dock accused of two murders. The main victim, her beautiful 21-year-old love-rival Mary Gerrard, had partaken of some sandwiches during an impromptu afternoon tea with Elinor and another character Nurse Hopkins, before falling ill and dying quietly in the sitting room. The sandwiches contained that war-time delicacy known appetisingly as 'paste' — on this particular occasion fish paste — and at that time the inclusion of fish in these pre-made sandwich fillings could lead to possible 'ptomaine poisoning'. (We don't use this term any more, but from 1883 'ptomaine' was a catch-all word which described what medics believed was the cause of food poisoning in rotting animal and vegetable matter, before it was discovered that it was just bacteria in the expired food which caused this poisoning rather than any other specific substance.) In the book, Elinor mentions this to the shopkeeper as she buys her groceries, saying, 'One used to be rather afraid of eating fish pastes. There have been cases of ptomaine poisoning from them, haven't there?' Unfortunately for her, this attempt to make idle conversation with the shopkeeper, as one sometimes does, looks rather suspicious in light of later events.

It seems, in the book, that the sandwich paste — and the risk of accidental 'ptomaine' poisoning from it — are possibly an effective cover for the real cause of the death of Mary: morphine hydrochloride. But is that really the case? The reason Agatha's knowledge of poisons is described as 'well to the fore' in this book is that she takes the time to illustrate that morphine poisoning doesn't share the symptoms of 'ptomaine' poisoning, and if the poisoner was trying to make *that* look like the cause of Mary Gerrard's death they could have chosen a substance which did. It's Poirot who points out, 'The symptoms of morphine are not in the least like those of food poisoning. Atropine, surely, would have been a better choice!'

After the death of Mary, the finger of suspicion points at Elinor Carlisle and asks questions of another recent death; that of her aunt Laura Welman whom it is now believed was also murdered by Elinor. On Ms Welman's exhumation, her tissues are found to contain vast amounts of morphine.

Ten years prior to the publication of *Sad Cypress*, the Hearn case was a real-life poisoning that had several features which may have inspired Agatha's plot: Sarah 'Annie' Everard (a.k.a. Annie Hearn) was accused of poisoning sandwiches she'd made for her married friends Alice and William Thomas. All three had gone to a tea shop in Cornwall after a day on the coast, and although they purchased their cups of tea there, they ate homemade sandwiches to save a few pennies. The sandwiches had been made by Annie and consisted of tinned salmon and homemade dressing. After they'd eaten them, Alice complained to her husband that she was feeling ill and had a foul taste in her mouth.

(Similar to something Amyas Crale said in *Five Little Pigs* after being poisoned with coniine — 'Everything tastes foul to me today' — indicating a bitter-tasting poison. As we've seen, a bitter taste can suggest an alkaloid, whereas arsenic has practically no taste.) Still ill once the couple reached home, they thought it best to call the local doctor, and after hearing they'd eaten salmon sandwiches that afternoon he diagnosed the expected 'ptomaine poisoning'. A week or so later, Annie Hearn came to visit the couple and help look after the ailing Alice by cleaning up and preparing meals. Shortly after this visit, Alice was dead. Subsequent analysis of her body showed that there were large quantities of arsenic present, the substance which mimics the symptoms of food poisoning.

Then, just as in *Sad Cypress*, the police began investigating the recent deaths of Hearn's relatives — namely her sister and aunt — and according to a Home Office report arsenic was found in significant quantities in both of their bodies.

The police wanted a word or two with Annie Hearn but she had already run away. When they finally tracked her down, she was calling herself 'Mrs Faithful' and working as a housekeeper — in Christie's native Torquay! No wonder Agatha knew the case so well.

Hearn was eventually brought to trial but there were too many unanswered questions which made the jury unsure of her guilt. Why did the victim Alice complain of having a foul taste in her mouth, if arsenic has no taste? How could Annie have poisoned the sandwiches and then distributed them in a way that would affect her intended target? (This was the exact question Hercule Poirot kept returning to in

Sad Cypress.) And how did no one notice the arsenic in the sandwiches, since at the time it was only available in weed-killer stained bright blue? In court, the defence actually prepared sandwiches with fish paste and weed-killer (delicious!) and passed them round to the members of the jury, who were horrified at the vivid blue colour oozing out of the white bread. Sarah 'Annie' Hearn was acquitted and no one was ever held accountable for the murder of Alice Thomas.

One particularly notable aspect of the death of Mary Gerrard in *Sad Cypress* is the technical detail Agatha goes into. We're told at the inquest, 'Death was due to poisoning of the 'foudroyante' variety.' When asked to explain what this means, the doctor obliges.

> Death from morphine poisoning might occur in several different ways. The most common was a period of intense excitement followed by drowsiness and narcosis, pupils of the eyes contracted. Another not so common form had been named by the French 'foudroyante'. In these cases deep sleep supervened in a very short time — about ten minutes; the pupils of the eyes were usually dilated . . .

This in-depth description of toxicological effects is one of the features which sets Agatha apart from other writers. The etymology of this 'foudroyante' term for the phenomenon described in *Sad Cypress* is from the French for 'violent' or 'sudden' and the word occurs so rarely in fact or fiction that several blogging fans have actually assumed that she made it up. In fact, it's mentioned in a poison manual written in 1895 by A. W. Blyth specifically for use by analytical chemists and experts. Agatha certainly was an expert, and her knowledge is just as in-depth for a variety of other toxic substances, no matter how different the symptoms.

* * *

In the same vein as *The Pale Horse*, another poisoning tale which Agatha has cleverly cloaked in the supernatural — this time in the form of seances and mediumship — is *Dumb Witness*. Just as in *The Pale Horse*, there is an atmosphere of foreboding and dread, ostensibly due to communication with the spirits of the dead and luminous auras manifesting around the seance table. But when Poirot comes to connect these luminous auras with a particular poison all becomes clear, and it's the accuracy of the toxicology which impresses rather more than the smoke and mirrors which begin the book.

Phosphorus is the rather unusual agent chosen by Christie to poison the unfortunate Mrs Emily Arundell in *Dumb Witness*, a conclusion that razor-sharp Hercule Poirot comes to as soon as he is told about the supposed 'luminous auras coming out of her mouth'. Phosphorus is unusual because it glows due to a process called *chemiluminescence*, although erroneously Poirot (and therefore, we can assume, Agatha) uses a slightly different but not outrageous term: 'Miss Arundell's breath was *phosphorescent*!' Poirot concludes:

> 'There are not many phosphorescent substances. The first and most common one gave me exactly what I was looking for. I will read you a short extract from an article on phosphorus poisoning.'

Poirot goes on to describe the phenomenon of glowing breath stated in the article, as well as the fact that this type of poisoning mimics the effects of liver failure, something Emily Arundell has suffered with for years. This would effectively mask the fact Emily was being poisoned — it's only the 'luminous haze' of the breath which gives it away — and suggests the murderer is aware of the similarity in the symptoms. This isn't very common knowledge, but the insinuation here is that anyone medical — or anyone with a connection to a medic — may be aware of the effects of phosphorus poisoning more than the average joe. And there is a doctor in the Arundell family . . .

* * *

There is something about poisoning someone which makes it seem exceedingly wicked, whether in Christie books or real life. When we find out who murdered Amyas Crale in *Five Little Pigs*, Poirot contemplates:

> 'For it is a devilish thing to do, to poison a man in cold blood. If there had been a revolver about and she caught it up and shot him — well, that might have been understandable. But this cold, deliberate, vindictive poisoning . . . '

It's left unsaid here, but the meaning is obvious. Often during poisonings, the crime itself is protracted; carried out over a long period of time in order to make it seem as though the victim is gradually deteriorating due to natural illness. The death therefore seems less suspicious. But this method means the poisoner has to carry out the act over and over again. It's not usually a crime of passion or a moment of madness which the person may immediately regret; it's systematic, deliberate and dispassionate, calculated and cruel. And it seems all the more cruel because often this cold, murderous desire comes from someone in very close proximity to the victim, as Christie says in *They Do It with Mirrors*: 'A slow poisoner is someone living in the intimacy of family life', just like Graham Young when he poisoned his father, sister, and stepmother at the kitchen table over family meals. This is what Colonel Johnson means in *Hercule Poirot's Christmas* when he says, 'Always an awkward business, a poisoning case.' It causes everyone to become distrustful of each other when carrying out perfectly natural processes like pouring a drink. There's something heinous about committing this crime at family meals, which are supposed to be about bonding, nourishment, and nurturing. Taking it a step further, it's very frequently people who are 'nursing' the victims that are also carrying out the poisoning, whether it's a doctor like Harold Shipman, nurses who are described as 'Angels of Mercy' or a family member ostensibly looking after an invalid and 'helping them recover'. It's cruel, and that's what makes it so terrifying.

* * *

Christie knew how to use poisons in her books because of her real-life experience at the dispensary, as well as her continued lifetime interest in the topic. She certainly wasn't working as a pharmacist when she wrote about thallium for the first time, in the 1960s (she was over seventy years old!), but she was well aware of its existence. This lifelong curiosity is what enabled her to be so accurate in her descriptions of the smells, colours and symptoms of a variety of substances; some rarer than others. The fact that poisons were so easily accessible at the beginning of Christie's writing career made it seem as though absolutely *anyone* could be the suspect. Yet as time marched on in her books, just as in real life, these substances became far more controlled, meaning that our poisoner was more likely to have specialist access. It really made the reader think about who could get their hands on these dangerous substances, as well as *why*. What sort of character were they? This leads to another interesting point about Christie's poison knowledge: it wasn't just their physical effects she was familiar with, but the psychology of the user: the cold, cruel mindset of someone dosing their loved one's food over a period of months, for example, just to get them out of the way.

Thankfully our modern toxicological techniques make these sorts of murders rarer than they once were in that 'Golden Age of Poisoning'. But let's not forget, it's not always tests and samples that solve poisoning cases. In the case of thallium, it was the words of Agatha Christie herself.

Conclusion

Zero Hour

This is the scene where Miss Marple, or Poirot, or any of Christie's other sleuths brings all the suspects into one place and sums up the investigation. Perhaps, right now, we're in an opulent drawing room in a stately home with glasses of sherry and a roaring fire? Perhaps we're huddled in the cold carriage of a stranded train, wrapped in furs to keep out the chill of the encroaching snowbanks, clutching veritable bowls of brandy? Or more likely we're curled up on the sofa in our pyjamas, with a cup of tea, curtains closed against the rain and slick city streets outside? For me in particular, this denouement is coming from a palatial pathology museum with rows of wooden shelves, where I'm lucky enough to be surrounded by medicolegal potted specimens collected by great forensic pathologists and surgical pioneers such as Bernard Spilsbury and James Paget, as I write. I'm sure Christie would be happy with any one of those scenarios. The summing-up scene is many people's favourite part of these mysteries and it's certainly the most satisfying part for me: when I see how all the puzzle pieces have been fitted together in the investigator's mind and I can finally find out who the culprit is and whether or not I guessed right.

Here, in our investigation, we've been able to fill in some of the scientific blanks and instead of Whodunnit, find out *How*dunnit. So, to sum up in true murder mystery style: Agatha did it — and here's how it was accomplished:

Agatha had good, working forensic knowledge even in her first book, 1920's *The Mysterious Affair at Styles*, but it certainly improved as she began to really 'accept' that her job was as an author of mostly crime stories. She references this late in her career in *The Clocks* when Hercule Poirot discusses his friend Ariadne Oliver, who shares many characteristics with Christie herself and is often used to cheekily inject her own thoughts into her books. Poirot says of Oliver:

> 'She has an original habit of mind, she makes an occasional shrewd deduction, and of later years she has learnt a good deal about things which she did not know before. Police procedure for instance. She is also now a little more reliable on the subject of firearms. What was even more needed, she has possibly acquired a solicitor or barrister friend who has put her right on certain points of the law.'

This is such a salient paragraph of Christie's and I believe she was directly describing herself here, and making the reader aware that she had learned more about the medicolegal system over the years — *The Clocks* was written in 1963, and she passed away only thirteen years later. We know (from previous chapters in this book) that she used to mix up the terms 'revolver' and 'automatic' which aren't the same type of gun, and that she pronounced the calibre of guns incorrectly in early books — but these sorts of mistakes never appeared later. She definitely became 'a little more reliable on the subject of firearms', as Poirot said. She also included in her stories novel forensic discoveries like the chemical luminol to detect the presence of latent blood, and illustrated ingenious ways to retrieve fingerprints. Conversely, she stopped referring to police procedures in her fiction as they fell out of favour in real life, such as the Bertillon System, and was well aware that some criminal theories — like the atavistic hypothesis of Cesare Lombroso — were outdated despite being interesting. She knew where they fit into the forensic puzzle.

When she was wrong, on rare occasions, like when she described using the contents of the stomach to determine time of death, she is only considered wrong by our contemporary standards — in that example because, at the time she was writing, it *was* considered to be a foolproof way of calculating when someone died.

In fact, Agatha was so *au fait* with the topic of forensics she was able to subvert it in order to point to who wasn't there rather than who was, or use its absence in a way that is much more significant than its presence. She imbued some of her murderers with the power to use forensics to frame others for their own crimes, and allowed her sleuths to trick criminals into admitting their misdeeds by planting 'fake' evidence.

When she was wrong about an aspect of medico-legal science, she wasn't really *wrong* — she tended to use artistic licence to create an unshakeable alibi or a dramatic mode of death, but she made it clear in other books or short stories that she knew the real details; she just chose — on occasion — to play a little fast and loose with the rules. We know she had this rebellious tendency from the time she was very nearly expelled from the Detection Club because of the ending of *The Murder of Roger Ackroyd*!

But something else Agatha was very familiar with from the start of her career was other detective fiction. In her humorous book *Partners in Crime* — part mystery puzzle, part thriller — in which she has husband and wife super team Tommy and Tuppence act out the roles of different famous fictional detectives, she even has Tommy dressed as a priest, like G. K. Chesterton's Father Brown. (According to G. C. Ramsey in 1968's *Mistress of Mystery*, Chesterton is said to have given her the idea for part of the plot of *The ABC Murders* when he said, 'Where to hide a tree, but in a forest?' If you've not already, you'll have to read the book to see how that inspired her.) Each story in *Partners in Crime* is not only a homage to a different detective and its creator, it also reads like that writer's own stories and takes on an air of their literary style, so the type of forensic evidence mentioned in each one is characteristic of those tales. This means we know she was inspired not only by real-life forensics but by the fiction of her contemporaries and — of course — the greats like Arthur Conan Doyle.

* * *

I've alluded to some important aspects of forensic science several times throughout the course of this book, such as the fact that many of the sciences and various pieces of evidence have to be used in conjunction to tell the story of, and ultimately solve, a case. Also, it's essential for the sciences to be used with common sense as well as experience and expertise. The fact that there is such an organisation as The Innocence Project, which currently works to reprieve people who have been wrongly convicted of crimes — usually due to faulty forensic evidence — tells us that forensic science IS fallible. Even in Christie's time this was the case, as illustrated by this quote from the forensically stuffed *Towards Zero*:

> ' . . . But facts are another. All the facts show that she's guilty.'
>
> 'All the facts showed that I was guilty two days ago!'

Faulty forensics may have been responsible for the wrongful imprisonment of Sam Sheppard following the murder of his wife Marilyn, and all the forensics in the world couldn't convince a jury that Adelaide Bartlett killed her husband with chloroform, because they just didn't know how it was done. Sir Bernard Spilsbury shot to fame via the case of Dr Crippen, who it now appears was wrongfully accused of murdering his wife because of Spilsbury's perhaps questionable expertise — and mistakes like that can't be rectified. In Crippen's case, was it an innocent man whose features were copied for the creation of a waxwork to be ogled in the 'Chamber of Horrors' at Madame Tussauds, along with genuine murderers like John Reginald Christie (no relation to Agatha!), a serial killer and necrophile active in 1940s and 1950s London? That part of Madame Tussauds was closed in 2016, but had been extremely popular, and Agatha references Crippen's waxwork in *Sleeping Murder*, the last work of detective fiction she had published.

Current TV shows such as *Exhibit A* on Netflix expose many of the mistakes which have occurred during forensic investigations, and the recent trace evidence study at Northumbria University has shown that it's even possible for traces from one person to innocently alight on another in the vicinity, which could effectively damn someone for a crime they didn't commit. Forensic science is fascinating, but its history is peppered with mistakes. As the sciences and related equipment progress and improve, evidence is becoming more and more minute — and therefore more complex and problematic. It's much easier for microscopic grains of pollen to blow from the clothing of the guilty to the innocent, for example, than for a person to change their fingerprints.

And when it comes to crime ftction, just how much should the public know? Consider a quote like this from *Crooked House*, where it is said of one of the characters that all they 'had to do was to avoid leaving fingerprints and the slightest knowledge of detective fiction would teach that'.

Whether through factual documentaries or accurate fictional stories, the developments in the forensic sciences are made accessible to those who, for various reasons, may not be privy to such information. In particular the advances made in these investigations can be especially fascinating. From using a fingerprint as a means to identify someone via the pattern left on a surface, to instead using minuscule amounts of DNA found within the sweat of that fingermark to identify the person *absolutely* is an impressive leap, it's like something from science fiction. But it is a double-edged sword. On the one hand, the public can be made aware of the amount of intricate and arduous work which goes into the experts' investigation of cases and this can generate a certain amount of admiration for those scientists on the front line every day, putting names to either victims or perpetrators, catching killers and in effect 'saving the world'. But on the other hand, if every development is reported in books and in podcasts and on TV, the criminals are able to keep up with the scientists' progress in order to avoid being caught. That is, of course, if we're being provided with that knowledge and kept up to date with each forensic advance in every single discipline. But this isn't an easy feat for most authors of crime fiction, and most real cases are reported retrospectively, so I'd urge every potential criminal out there who thinks they can beat the system to ask themselves one question: 'Are we?'

Use the examples of Roland Roussel and Mahin Qadiri as warnings — they tried to copy Agatha's fiction and got caught. Leave the criminal tendencies in the world of fiction, because the landscape of forensic science is changing every day. In fact, the criminals will never be able to keep up, no matter how hard they try.

Appendix 1

Murder Methods Table

Name of Book	Date	Murder Methods
The Mysterious Affair at Styles	1920	
The Secret Adversary	1922	
Murder on the Links	1923	
The Man in the Brown Suit	1924	
The Secret of Chimneys	1925	
The Murder of Roger Ackroyd	1926	
The Big Four	1927	
The Mystery of the Blue Train	1928	
The Seven Dials Mystery	1929	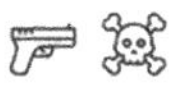
The Murder at the Vicarage	1930	
The Sittaford Mystery	1931	
Peril at End House	1932	

Lord Edgware Dies	1933	
Murder on the Orient Express	1934	
Why Didn't They Ask Evans?	1934	
Three Act Tragedy	1934	
Death in the Clouds	1935	
The ABC Murders	1936	
Murder in Mesopotamia	1936	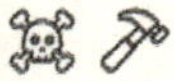
Cards on the Table	1936	
Dumb Witness	1937	
Death on the Nile	1937	
Appointment with Death	1938	
Hercule Poirot's Christmas	1938	
Murder Is Easy	1939	
And Then There Were None	1939	
Sad Cypress	1940	
One, Two, Buckle My Shoe	1940	
Evil Under the Sun	1941	
N or M?	1941	
The Body in the Library	1942	
Five Little Pigs	1942	
The Moving Finger	1942	

Towards Zero	1944
Death Comes as the End	1944
Sparkling Cyanide	1945
The Hollow	1946
Taken at the Flood	1948
Crooked House	1949
A Murder Is Announced	1950
They Came to Baghdad	1951
Mrs McGinty's Dead	1952
They Do It with Mirrors	1952
After the Funeral	1953
A Pocket Full of Rye	1953
Destination Unknown	1954
Hickory Dickory Dock	1955
Dead Man's Folly	1956
The 4:50 from Paddington	1957
Ordeal by Innocence	1958
Cat Among the Pigeons	1959
The Pale Horse	1961
The Mirror Crack'd from Side to Side	1962
The Clocks	1963

A Caribbean Mystery	1964
At Bertram's Hotel	1965
Third Girl	1966
Endless Night	1967
By the Pricking of My Thumbs	1968
Halloween Party	1969
Passenger to Frankfurt	1970
Nemesis	1971
Elephants Can Remember	1972
Postern of Fate	1973
Curtain (Poirot's Last Case)	1975

Key

= Gunshot
= Poison
= Stabbing
= Sepsis
= Heart attack
= Electrocution
= Hit and run
= Blow to head
= Strangling
= Cut throat

 = Drowning

 = Pushed/falling

 = Hanging

 = Body burnt

 = Crushed

 = Axe/hatchet

Appendix 2

Maps and Floorplans

The Murder of Roger Ackroyd
'Murder in the Mews'/'Dead Man's Mirror'
Murder on the Orient Express
Towards Zero
The Murder at the Vicarage
Evil Under the Sun
They Do It with Mirrors
The Mysterious Affair at Styles
Death in the Clouds
'The Jewel Robbery at the Grand Metropolitan' (short story)
The Unexpected Guest (play)

Agatha Christie References

A Caribbean Mystery (London: HarperCollins, 2006)
A Murder Is Announced (London: HarperCollins, 2005)
A Pocket Full of Rye (London: HarperCollins, 2006)
After the Funeral (London: HarperCollins, 2014)
And Then There Were None (London: HarperCollins, 2003)
Appointment with Death (London: Fontana, 1960)
At Bertram's Hotel (London: HarperCollins, 2006)
Black Coffee, Agatha Christie and Charles Osborne (London: HarperCollins, 2007)
By the Pricking of My Thumbs (London: Fontana, 1975)
Cards on the Table (London: HarperCollins, 2006)
Cat Among the Pigeons (London: HarperCollins, 1985)
Crooked House (London: Fontana, 1959)
Curtain: Poirot's Last Case (London: HarperCollins, 2002)
Dead Man's Folly (London: Pan, 1966)
Death in the Clouds (London: HarperCollins, 2006)
Death on the Nile (London: Fontana, 1988)
Destination Unknown (London: HarperCollins, 2007)
Dumb Witness (London: Pan, 1978)
Elephants Can Remember (London: HarperCollins, 2016)
Endless Night (London: HarperCollins, 2017)
Evil Under the Sun (London: Pan, 1941)
Five Little Pigs (London: Fontana, 1976)
4.50 from Paddington (London: HarperCollins,

2005)
Halloween Party (London: HarperCollins, 2015)
Hercule Poirot's Christmas (London: HarperCollins, 2001)
Hickory Dickory Dock (London: HarperCollins, 1984)
Lord Edgware Dies (London: Fontana, 1965)
Miss Marple's Final Cases (London: Fontana, 1981)
Mrs McGinty's Dead (London: Fontana, 1988)
Murder in Mesopotamia (London: HarperCollins, 2016)
Murder in the Mews (London: Fontana, 1964)
Murder Is Easy (London: HarperCollins, 2017)
Murder on the Orient Express (London: HarperCollins, 2017)
Nemesis (London: HarperCollins, 2006)
N or M? (London: HarperCollins, 2007)
One, Two, Buckle My Shoe (London: Fontana, 1970)
Ordeal by Innocence (London: Fontana, 1963)
Partners in Crime (London: HarperCollins, 1988)
Peril at End House (London: HarperCollins, 2015)
Poirot's Early Cases (London: Fontana, 1983)
Poirot Investigates (London: Pan, 1955) Postern of
Fate (London: Fontana, 1976)
Sad Cypress (London: Pan Books, 1981)
Sleeping Murder: Miss Marple's Last Case (London: HarperCollins, 2006)
Sparkling Cyanide (London: Fontana, 1966)
Spider's Web, Agatha Christie and Charles Osborne (London: HarperCollins, 2003)
Taken at the Flood (London: HarperCollins, 2015)
The ABC Murders (London: HarperCollins, 2018)
The Adventure of the Christmas Pudding (London: HarperCollins, 2016)
The Big Four (London: HarperCollins, 1986)

The Body in the Library (London: HarperCollins, 2005)
The Clocks (London: Fontana, 1967)
The Hollow (London: Fontana, 1961)
The Labours of Hercules (London: Fontana, 1963)
The Listerdale Mystery (London: HarperCollins, 1982)
The Man in the Brown Suit (London: Pan, 1953)
The Mirror Crack'd from Side to Side (London: HarperCollins, 2006)
The Moving Finger (London: HarperCollins, 2005)
The Murder at the Vicarage (London: HarperCollins, 2005)
The Murder of Roger Ackroyd (London: HarperCollins, 2016)
The Murder on the Links (London: HarperCollins, 2001)
The Mysterious Affair at Styles (London: HarperCollins, 2007)
The Mystery of the Blue Train (London: Fontana, 1976)
The Pale Horse (London: HarperCollins, 2017)
The Secret Adversary (London: Pan, 1955)
The Secret of Chimneys (London: Pan, 1956)
The Seven Dials Mystery (London: Fontana, 1971)
The Sittaford Mystery (London: HarperCollins, 2017)
The Thirteen Problems (London: HarperCollins, 2005)
The Unexpected Guest, Agatha Christie, and Charles Osborne (London: HarperCollins, 2000)
They Do It with Mirrors (London: Fontana, 1983)
Third Girl (London: Fontana, 1969)
Three Act Tragedy (London: Fontana, 1972)
Towards Zero (London: Fontana, 1983)
Why Didn't They Ask Evans (London: Fontana, 1959)

Image Credits

Mr. Galton's types of finger-prints: Middle Temple Library/Science Photo Library

A photograph of a basic microscope as used in Christie's era: iStock

A photograph of Nancy Titterton: TopFoto

A photograph of a typical vintage revolver: Shutterstock

A photograph of bullets of various calibres: iStock

A photograph of Robert Churchill and the comparison microscope: General Photographic Agency/Stringer/Getty Images

One of the Nutshell Studies of Unexplained Death created by 'real-life Miss Marple' Frances Glessner Lee: Spencer Grant/Alamy Stock Photo

Frances Glessner Lee, the real-life Miss Marple: Courtesy of the Glessner House Museum

A photograph of Isabella Ruxton's face superimposed over the image of her skull: TopFoto

A photograph of Ruby Keen: Central Press/Stringer/Getty Images

Evidence from the Ruby Keen case at Scotland Yard Museum: Reproduced by kind permission of the Museum of London/Metropolitan Police Service

A diagram of blood drops hitting a surface from dif ferent angles: Jo Millington

A photograph of Sir Bernard Spilsbury: Topical Press Agency/Stringer/Getty Images

A diagram of the apparatus used in the Marsh test for arsenic: Universal History Archive/Getty Images

Photograph of Graham Young: PA Images/Alamy Stock Photo

Acknowledgements

This book was so different to my last one, *Past Mortems*, in that I previously wrote about my own life and yet in this one I wrote about someone else's. In fact, apart from Agatha Christie I wrote about the lives of various perpetrators, victims and investigators of crime in the first half of the twentieth century, making this a much more arduous and complex process.

They say 'it takes a village' and in this case it took several. I couldn't have completed this work without the guidance of many forensic professionals who were kind enough to go over my chapters on the specific disciplines which I'd touched upon in my studies — and experienced during my cases — yet was by no means an authority on. These include: Jonathan Ferguson, Keeper of Firearms & Artillery, based at the National Firearms Centre in Leeds; Jo Millington, a forensic scientist who is an expert in bloodstain pattern analysis; Diane Ivory, a fingerprint examiner and founder of Forensic Minds; Dr Suzy Lishman CBE, a histopathologist and former president of the Royal College of Pathologists, and Dr Kathryn Harkup, chemist, science communicator and author.

Further thanks is to be extended to the curator of the Scotland Yard Crime Museum, Paul Bickley, who allowed me to carry out research at this elusive collection, kept in London for law enforcement professionals and forensic investigators.

In addition to my formal research of Agatha Christie I also educated and entertained myself with several podcasts which I feel deserve a mention for bringing facts to me which I hadn't previously considered, at the same time as being thoroughly enjoyable. My favourites are *Shedunnit*, *The Poisoner's Cabinet* and — of course — *All About Agatha*, all of which can be found wherever you listen to your podcasts.

Thanks, as ever, to my wonderful editor Rhiannon Smith, who either reined me in or pushed me further depending on what the situation required, and for simply being a friend.

Thanks to the team at Diane Banks Associates, particularly Martin Redfern. And thanks to fellow Agatha Christie enthusiasts, authors and professionals who helped guide me through my dream of writing this book: Agatha Christie Limited (especially Sarah Thrift), Nicola Crane, Tina Hodgkinson, author Martin Edwards, Amber Butchart and Eric Ray.

The one person who has without a doubt spurred me on to complete this book is my beautiful son, Caleb, who — in the early days — would lie asleep in my arms as I furiously read every book Agatha penned and highlighted various excerpts with colour-coded neon highlighters and Post-its.

Finally, none of this would have been possible without my followers, family and friends. I'm forever grateful to my husband, Jonny, and his parents, Margaret and Les — as well as my fairy godmother Catharine Long — who have all been there throughout the most difficult parts of this process; whether because of tight deadlines, COVID, or whatever the last year or two decided to throw at us.

After a tough time, and lots of delving into the past,

I'm looking to the future and hoping to meet as many of you as possible out there in the world and away from the computer screen!

Other titles published by Ulverscroft:

A PASSION FOR POISON

Carol Ann Lee

In the summer of 1962, fourteen-year-old Graham Young stood in the Old Bailey dock charged with poisoning family members and a schoolfriend by methodically lacing their food and drink with such substances as thallium and antimony. Diagnosed with 'a psychopathic disorder', he was detained under the Mental Health Act and committed to Broadmoor, the youngest patient there since 1885.

Nine years later, Graham was released, believed to be no longer a danger to others. He found employment at Hadlands, a photographic supplies firm. In his role as an assistant storekeeper, Graham's duties included collecting and serving his colleagues' morning and afternoon tea. Very soon, members of staff began falling ill, experiencing debilitating pain — and dying . . .

LEARWIFE

J. R. Thorp

Word has come. Care-bent King Lear is dead, driven mad and betrayed. His three daughters too, broken in battle. But someone has survived: Lear's queen. Exiled to a nunnery years ago, written out of history, her name forgotten. Now she can tell her story.

Though her grief and rage may threaten to crack the earth open, she knows she must seek answers. Why was she sent away in shame and disgrace? What has happened to Kent, her oldest friend and ally? And what will become of her now, in this place of women? To find peace, she must reckon with her past and make a terrible choice — one upon which her destiny, and that of the entire abbey, rests.

THE MITFORD VANISHING

Jessica Fellowes

1937. War with Germany is looming, and a civil war already raging in Spain. Split across political lines, the six Mitford sisters are more divided than ever. Meanwhile their former maid Louisa Cannon is now a private detective, working with her ex-policeman husband Guy Sullivan.

Louisa and Guy are surprised when a call comes in from novelist Nancy Mitford requesting that they look into the disappearance of her Communist sister Jessica, nicknamed Decca. It quickly becomes clear that Decca may have made for the war in Spain — and not alone.

As a second, separate missing person case is opened, Louisa and Guy discover that every marriage has its secrets — but some are more deadly than others . . .